Doors to Elsewhere

Also available from The Alchemy Press

Astrologica: Stories of the Zodiac (autumn 2013)

Beneath the Ground

Invent-10n

Rumours of the Marvellous

Sailor of the Skies (ebook)

Sex, Lies and Family Ties

Shadows of Light and Dark

Swords Against the Millennium

In the Broken Birdcage of Kathleen Fair (ebook)

The Alchemy Press Book of Ancient Wonders

The Alchemy Press Book of Pulp Heroes

The Alchemy Press Book of Pulp Heroes 2 (autumn 2013)

The Alchemy Press Book of Urban Mythic (autumn 2013)

The Komarovs (ebook)

The Paladin Mandates

Where the Bodies are Buried

www.alchemypress.co.uk

Doors to Elsewhere

Mike Barrett

Introduction by Ramsey Campbell

The Alchemy Press

Doors to Elsewhere © Mike Barrett 2013

Introduction © Ramsey Campbell 2013

Cover painting © Bob Covington 2013

Published © The Alchemy Press 2013

Production by Peter Coleborn

By arrangement with the author

All rights reserved

First edition

ISBN 978-0-9573489-0-5

The Alchemy Press, Cheadle, Staffordshire
www.alchemypress.co.uk

The views expressed in these essays do not necessarily reflect those of The Alchemy Press

ACKNOWLEDGEMENTS

"Arkham House: Sundry Observations" first appeared in *Dark Horizons*, March 2010, and has been expanded for its appearance here © Mike Barrett 2010, 2013

"Weaver of Weird Tales" first appeared in slightly different form in *The New York Review of Science Fiction*, August 2008 © Mike Barrett 2008, 2013

"Narratives out of Nightmare" first appeared in *Wormwood*, Spring 2009, and has been expanded for its appearance here © Mike Barrett 2009, 2013

"From Simorgya to Stardock" first appeared in *The Silver Eel* in 1978 as "The Two Greatest Heroes in Lankhmar", and was substantially revised for its appearance in *Fantasy Commentator*, Summer 2004. It has been expanded for its appearance here ©Mike Barrett 1978, 2004, 2013

"Otherworldly Presences" first appeared in *The New York Review of Science Fiction*, June 2009, as "Entrances to Elsewhere" © Mike Barrett 2009, 2013

"Screaming Skulls and Dead Smiles" first appeared in *Wormwood*, April 2012 © Mike Barrett 2012, 2013

"Dark and Sinister Shades" first appeared in *The New York Review of Science Fiction*, July 2010 © Mike Barrett 2010, 2013

"Mostly in Shadow" first appeared in *The New York Review of Science Fiction*, April 2009 © Mike Barrett 2009, 2013

"Opportune Recitals at Convenient Intervals" first appeared in *The New York Review of Science Fiction*, August 2007, and has been expanded for its appearance here © Mike Barrett 2007, 2013

"West Indian Frights" first appeared in slightly different form in *The New York Review of Science Fiction*, May 2007 © Mike Barrett 2007, 2013

"The Passion, the Magic, and the Outrageous" first appeared in *Dark Horizons* in 1978, and was substantially revised for its appearance in *The New York Review of Science Fiction*, February 2010 © Mike Barrett 1978, 2010, 2013

"A Forgotten Disciple" and "Another Forgotten Disciple" first appeared as the one article "Two Forgotten Disciples" in *Dark Horizons*, September 2009 © Mike Barrett 2009, 2013

"Tales in a Major Key" appears here for the first time © Mike Barrett 2013

"Shapes and Sounds" first appeared as "A Primate of Pure Prose" in *Shiel in Diverse Hands*, 1983, and was substantially revised for its appearance in *The New York Review of Science Fiction*, January 2007 © Mike Barrett 1983, 2007, 2013

"Things of Darkness" first appeared in *Wormwood*, Autumn 2009 © Mike Barrett 2009, 2013

"The Final Resting Place" first appeared in *The New York Review of Science Fiction*, December 2008 © Mike Barrett 2008, 2013

Mike Barrett first discovered the worlds of imaginative fiction at school, when a friend lent him a battered paperback edition of *The Golden Apples of the Sun* by Ray Bradbury. His first foray into writing was an article on MP Shiel for the British Fantasy Society's publication *Dark Horizons* in the 1970s, and while several more contributions followed over the next few years he reverted to reading rather than writing. It was not until 2003, when he joined the SSWFT amateur press association, that his interest was rekindled, and since then he has had twenty pieces published in *The New York Review of Science Fiction*, nine in *Dark Horizons*, five in *Wormwood*, and has also appeared in *Science Fantasy Commentator* and *Studies in Fantasy Literature*. He lives in Kent and commutes to London each day, where he works in the Financial Services industry; the one and only attraction of commuting is the time it gives him to read the books in his ever increasing collection.

CONTENTS

Introduction by Ramsey Campbell	9
Arkham House: Sundry Observations	17
Weaver of Weird Tales: Greye La Spina	45
Narratives Out of Nightmare: Edward Lucas White	63
From Simorgya to Stardock: Fritz Leiber	75
Otherworldly Presences: Mary E Wilkins Freeman	95
Screaming Skulls and Dead Smiles: F Marion Crawford	109
Dark and Sinister Shades: Marjorie Bowen	119
Mostly in Shadow: Mary Elizabeth Counselman	141
Opportune Recitals at Convenient Intervals: Ernest Bramah	155
West Indian Frights: Henry S Whitehead	183
The Passion, the Magic, & the Outrageous: Theodore Sturgeon	195
A Forgotten Disciple: C Hall Thompson	211
Another Forgotten Disciple: Clifford Ball	221
Tales in a Major Key: CL Moore	229
Shapes and Sounds: MP Shiel	243
Things of Darkness: GG Pendarves	269
The Final Resting Place: Lord Dunsany	279

BEYOND THE DOORS:
INTRODUCTION BY RAMSEY CAMPBELL

ARKHAM HOUSE! *WEIRD Tales*! Names to conjure with – names that conjure much of the history of modern fantasy and horror fiction. I venture to suggest, however, that many more readers in these fields know of them than have read those books and magazines. Those who haven't encountered them yet have a feast of treats ahead, and for years Mike Barrett has been quietly but diligently publishing celebrations of them and their authors, together with essays on important writers whose work appeared elsewhere. This collection is a fine guide for folk who are eager to broaden their reading, and a useful reappraisal for us who think we know the fields.

Arkham House (now apparently moribund, alas) represented something of a history of them. Mike brings out this quality in his celebration of the publisher and reminds us how much the house owed to the enthusiasm of August Derleth. The publisher has been the subject of several book-length commemorations, and Mike usefully compares them. There's fascinating stuff in his miscellany about the house, and I'm unmaliciously glad to be able to expand on one of his references. While Frank Utpatel did indeed produce nearly all the 1964 covers, he was close to being ousted from one of them by another artist. On 9 August 1963 Derleth wrote to me about *The Inhabitant of the Lake*: "I won't do anything about a title anyway until the MS. is fully ready for the printer, and then I'll have a dummy made for the artist to work on—probably Lee Brown Coye."

Greye La Spina had one Arkham volume to her name, *Invaders from the Dark*. Like many Arkham titles – of short stories too, not only books – it can evoke a good deal in itself, and some readers may even be disappointed to learn that it's a werewolf novel (as with another haunting title, *The Door of the Unreal*). Mike gives us an intriguing history of her career and a balanced overview of her work, which certainly prompts me to seek out some of the examples I haven't read. Sadly, the Arkham House omnibus that Mike names as forthcoming is now at best in limbo. Let's hope it appears from some source.

"Lukundoo" is a tale every horror reader ought to know, with a theme so powerful that Donald Wandrei borrowed it to write a partial variation ("It Will Grow on You"), but how many can identify its author? Like many contributors to our great tradition, Edward Lucas White was best known in his lifetime for his mainstream work (in his case, historical), but it's the horror stories that have stood the test of time. While "The House of the Nightmare" (a quintessential White title) is anthologised now and then, many tales other than "Lukundoo" have only recently been revived. They're an experience worth seeking out.

Surely nobody with a serious interest in fantasy or science fiction, let alone horror, can be unfamiliar with Fritz Leiber. Perhaps this is a naïve assumption on my part, in which case it's good that we have books like Mike's to rectify the situation. His essay confines itself to relishing Leiber's fantasy – specifically the tales of Fafhrd and the Grey Mouser – but it doesn't seem at all confined, given the range and inventiveness Fritz displays in that series of stories. I can't imagine anyone who hasn't read them not resolving to do so on the basis of Mike's affectionate and evocative account of them.

Mary E Wilkins Freeman takes us back to Arkham House, who published her collected ghost stories (or rather a selection, as Mike reminds us). Derleth regarded her as a major influence on his own spectral tales, and Lovecraft ranked her alongside Washington Irving as the other great exponent of New England supernaturalism; I'm surprised Robert Aickman found no tale to reprint in his Fontana series. While some of her tales are poignant in the Victorian way, Lovecraft enthused about her sense of horror, however delicately conveyed. I second Mike's call for a complete edition of her ghostly tales, and I'm sure others of our readers will.

Another writer who deserves revival is F Marion Crawford. It was HP Lovecraft who pointed out in his essay *Supernatural Horror in Literature* that whereas "the older stock ghosts were pale and stately, and apprehended chiefly through the sense of sight", a spectre summoned up by MR James was likely to be altogether less polite in shape and behaviour, not least because it was "usually *touched* before it is *seen*". One crucial precursor of this physicality is Crawford's fine tale "The Upper Berth", singled out by James in *The Bookman* as a "horrid story" that "stands high among ghost stories in general". Crawford also wrote the definitive screaming skull tale and, as Mike shows, was enviably inventive in his other stories of the supernatural (for instance, the hauntingly moonlit "For the Blood is the Life"). At the time of writing a complete edition of *Wandering Ghosts* (including "The King's Messenger") can be had from Wildside Press.

Marjorie Bowen is more than due for reappraisal and more widespread appreciation. She was a highly individual writer, often unsettlingly bleak, and Mike brings out the scope of her work. Arkham House revived her work under the editorship of James Turner, who put together *Kecksies* and contributed a typically enthusiastic and insightful blurb. It's worth noting that she edited (as far as I can tell) the earliest anthology to announce in its title – *Great Tales of Horror* – that it consists of horror fiction. (In fact, even by my very broad definition of the field, it doesn't entirely.) Her work is well worth tracking down, and readers may be mystified as to why Peter Penzoldt accused her in his monograph *The Supernatural in Fiction* of writing "the worst type of horror tale: that containing descriptions of sadism" – specifically, "Marjorie Bowen's disgusting stories in *The Bishop of Hell*". Still, he found Thomas Burke and Rudyard Kipling guilty too.

Mary Elizabeth Counselman was an underrated original. Readers of her early horror story "The Accursed Isle" may be reminded of the ending of a John Carpenter film – as radical in popular cinema as her payoff was in *Weird Tales*. "The Three Marked Pennies" is a splendid conte cruel, and she had an individual way with ghostly themes. Find both her books!

Ernest Bramah is perhaps the most forgotten of Mike's trove of writers. A gentler Orientalist than most, he may have influenced Frank Owen, contributor of many Chinese fantasies to *Weird Tales*, and even Peter Cheyney, among others. Mike's voluminous appreciative piece is timely, since a number of Bramah titles are in print or imminent just now. Sip and savour their elegance (and don't forget the Max Carrados tales, often overlooked when detective fantasies are discussed).

Henry S Whitehead was one of the most literate contributors to *Weird Tales*, and admired by his friend HP Lovecraft. His tales are firmly rooted in personal knowledge of (though not necessarily encounters with) the Caribbean supernatural. He was a clergyman, and as Mike points out, brings an unusually gentle Christian resolution to his tale "Cassius". As Mike says, few authors would have taken this route; Lovecraft, who gave Whitehead the idea, certainly wouldn't. He'd noted it in his commonplace book ("Man has miniature shapeless Siamese twin—exhib. in circus—twin surgically detached—disappears—does hideous things with malign life of his own") and had planned to develop the basic idea in a quite different and more gruesome way – indeed, two partial plots occurred to him – but when Whitehead proposed a collaboration, Lovecraft simply donated the idea. Later he thought of a development sufficiently unlike Whitehead's that he was tempted to write the tale, but – like Derleth's "The Survivor" – it remained unwritten by Lovecraft, alas.

Theodore Sturgeon used to be described by hard-core science fiction fans as writing "human interest" tales. We may wonder who else they expected the stories to interest. The term is a spectacularly inadequate way of summing up the psychological depth of many Sturgeon tales, which often immerse themselves in viewpoints as warped and obsessive as any in Poe but more compassionately, sometimes poignantly, observed. Like Leiber, he was as much at home in Campbell's *Unknown* as in the magazine to which it was conceived as a riposte, *Weird Tales* – indeed, his range rivals Fritz's. He famously used to advise us to ask the next question (and perhaps more famously, and certainly more sadly – unfairly, even – was the model on whom his friend Kurt Vonnegut based Kilgore Trout). He deserves to be remembered most for his work, and history is on his side.

For a while C Hall Thompson was a virtually lost Lovecraftian writer, brought to a halt by August Derleth. In August 1964 Derleth wrote to me "He borrowed flagrantly from HPL's work, and we stopped it by writing to his editors pointing out his invasion of proprietary interests, though we would probably have given him the green signal to go ahead if he had submitted his work to us first. This he did not do; so it had to stop...." Ironically, Thompson's vision was closer to Derleth's reduction of the Lovecraft mythos to a standard conflict between good and evil. Where Thompson's primary influence was Lovecraft, Clifford Ball found a model in Robert E Howard, and some *Weird Tales* readers enjoyed these echoes just as much. Like Thompson, Ball moved on to pen less obviously derivative tales, and Mike's essay is a welcome reminder.

CL Moore remains one of the greats of *Weird Tales*. Her tales there often convey Lovecraft's sense of alien terror and Clark Ashton Smith's exotic dread, but she's a great deal more like herself than either. Is her Mars not resurrected in Ray Bradbury's Martian fantasies? Her later tales with Henry Kuttner are often considerable too, but her *Weird Tales* contributions form a major body of work, the best of which is uniquely haunting.

And so to MP Shiel, who is to almost any other writer here what absinthe is to wine. Mike celebrates his short stories, which are often even richer in their prose than the novels. It seems likely that Chesterton read Shiel and may in particular have been inspired by one Zaleski tale, "The Race of Orven". But Shiel was also adept at conveying horror and awe. As Mike says, his last work – *Jesus* – remains unpublished. We may wonder what we've lost, given this note from a correspondent of Shiel's:

My dear Shiel,

I've got your manuscript [Jesus] and letter and I began to read the first chapter of the former. I found it very interesting and then gave way to fatigue. The fact is at present I am scarcely existent mentally, I've got acute neuritis and I find it almost impossible to keep my attention steady on anything for more than five to ten minutes. Everybody says this will pass off presently but meanwhile I just cannot tackle the problems your book raises. My impression is that you've got something very important to say and that you have massed your evidence upon it instead of using supplements and notes to make it very difficult reading for the ordinary man of intelligence. What shall I do about it? I know someone who might show it to the Cresset Press and beyond that I cannot think of anything to further your desire for publication. What shall I do with the manuscript?

Forgive this rambling letter. I've always regarded you as an outstanding worthwhile writer.

The correspondent was HG Wells.

GG Pendarves was a *Weird Tales* contributor who ended her life in Wallasey, not half a mile from where I'm writing this. No plaque graces Sovereign Cars in Seabank Road – in the thirties, an accommodation she shared with her sister – and, more disturbingly, her little stone in Rake Lane Cemetery had disappeared from the Trenery family grave the last time I looked for it. Her story "Thing of Darkness" uses the same setting, though renamed, as my tale "The Ferries" (Parkgate on the Wirral). She and other writers for the magazine may have followed Lovecraft's lead in being known just by initials and a surname. She seems to have been versed in the history of her field; I take Monk's Rock and Father Ambrosius in "The Devil's Graveyard" to be conscious references to MG Lewis's *The Monk* (and possibly Bierce's *The Monk and the Hangman's Daughter* as well).

Lord Dunsany – carried high by admirers, I hope – rounds off the parade. Mike celebrates his many splendid qualities and then introduces an unusually personal element – Dunsany remembered and revisited. The poem from the stone is certainly worthy of him and of reproduction here, and this moving memoir brings Mike's collection of appreciations to a fitting end.

One last thought. I've had the privilege of meeting many of the masters of pulp fantasy. At the first World Fantasy Convention (Providence, 1975) I had the splendid experience of hearing a panel consisting of Joseph Payne Brennan, Robert Bloch, Frank Belknap Long and Manly Wade Wellman, with that young chap Gahan Wilson as the moderator. Now you can hear it too (http://archive.org/details/FirstWorldFantasyConvention1975). It keeps an important tradition alive, and so does Mike's book. Here's to the keepers of tradition!

Ramsey Campbell
Wallasey, Merseyside
12 August 2013

ARKHAM HOUSE: SUNDRY OBSERVATIONS

HISTORY

ARKHAM HOUSE PUBLISHERS was set up by August Derleth and Donald Wandrei with the express intention of collecting HP Lovecraft's work in durable book form. It not only massively succeeded in that original objective, but has moved a long way beyond its original expectations. More than seventy years later the firm is still in existence, and has become a by-word for the successful and respected small press publisher.

Arkham's first publication was *The Outsider and Others* in 1939; 1,268 copies were printed at what was then a fairly high retail price of five dollars (three dollars for pre-publication orders, though such orders were few). The book took four years to sell out, not a particularly auspicious start for the fledgling publisher.

This initial book was followed in 1941 by *Someone in the Dark*, a collection of seventeen short stories by August Derleth – not a Lovecraft volume. Although it sounds as though this may have been a vanity publication, that was not the case; Derleth produced it under the Arkham House logo at the suggestion of the publishers of his other fiction at the time, Charles Scribner's Sons. The book had a small print run – 1,115 copies – but it sold more quickly than *The Outsider and Others*, although this was almost certainly due to the fact that it was a far shorter book and priced accordingly at a more affordable two dollars.

By 1942 Donald Wandrei had reduced his commitment when he was called up into the Army, and Derleth was effectively in full control of Arkham House. Wandrei still had the editorial responsibilities for the preparation of the Lovecraft titles, particularly the *Selected Letters*. This latter project was originally envisaged as being a single volume, but eventually comprised five sizeable books.

With *Someone in the Dark* recouping its production costs before *The Outsider and Others*, Derleth felt encouraged to expand – and with the gusto and determination that typified much of what he devoted himself to, this is just what he did. The publications up to the end of the World War II became sought after and highly praised. These included Clark Ashton Smith's *Out of Space and Time* (1942) and *Lost Worlds* (1944); Lovecraft's *Beyond the Wall of Sleep* (1943) and *Marginalia* (1944); Henry S Whitehead's *Jumbee and Other Uncanny Tales* (1944); and Robert Bloch's first book, *The Opener of the Way*, in 1945. All of these were produced in editions averaging less than 2,000 copies. There were larger printings in the late 1940s – three successive books had print runs exceeding 4,000 copies – but Derleth came to realise that 2,000 was a more practical figure. He not only had the problem of financing the books but also of finding the space to store them all.

Not all the Arkham House publications sold well; some titles took a *long* time to move. The summer 1967 issue of *The Arkham Collector* listed six books from the 1940s that were still in print, although "low in stock". The spring 1971 issue of *The Arkham Collector* listed some titles as "soon to go out of print", including Evangeline Walton's *Witch House* (1945) and Algernon Blackwood's *The Doll and One Other* (1946). These books, which had printings of 2,949 and 3,490 respectively, therefore took over a quarter of a century to sell out, and there were several other slow movers.

Two new imprints were introduced in 1945. The first of these was Mycroft & Moran, intended for detective stories and mysteries, most notably Derleth's own Solar Pons series. There were a few examples of weird fiction as well: William Hope Hodgson's *Carnacki the Ghost Finder* (1947), Seabury Quinn's *The Phantom Fighter* (1966) and Margery Lawrence's *Number Seven, Queer Street* (1969).

A later volume was *In Lovecraft's Shadow* (1998). This was a collection of August Derleth's Cthulhu Mythos stories, and while this is a particularly attractive book, excellently and lavishly illustrated by Stephen Fabian, it hardly seems to belong under the Mycroft & Moran banner. In fact it was published by George A Vanderburgh under a special licensing agreement. This was also the case with Derleth's *The Final Adventures of Solar Pons* and *The Original Text Solar Pons Omnibus Edition* (1998 and 2001 respectively), but this time the titles *were* correctly included in the Mycroft & Moran stable.

The second new imprint was Stanton & Lee, created primarily to publish books of cartoons and to reprint Derleth's mainstream fiction. Several volumes of poetry also appeared under this impression.

Poetry was also a regular feature of the Arkham House imprint. The first such volume was *Dark of the Moon* (1947), an outstanding 400-page selection of weird and macabre verse from the Middle Ages through to the 1940s. This volume had a print run of 2,634 copies, much the same as the fiction that was published at the same time, but verse did not have the popularity or the selling power of fiction, and future poetry books were printed in significantly lower numbers, usually well below 1,000 copies.

Derleth continued to use Arkham House to publish hardbacks of pulp writers for the rest of his life, including books by E Hoffman Price, Frank Belknap Long, Seabury Quinn, Greye La Spina, Arthur J Burks, Donald Wandrei and Carl Jacobi. Books by well-known "non-pulp" authors such as Lord Dunsany, J Sheridan le Fanu, Algernon Blackwood and Cynthia Asquith also appeared – but Derleth was interested in fostering new talent too. Consequently, the Arkham House imprint saw the first books by Robert Bloch, Fritz Leiber and Ray Bradbury, as well as those of Ramsey Campbell and Brian Lumley in later years.

With *Night's Yawning Peal* (1952), Derleth instituted a series of anthologies that collected macabre tales "never before published in book form". Although this was not quite correct – the book included Lovecraft's *The Case of Charles Dexter Ward*, which had previously been included in *Beyond the Wall of Sleep* (1943) – the periodic publication of anthologies of original tales was maintained. That first book was followed by *Dark Mind, Dark Heart* in 1962, a volume notable for including Ramsey Campbell's first published story, "The Church in High Street". Other anthologies in the series were *Over the Edge* (1964), *Travellers by Night* (1967) and *Dark Things* (1971). An attempt to continue this tradition was made in 1975 with *Nameless Places*, edited by Gerald W Page.

Arkham House never appeared to flourish financially during Derleth's lifetime, and he continued subsidising it throughout, never making any significant money out of publishing. Not that this bothered him. Throughout his life he seemed to almost revel in the difficulties that Arkham House consistently presented. In *Thirty Years of Arkham House* (1970), he said that "…in no single year since its founding have the earnings of Arkham House met the expenses, so that it has been necessary for my personal earnings to shore up Arkham House finances".

This makes the decades during which he ran the imprint all the more remarkable: it really was a labour of love as far as he was concerned. Much of the mediocre fiction that he is accused of writing was almost certainly penned to finance Arkham House, and one has to say that his own reputation as a writer suffered unjustly as a result.

A direct consequence of the financial and storage problems, as well as the demands on Derleth's time and the ill health that dogged him in his later years, was that many books were optimistically announced for publication and then took years to appear. The contract for MP Shiel's *Xélucha and Others* was, for instance, signed in 1947; but the book was not published during Derleth's lifetime, eventually appearing in 1975. Other titles were announced as forthcoming but never appeared, and some were eventually published elsewhere.

Following Derleth's death in 1971, much of the backlist eventually appeared. Once that had been achieved, the new editors branched out; science fiction books began to be published. Derleth had printed one such title himself – *Slan* by AE Van Vogt in 1946 – but it is probably unlikely that he would have sanctioned the plethora of SF books that appeared throughout the 1980s and 90s. But Arkham House as a publisher needed to diversify to maintain its position, and it seemed to have done so with some success. Although little has appeared under the imprint in recent years, they now distribute books published by Fedogan & Bremer, which has produced a number of titles that might have been expected to appear from Arkham House. These include some that had actually been announced but had never appeared, such as *Colossus* by Donald Wandrei, *The Black Death* by Basil Copper and

Time Burial by Howard Wandrei.

In 2009, George Vanderburgh and Robert Weinberg took over the editorial duties at Arkham House. In 2010 there was a two-volume facsimile reissue of the four issues of *The Arkham Sampler*, a magazine that appeared from the publisher in 1948 and 1949; a number of other titles were also announced.

HISTORIES OF THE HISTORY

THERE HAVE BEEN several books covering the history of Arkham House, although they are essentially bibliographic. One of these is *Thirty Years of Arkham House*, written by August Derleth and published in 1970, which gives comprehensive details of all the titles published by Arkham up to 1969 – an update of the author's *Arkham House: The First Twenty Years* (1959). The book features an interesting if brief introduction by Derleth, which mentions that in the first decade of the publishing house's existence, its founder had to subsidise it to the tune of no less than $25,000. In those days, this was a huge amount of money, and thus we should be thankful that Derleth was such a prolific writer so that he could pay the bills.

Thirty Years of Arkham House was updated in *Sixty Years of Arkham House* by ST Joshi (1999), but the text suggests Joshi may not have seen all of the titles commented on. For instance, he says that Derleth's *Mr Fairlie's Final Journey* has "an engaging map of the locale of the crime on the endpapers"; this is erroneous – the map is on the dust-wrapper. He provides a synopsis of *Lord Kelvin's Machine* by

James P Blaylock which is incorrect, and also states that the book is a sequel to *The Digging Leviathan*, which it is not. He indicates that *The Web of Easter Island* is a Cthulhu Mythos novel, which is disputable, and that MP Shiel's *Prince Zaleski and Cummings King Monk* comprises "supernatural adventure stories", which is not the case. He also describes Basil Copper as "a young and dynamic Arkham House author", and although Copper may well have been dynamic he was nearly fifty when Arkham published his first book.

Arkham House Books: A Collector's Guide by Leon Nielsen (2004) is also bibliographical rather than historical. The book is primarily aimed at collectors; consequently it includes estimated values of all the titles, although some of these are open to dispute. For instance, when the book was published it was unlikely that a fine copy of *The Outsider and Others* lacking a dust-wrapper could have been purchased for $400. The book covers the same ground as the Joshi volume but is naturally five years more up to date. Nielsen includes excellent reproductions of the covers of many of the titles, together with full contents listings and indices of the rarest and most valuable titles, and even gives details of stock lists and catalogues. He also includes fascinating details on many aspects of book collecting – all in 200 pages. There are some inaccuracies, such as again describing MP Shiel's *Prince Zaleski and Cummings King Monk* as collecting "the author's supernatural adventure/detective stories", but overall Nielsen's book is accessible and informative.

An earlier book was *The Arkham House Companion* by Sheldon Jaffery, which appeared in 1989. This is also a bibliographical history and collectors' price guide, but it is inevitably dated concerning the market prices of out of print books.

More peripheral is Peter Ruber's *Arkham's Masters of Horror* (1999), which is basically a collection of lesser-known writings by a variety of Arkham House stalwarts. While most of the stories are acceptable enough, it is the editor's introductory essays, prefacing both the collection as a whole and the individual stories, that makes the book particularly interesting. These introductions cast new light on the actual modus operandi of Arkham House and its owner's interaction with the writers. The book also includes Ruber's spirited and insightful article "The Un-Demonising of August Derleth", which is recommended reading, particularly for anyone whose opinion of Derleth remains low.

RARITIES

- The *rarest* Arkham title is difficult to determine. Much depends from which point of view one looks. As far as desirability and collectability is concerned, it is probably *The Outsider and Others;* a particularly good copy in an excellent dust-wrapper was sold on eBay for over $5,500 within the last decade. With a printing of 1,268 copies, it is, however, far from the rarest in terms of the number of books produced. Indeed, the second Lovecraft collection, *Beyond the Wall of Sleep* in 1943, had an even lower print run of 1,217 copies.

- The honour of the lowest overall number of copies produced by Arkham belongs to HP Lovecraft's *The Shunned House*. This volume was first printed in 1928 by W Paul Cook and it was not until 1961 that Arkham bound 100 copies with their imprint on the spine; 50 unbound copies were sold by them two years earlier. This is certainly the rarest of all the titles associated with the publisher, even if it is not strictly an Arkham House book.

- Although 815 copies of August Derleth's *Arkham House: The First Twenty Years* were printed in 1959, only 80 were bound – the rest were sold with wrappers. Thus *The First Twenty Years* had the fewest bound copies of all Arkham books. *100 Books by August Derleth* (1962) had 200 copies bound in boards, with an additional 925 copies in wrappers. It is probable that these small numbers of hardback copies were intended for libraries and/or presentation.

- Only a very small number of the poetry volume *A Hornbook for Witches* by Leah Bodine Drake (1950) were offered for sale. Although 553 copies were printed, 300 of these went to the author (who subsidised the cost), leaving a mere 253 copies available to buy.

- Several titles had printings in the region of 500-600 copies. Most of these were books of verse: Clark Ashton Smith's *The Dark Chateau* (1951), 563 copies, and *Spells and Philtres* (1958), 519 copies, together with Robert E Howard's *Always Comes Evening* (1957), 636 copies, appearing to be the rarest of these. They are infrequently offered for sale and command high prices when they do appear.

- A title with just a 500 copy print run is *Autobiography: Some Notes on a Nonentity* by HP Lovecraft. This essay, which first appeared in *Beyond the Wall of Sleep,* was reprinted as a seventeen-page booklet in 1963 with annotations by August Derleth.

- Although the majority of the publications did (and still do) include a limitation notice at the back of each book detailing the approximate numbers produced, some print runs are unknown. Derleth's anthology *Night's Yawning Peal* (1952) is an example of the second printing being far rarer than the first. At the time of writing, this rarity is reflected by the several copies of the first edition that are available via Abe Books, signed, at around $250; but there is only one copy of the second printing, unsigned, at $560.

MISCELLANY

- There has been a marked slowdown in the production of books in the last decade or so, with just one new title appearing each year between 2002 and 2006, and nothing else until 2010, with the reprinting of *The Arkham Sampler*. This represents the least productive period in the publisher's history. Prior to this, there were only three years during which no new titles were published: 1940, 1955 and 1997 – although 1956 came close when just a single thirty-two page promotional pamphlet appeared.

- The peak years were 1946, which saw nine titles appear, all from Arkham House, and 1948 when the same number was published, six from Arkham and three from Stanton & Lee. In later years the most fruitful was 1971 which, in the wake of August Derleth's death, saw eight Arkham books published.

- In terms of actual numbers of books produced, the overall print run in 1975 tops the list with 36,330, followed by 27,271 in 1946 and 25,182 in 1971. The latter year's figures included several reprinted titles.

- As mentioned previously in this article, some books took a long time to sell out their whole print run. This is still the case – at the time of writing, the Arkham House website lists the following titles as still in print, more than thirty years after their original publication:

Collected Ghost Stories by Mary E Wilkins-Freeman (1974)
The Purcell Papers by J Sheridan Le Fanu (1975)
Harrigan's File by August Derleth (1975)
Kecksies and Other Twilight Tales by Marjorie Bowen (1976)

- Even a book such as Robert E Howard's *Always Comes Evening*, with a print run of only 636 copies, took nearly eight years to sell out. On average, that means less than two copies a week were sold.

- There are likely to be future Mycroft & Moran (M&M) titles. George A Vanderburgh has announced *The Complete Adventures of Judge Peck* by August Derleth, under a licensing agreement with M&M. It would appear that there are other recent Mycroft & Moran books already issued by Vanderburgh: their website lists a number of August Derleth's juvenile detective novels, the Mill Creek Irregulars series.

- Two titles were subsidised by their authors for publication: Seabury Quinn's *Roads* (1948) and Leah Bodine Drake's *A Hornbook for Witches* (1950), while Robert E Howard's *Always Comes Evening* (1957) was funded by Glenn Lord.

- The vast majority of the books were printed by the Collegiate Press, George Banta Publishing Company, of Wisconsin, and bound in Holliston Black Novelex. There are exceptions: two 1952 titles, David H Keller's *Tales from Underwood* and the Derleth-edited anthology *Night's Yawning Peal* were produced for Arkham House by Pellegrini & Cudahy with bindings that were brown and grey respectively.

- Villiers Publications Ltd in England also printed and published several titles for Arkham. These were the booklet *Autobiography: Some Notes on a Nonentity* by HP Lovecraft (1963); and the three verse collections *Nightmare Need* (1964) by Joseph Payne Brennan, which has a red cloth binding; Stanley McNail's *Something Breathing* (1965), with a green binding; and L Sprague de Camp's *Demons and Dinosaurs* (1970), which has the traditional black cloth. The last Stanton & Lee book, Meridel Le Sueur's *Corn Village: A Selection* (1970) was also printed by Villiers Publications.

- Evangeline Walton's *Witch House* (1945) seems to be the only title with *green* lettering on the book's spine, rather than the normal gold. *Witch House* was also the first original novel that appeared under the Arkham imprint. It was announced as the beginning of the "Library of Arkham House Novels of Fantasy and Terror", but the series was short lived. Other titles were announced as forthcoming, and the majority of them did eventually appear, but only one further volume appeared under the designated "Library" heading: *The Lurker at the Threshold* by HP Lovecraft and August Derleth (1945).

- Joseph Payne Brennan's *Nine Horrors and a Dream* (1958) is titled simply *Nine Horrors* on the dust-wrapper's cover and spine, as well as on the spine of the book itself. Apparently the book was originally intended to be called *Nine Horrors*, and it was late in the day that the decision was taken to include an extra story.

- *3 Tales Of Horror* (1967) by HP Lovecraft was originally titled *3 Arkham Tales* until it was realised that one of the stories in question was "The Dunwich Horror".

- Seabury Quinn's *The Phantom Fighter* (1966) indicates that the publisher is Arkham House on the dust-wrapper but as Mycroft & Moran on both the spine of the book and the copyright page.

- There is also a discrepancy in the two volume collection *The Solar Pons Omnibus* (1982) by August Derleth. The spine and the title page show Arkham House as the publisher, but the first page and the copyright details indicate it as a "Mycroft & Moran book".

- Clark Ashton Smith's *Out of Space and Time* (1942) was the third Arkham title to be published. Smith had wanted the volume to be titled *The End of the Story and Other Tales*. Derleth's original choice for the title was *Out of Space, Out of Time*.

- Other books that had title changes include Ramsey Campbell's *The Inhabitant of the Lake and Less Welcome Tenants* (1964), which was originally announced as *The Box In The Priory* (although Campbell's preferred title was *The Render of the Veils*), and the same author's *Demons by Daylight* (1973), originally *Gardens of Night*.

- One title was never copyrighted: August Derleth's book *Some Notes on HP Lovecraft* (1959).

- *New Horizons*, an anthology compiled by Derleth in the 1960s, was published in June 1999, although the book shows the date as 1998.

- Apart from the several Lovecraft volumes, there were only two other titles that were reprinted during Derleth's lifetime. These were his own *Someone in the Dark* (1941, reprinted 1965) and his anthology *Night's Yawning Peal* (1952, reprint date unknown).

- There have been four other reprints in the last twenty-five years, excluding Lovecraft titles. These were Basil Copper's *Necropolis* (1980, reprinted 1981), Greg Bear's *Wind From a Burning Woman* (1982, 1983), Clark Ashton Smith's *Rendezvous in Averoigne* (1988, 2003), and Lucius Shepard's *The Jaguar Hunter* (1987, 1987).

- None of the Mycroft & Moran titles were reprinted, but two of Derleth's Stanton & Lee books were: *Bright Journey* (1953) and *Wind over Wisconsin* (1957).

- The *four* printings of *Bright Journey* between 1953 and 1968, totalling 6,531 copies in all, make it arguably the most successful non-Lovecraft book produced by any of the three imprints during Derleth's lifetime.

- *Tales of the Cthulhu Mythos* has been printed twice (1969 and 1990), but the later version, edited by James Turner, was a revised edition of the original August Derleth-edited anthology, with some stories omitted and others added.

- The highest individual print run of any Arkham House book to date is the 7,015 for the initial printing of the revised *Tales of the Cthulhu Mythos* in 1990. The highest combined figure, taking into account reprints, is Lovecraft's *The Dunwich Horror and Others*, totalling in excess of 40,000. The runners up are the same author's *At the Mountains of Madness and Other Novels* and *Dagon and Other Macabre Tales*.

- *Dark of the Moon* (1947) had one printing but two dust-wrappers. The photographic jacket was lettered by Frank Utpatel but later redesigned by Gary Gore. The second state actually looks a lot better; the lettering on the original version is dark green and merges too much with the dark background. *Dark of the Moon* is also the only book for which an errata slip was prepared; several of the poems had been incorrectly credited on the copyright page.

- Two paperback books have been published by Arkham House – *The Black Book of Clark Ashton Smith* (1979) and Richard Tierney's *Collected Poems* (1981) – although a number of the earlier titles were in the form of booklets or bound with paper wrappers.

- The well-known Arkham House colophon, designed by Frank Utpatel, was not present from the start. It first appeared in Donald Wandrei's *The Eye and the Finger* in 1944.

- The Mycroft & Moran colophon, designed by Ronald Clyne, was used from the very first book, August Derleth's *In Re: Sherlock Homes* (1945). Clyne also designed the main Stanton & Lee colophon, although the original version, which was used in Derleth's *Evening in Spring* (1945), was produced by Howard Wandrei.

- Arkham's first four-colour dust-wrapper (by Hannes Bok) appeared in 1946 for *The House on the Borderland* and the first Arkham book containing interior illustrations was Seabury Quinn's Roads in 1948, with artwork by Virgil Finlay.

- The artists responsible for the most covers for all three imprints were Frank Utpatel, with a total of forty-seven, followed by Ronald Clyne with thirty-one. Utpatel's first cover was in 1941 for

Derleth's *Someone in the Dark*. He was responsible for six out of the seven for 1964 (the interloper was Lee Brown Coye).

- Clyne made his debut with Derleth's *Something Near* in 1945. He produced all five Arkham House covers in 1945. Stephen Fabian did eight out of eleven covers between 1976 and 1981.

FINIS

OVER THE YEARS, Arkham House had become something of an institution. Its achievement far surpassed anything that could possibly have been anticipated by its founders in 1939, with many of the books acquiring near-legendary status in weird fiction.

Nevertheless, although its diversification into other areas has led to its becoming more successful than it ever was in August Derleth's time, this author argues that the imprint has lost much of its charisma since its founder's death, and it no longer has the appeal it once possessed. It has become just another specialty publisher with little to distinguish it from its competitors. Even so, Arkham House has historically established its own important niche in the development of the literature of the weird. The inspiration for its formation was HP Lovecraft, and if Derleth and Wandrei had never done anything about their youthfully enthusiastic idea of preserving his work back in the 1930s, then we would be all the poorer for the lack of many fine books from many fine writers.

BIBLIOGRAPHY

Arkham House

The Outsider and Others – HP Lovecraft 1939

Someone in the Dark – August Derleth 1941

Out of Space and Time – Clark Ashton Smith 1942

Beyond the Wall of Sleep – HP Lovecraft 1943

The Eye and the Finger – Donald Wandrei 1944

Jumbee and Other Uncanny Tales – Henry S Whitehead 1944

Lost Worlds – Clark Ashton Smith 1944

Marginalia – HP Lovecraft 1944

Something Near – August Derleth 1945

The Opener of the Way – Robert Bloch 1945

Witch House – Evangeline Walton 1945

Green Tea and Other Ghost Stories – J Sheridan Le Fanu 1945

The Lurker at the Threshold – HP Lovecraft and August Derleth 1945

The Hounds of Tindalos – Frank Belknap Long 1946

The Doll and One Other – Algernon Blackwood 1946

The House on the Borderland and Other Novels – William Hope Hodgson 1946

Skull-Face and Others – Robert E Howard 1946

West India Lights – Henry S Whitehead 1946

August Derleth: Twenty Years of Writing – August Derleth 1946

Fearful Pleasures – AE Coppard 1946

The Clock Strikes Twelve – H Russell Wakefield 1946

Slan – AE Van Vogt 1946

This Mortal Coil – Cynthia Asquith 1947

Dark of the Moon – edited by August Derleth 1947

Dark Carnival – Ray Bradbury 1947

Revelations in Black – Carl Jacobi 1947

Night's Black Agents – Fritz Leiber 1947

The Arkham Sampler – edited by August Derleth 1948/9 (8 issues)

The Travelling Grave and Other Stories – LP Hartley 1948

The Web of Easter Island – Donald Wandrei 1948

The Fourth Book of Jorkens – Lord Dunsany 1948

Roads – Seabury Quinn 1948

Genius Loci and Other Tales – Clark Ashton Smith 1948

Not Long for this World – August Derleth 1948

Something About Cats and Other Pieces – HP Lovecraft 1949

The Throne of Saturn – S Fowler Wright 1949

A Hornbook for Witches – Leah Bodine Drake 1950

August Derleth: Twenty-Five Years of Writing – August Derleth 1951

The Dark Chateau – Clark Ashton Smith 1951

Tales from Underwood – David H Keller 1952

Night's Yawning Peal – edited by August Derleth 1952

The Curse of Yig – Zealia B Bishop 1953

The Feasting Dead – John Metcalfe 1954

August Derleth: Thirty Years of Writing – August Derleth 1956

The Survivor and Others – HP Lovecraft and August Derleth 1957

Always Comes Evening – Robert E Howard 1957

Spells and Philtres – Clark Ashton Smith 1958

The Mask of Cthulhu – August Derleth 1958

Nine Horrors and a Dream – Joseph Payne Brennan 1958

Arkham House: the First Twenty Years – August Derleth 1959

Some Notes on HP Lovecraft – August Derleth 1959

The Shuttered Room and Other Pieces – HP Lovecraft and Divers Hands 1959

The Abominations of Yondo – Clark Ashton Smith 1960

Pleasant Dreams – Robert Bloch 1960

Invaders from the Dark – Greye La Spina 1960

Strayers from Sheol – H Russell Wakefield 1961

Fire and Sleet and Candlelight – edited by August Derleth 1961

The Shunned House – HP Lovecraft 1961

Dreams and Fancies – HP Lovecraft 1962

Lonesome Places – August Derleth 1962

Dark Mind, Dark Heart – edited by August Derleth 1962

100 Hundred Books by August Derleth – August Derleth 1962

The Trail of Cthulhu – August Derleth 1962

The Dunwich Horror and Others – HP Lovecraft 1963

Collected Poems – HP Lovecraft 1963

Who Fears the Devil? – Manly Wade Wellman 1963

Mr George and Other Odd Persons – Stephen Grendon 1963

The Dark Man and Others – Robert E Howard 1963

The Horror from the Hills – Frank Belknap Long 1963

Autobiography: Some Notes on a Nonentity – HP Lovecraft 1963

AH 1939-1964: 25th Anniversary – August Derleth 1964

The Inhabitant of the Lake and Less Welcome Tenants – J Ramsey Campbell 1964

Poems for Midnight – Donald Wandrei 1964

Over the Edge – edited by August Derleth 1964

At the Mountains of Madness and Other Novels – HP Lovecraft 1964

Portraits in Moonlight – Carl Jacobi 1964

Tales of Science and Sorcery – Clark Ashton Smith 1964

Nightmare Need – Joseph Payne Brennan 1964

Selected Letters I – HP Lovecraft 1965

Poems in Prose – Clark Ashton Smith 1965

Dagon and Other Macabre Tales – HP Lovecraft 1965

Something Breathing – Stanley McNail 1965

The Quick and the Dead – Vincent Starrett 1965

Strange Harvest – Donald Wandrei 1965

The Dark Brotherhood and Other Pieces – HP Lovecraft and Divers Hands 1966

Colonel Markesan and Less Pleasant People – August Derleth and Mark Schorer 1966

Black Medicine – Arthur J Burks 1966

Deep Waters – William Hope Hodgson 1967

Travellers by Night – edited by August Derleth 1967

The Arkham Collector – edited by August Derleth 1967/71(10 issues)

The Mind Parasites – Colin Wilson 1967

3 Tales of Horror – HP Lovecraft 1967

Strange Gateways – E Hoffmann Price 1967

The Green Round – Arthur Machen 1968

Selected Letters II – HP Lovecraft 1968

Nightmares and Daydreams – Nelson Bond 1968

Tales of the Cthulhu Mythos – HP Lovecraft and Others 1969

The Folsom Flint and Other Curious Tales – David H Keller 1969

Thirty Years of Arkham House – August Derleth 1970

Demons and Dinosaurs – L Sprague de Camp 1970

Other Dimensions – Clark Ashton Smith 1970

The Horror in the Museum and Other Revisions – HP Lovecraft 1970

Selected Poems – Clark Ashton Smith 1971

The Face in the Mirror – Denys Val Baker 1971

Eight Tales – Walter de la Mare 1971

Dark Things – edited by August Derleth 1971

Songs and Sonnets Atlantean – Donald S Fryer 1971

Selected Letters III – HP Lovecraft 1971

The Caller of the Black – Brian Lumley 1971

The Arkham Collector: Volume 1 – edited by August Derleth 1971

Disclosures in Scarlet – Carl Jacobi 1972

The Rim of the Unknown – Frank Belknap Long 1972

Stories of Darkness and Dread – Joseph Payne Brennan 1973

Demons by Daylight – Ramsey Campbell 1973

From Evil's Pillow – Basil Copper 1973

Beneath the Moors – Brian Lumley 1974

The Watchers Out of Time and Others – HP Lovecraft and August Derleth 1974

Collected Ghost Stories – Mary E Wilkins-Freeman 1974

Howard Phillips Lovecraft: Dreamer on the Nightside – Frank Belknap Long 1975

The House of the Worm – Gary Myers 1975

Nameless Places – edited by Gerald W Page 1975

The Purcell Papers – J Sheridan Le Fanu 1975

Dreams from R'lyeh – Lin Carter 1975

Harrigan's File – August Derleth 1975

Xélucha and Others – MP Shiel 1975

Literary Swordsmen and Sorcerers – L Sprague de Camp 1976

The Height of the Scream – Ramsey Campbell 1976

Dwellers in Darkness – August Derleth 1976

Selected Letters IV – HP Lovecraft 1976

Selected Letters V – HP Lovecraft 1976

Kecksies and Other Twilight Tales – Marjorie Bowen 1976

The Horror at Oakdeene and Others – Brian Lumley 1977

And Afterwards, the Dark – Basil Copper 1977

In Mayan Splendor – Frank Belknap Long 1977

Half in Shadow – Mary Elizabeth Counselman 1978

Born to Exile – Phyllis Eisenstein 1978

The Black Book of Clark Ashton Smith – Clark Ashton Smith 1979

The Princess of All Lands – Russell Kirk 1979

In the Mist and Other Uncanny Encounters – Elizabeth Walter 1979

New Tales of the Cthulhu Mythos – edited by Ramsey Campbell 1980

Necropolis – Basil Copper 1980

The Third Grave – David Case 1981

Tales from the Nightside – Charles L Grant 1981

Collected Poems – Richard L Tierney 1981

Blooded on Arachne – Michael Bishop 1981

The Darkling – David Kesterton 1982

The Wind from a Burning Woman – Greg Bear 1982

The House of the Wolf – Basil Copper 1983

The Zanzibar Cat – Joanna Russ 1983

One Winter in Eden – Michael Bishop 1984

Watchers at the Strait Gate – Russell Kirk 1984

Who Made Stevie Cry? – Michael Bishop 1984

Lovecraft's Book – Richard A Lupoff 1985

Tales of the Quintana Roo – James Tiptree Jr 1986

Dreams of Dark and Light – Tanith Lee 1986

The Jaguar Hunter – Lucius Shepard 1987

Polyphemus – Michael Shea 1987

A Rendezvous in Averoigne – Clark Ashton Smith 1988

Memories of the Space Age – JG Ballard 1988

Crystal Express – Bruce Sterling 1989

Her Smoke Rose up Forever – James Tiptree Jr 1990

Tales of the Cthulhu Mythos (revised) – edited by James Turner 1990

Gravity's Angels – Michael Swanwick 1991

The Ends of the Earth – Lucius Shepard 1991

Lord Kelvin's Machine – James P Blaylock 1992

Meeting in Infinity – John Kessel 1992

The Aliens of Earth – Nancy Kress 1993

Alone with the Horrors – Ramsey Campbell 1993

The Breath of Suspension – Alexander Jablokov 1994

Cthulhu 2000 – edited by James Turner 1995

Miscellaneous Writings – HP Lovecraft 1995

Synthesis & Other Virtual Realities – Mary Rosenblum 1996

Voyages by Starlight – Ian R McLeod 1996

Flowers from the Moon and Other Lunacies – Robert Bloch 1998

Lovecraft Remembered – edited by Peter Cannon 1998

New Horizons – edited by August Derleth 1999

Dragonfly – Frederic S Durbin 1999

Sixty Years of Arkham House – edited by ST Joshi 1999

Arkham's Masters of Horror – edited by Peter Ruber 1999

In the Stone House – Barry N Malzberg 2000

Book of the Dead – E Hoffman Price 2001

The Far Side of Nowhere – Nelson Bond 2001

The Cleansing – John D Harvey 2002

Selected Letters of Clark Ashton Smith – edited by David E Schultz and Scott Connors 2003

Cave of a Thousand Tales: the Life and Times of Hugh B Cave – Milt Thomas 2004

Other Worlds than Ours – Nelson Bond 2005

Evermore – edited by James Robert Smith and Stephen Mark Rainey 2006

Mycroft & Moran

In Re: Sherlock Holmes – August Derleth 1945

Carnacki, the Ghost-Finder – William Hope Hodgson 1947

The Memoirs of Solar Pons – August Derleth 1951

Three Problems for Solar Pons – August Derleth 1952

The Return of Solar Pons – August Derleth 1958

The Reminiscences of Solar Pons – August Derleth 1961

The Casebook of Solar Pons – August Derleth 1965

The Phantom-Fighter – Seabury Quinn 1966

A Praed Street Dossier – August Derleth 1968

The Exploits of the Chevalier Dupin – Michael Harrison 1968

Wisconsin Murders – August Derleth 1968

The Adventure of the Unique Dickensians – August Derleth 1968

Mr Fairlie's Final Journey – August Derleth 1968

Number Seven, Queer Street – Margery Lawrence 1969

The Chronicles of Solar Pons – August Derleth 1973

Prince Zaleski and Cummings King Monk – MP Shiel 1977

The Solar Pons Omnibus – August Derleth 1982

The Final Adventures of Solar Pons – August Derleth 1998

In Lovecraft's Shadow – August Derleth 1998

The Original Text Solar Pons Omnibus – August Derleth 2001

Baker Street Irregular – Jon Lellenberg 2010

Stanton & Lee

Bill's Diary – Clare Victor Dwiggins 1945

Evening in Spring – August Derleth 1945

Oliver, the Wayward Owl – August Derleth 1945

A Boy's Way – August Derleth 1947

Wisconsin Earth: A Sac Prairie Sampler – August Derleth 1948

Sac Prairie People – August Derleth 1948

It's a Boy's World – August Derleth 1948

Bright Journey – August Derleth 1953

Wind over Wisconsin – August Derleth 1957

Wilbur, the Trusting Whippoorwill – August Derleth 1959

Restless is the River – August Derleth 1965

A Wisconsin Harvest – edited by August Derleth 1966

The House on the Mound – August Derleth 1966

Eyes of the Mole – Jane Stuart 1967

New Poetry out of Wisconsin – edited by August Derleth 1969

Corn Village: A Selection – Meridel Le Sueur 1970

44 / Doors to Elsewhere

WEAVER OF WEIRD TALES
GREYE LA SPINA

ALTHOUGH LARGELY FORGOTTEN today, Greye La Spina was the author of many fine stories in the supernatural genre. The bulk of these were published in pulp magazines. In the 1920s she became the first regular female contributor to *Weird Tales*, continuing to feature in its pages for nearly three decades. Much of her longer fiction, which was in the Gothic tradition, was of consistently good quality; and some of her shorter pieces – "The Wax Doll", "The Dead-Wagon", "The Rat Master" and "A Suitor from the Shades" for instance – are just as fresh today as they were when they first appeared.

Her most renowned work, the novel *Invaders from the Dark*, was one of a number of skilfully crafted werewolf stories. In addition, she utilised the themes of vampirism, devil worship, Voodoo and possession, as well as traditional ghost stories encompassing such subject matter as family curses, hauntings, and post-mortem revenge. However, much of her writing was far from traditional, and in many instances her perspective was distinctly inventive.

La Spina wrote four serials for *Weird Tales* between 1925 and 1930; each covered standard themes but in more imaginative ways than the fiction of many of her contemporaries. This is particularly demonstrated in *Invaders from the Dark*, which features a beautiful and seductive female werewolf, thus utilising a standard vampire motif, but in a lycanthropy setting. When vampires do appear, as in the serial *Fettered*, the story progresses in a far from orthodox manner. Likewise, the plots of *The Gargoyle* and *The Portal to Power* incorporate distinct departures from the normal pattern of such tales.

Her sometimes melodramatic style is admittedly a little old-fashioned by today's standards, but this is simply an indication of the times in which her tales were written. This dated aspect is present in varying areas – few modern books have heroines with names such as Portia Differman or Bessie Gillespie, or characters who say, "I cannot deny that your words are couched in a sophistry that carries reluctant conviction to my intellect", and even fewer have scenes in which someone inadvertently says, "Damn", and is highly embarrassed at her use of that sort of language. This reflection of the style and the literary attitudes prevalent in the 1920s does generate a certain nostalgic appeal to the writing, but the verve of the narratives and their created moods make the tales memorable in their own right. Ultimately they preserve their ability to entertain not simply because they are period pieces, but because they tell interesting stories in interesting ways and, most important of all, they are thoroughly enjoyable.

BORN FANNY GREYE Bragg on 10 July 1880 in Wakefield, Massachusetts, Greye La Spina led what seems to have been an eventful early life. She was married at eighteen, a mother at twenty and a widow at twenty-one, having already travelled much of the world. She was reputedly the first woman newspaper photographer in New York and was a self-taught master weaver – her publishing debut was the article "Popular Venetian Crochet", which appeared in the December 1915 edition of *McCalls* magazine. She was by this time married to an Italian aristocrat named Robert La Spina and had as a consequence become the Baroness di Savuto in 1910.

Her first work of fiction was "Wolf of the Steppes" for which she received $50. Originally submitted to *The Popular Magazine* in 1918, it became the cover story for the initial issue of a new title from the same publisher, *The Thrill Book*, in 1919. This twice-monthly periodical did not last for long, but was very much a forerunner to

Weird Tales. Featuring "strange, bizarre, occult, mysterious tales", it was probably the earliest magazine to print primarily science fiction and fantasy; published authors included pulp stalwarts such as Seabury Quinn, Murray Leinster and H Bedford-Jones. Clark Ashton Smith also appeared in its pages with the poem "Dissonance".

According to the author, "Wolf of the Steppes" was the first professional story that she wrote and sold, but it does not appear to have been the first of her fiction to be published, for a tale entitled "In the Fable's Heart" by Baroness di Savuto appeared in *Top-Notch Magazine* for 15 October 1918. *Top-Notch* was a Street & Smith publication (as were *The Popular Magazine* and *The Thrill Book*), so La Spina could well have decided that she would try her luck with the same publisher which had already accepted her first submission. The Baroness di Savuto was of course La Spina's aristocratic name, and it seems highly unlikely that there would have been a similarly-titled lady contributing to a Street & Smith periodical at the same time. Although the appearance of "In the Fable's Heart" pre-dates "Wolf of the Steppes", the latter story could perhaps have been deliberately held over for the launch of *The Thrill Book* several months later.

Whatever the facts of the matter, she was still an unknown author and it seems surprising that the cover of the premiere issue of *The Thrill Book* was given over to her. "Wolf of the Steppes" did not, however, disappoint. It is an accomplished story of lycanthropy, told in an epistolary form through extracts from letters and journals, and revolves around a beautiful young girl who is being menaced by grim forces, and who is eventually rescued by an occult expert who is able to combat the dangers. Well written and intriguing, with appealing characters and a compelling storyline, this was an auspicious debut which boded well for the future.

The editor of *The Thrill Book*, Harold B Hersey, clearly liked La Spina's work, and a number of her contributions followed, in both her own name and using pseudonyms. Three very short pieces were published under the name of Isra Putnam, while a longer story, "The Wax Doll", had the almost identical by-line of *Ezra* Putnam. In any event, the author's identity in the latter case was not exactly hidden – the issue preceding "The Wax Doll" mentions it as forthcoming, but as being "by Greye La Spina"! All of these tales featured elements of the fantastic: "From Over the Border" tells of a murderously bizarre method of revenge from beyond the grave; "The Ultimate Ingredient" is about an unscrupulous scientist who makes himself invisible by using human blood; and "The Haunted Landscape" concerns a dead artist who animates one of his own paintings to show that his supposed suicide was no suicide at all.

The best of these early stories was certainly "The Wax Doll", an affecting tale of a lonely child whose intense love for her only plaything outlasts her cheerless life. Touching and eerie, it is outstandingly well told, its atmosphere of uncanny tragedy firmly established in the opening lines and expertly sustained throughout. The Butterworths' religious fanaticism and its dire consequences are starkly conveyed, and Anice is a sad little character whose presence stays with the reader long after the narrative is concluded.

The Thrill Book lasted for only sixteen issues. After its demise La Spina made use of another market, *Black Mask* magazine, and her lightweight piece "The Seventh Step" appeared in the second issue in 1920. This tale of a missing will was fairly straightforward but incorporated a ghostly element that was uncommon for the magazine and which demonstrated the author's affinity for that type of fiction. In 1921 she won second place in *Photoplay's* short story contest for the mainstream offering "A Seat on the Platform", gaining a handsome prize of $2,500. During this same period, she also had non-weird fiction published in *Action Stories* ("The Winged Death", for example, was in the debut issue of that publication) and various other periodicals, including *Telling Tales* and *Metropolitan*, although as she later told August Derleth, she "liked the occult and supernatural best".

THE ADVENT OF *Weird Tales* in 1923 must therefore have been of great appeal to her, since it published the sort of stories that La Spina preferred to write. However, when she sent *Invaders from the Dark* to the new periodical, it was rejected as being "too commonplace" by the then editor Edwin Baird. This did not stop her from continuing to submit stories, and her first accepted contribution was "The Tortoise-Shell Cat", which appeared in November 1924, marking the beginning of a productive period that saw her become a regular contributor to the magazine.

"The Tortoise-Shell Cat" was an account of shape-shifting, and as with "Wolf of the Steppes", uses an epistolic format. It tells of the friendship between Althea Benedict and the beautiful but strange Vida di Monserreau, whose life is controlled and dominated by the powers of a vengeful Voodoo priestess. While the ending is somewhat contrived, depending a little too much on coincidence, the story has force and is written with style and assurance.

Several more short stories followed, and within six months *Invaders from the Dark* appeared as a three-part serial, having been accepted on resubmission by the new editor Farnsworth Wright. This proved to be very popular, with such authors as Arthur J Burks, CM

Eddy Jr and Seabury Quinn singing its praises; it is indeed a fine work. Set in Brooklyn (thinly disguised as *Lynbrook*) a few years before the First World War, it tells of the appearance of the mysterious Princess Tchernova and her attempts to seduce Owen Edwardes into becoming her wolf-lover. Her adversary is Portia Differman, who is in love with Owen herself and who is an expert on occult lore, but who naturally finds it difficult to persuade the townsfolk that there is a werewolf in their midst. Aided only by her initially sceptical Aunt Sophie, she sets about combating the menace; but the deaths begin and the Princess seems to be too powerful for Portia to defeat, although needless to say her efforts are ultimately not in vain.

Although written in the 1920s, and slightly revised for its book publication by Arkham House in 1960, it is still very readable today. The characters are strongly defined, the pacing of the story is astutely controlled, and the descriptive passages are well wrought. The plot is compelling, unfolding at a steadily increasing tempo, and achieves its chilling effect through skilful use of atmosphere rather than any recourse to explicit description. There are only limited graphic scenes, with much of the horror implicit – the Princess's meat order for instance is drastically reduced whenever one of the townsfolk goes missing…

The book moves soundly towards its conclusion, which resolves matters with two separate climaxes. The first takes place off-stage, related by a third party, but is none the less powerful for that, with the final scenes in the Burnham House impressive in their dramatic imagery. This is followed by an equally commanding aftermath as Portia struggles against the evil powers holding Owen in thrall. There is thus a dual culmination to the main plot, with a fiery finale on the physical plane followed by a supernatural coda that merges seamlessly with preceding events and avoids any sense of anticlimax. Even then, the story is not over, for the final chapter completes the circle and takes the reader back to the opening pages, but this time from a different character's viewpoint.

The combined themes of horror and romance are of course staple ingredients of the Gothic novel, but *Invaders from the Dark* never becomes overly melodramatic; the romantic element is also subdued, overshadowed by plot development and the confrontation between good and evil. The book furthermore lacks the stereotypical Gothic-lead characters. Portia, with her mystical expertise, is hardly a typical heroine and her strength of character and moral conviction are such that she even accepts that she may need to stand by and sacrifice Owen for the greater good.

There is an interesting element of spirituality as an undercurrent to the story, and an emphasis that the incidents being related are simply a part of the ongoing struggle against Evil. The closing chapter, sad but uplifting, signifies the end of a battle that has been successfully fought but which gives little respite to its participants – triumph can only be savoured to a limited degree, for the war continues, and the fate of one individual matters little in this arena.

WITHIN A FEW months of *Invaders from the Dark*, a second La Spina serial, *The Gargoyle*, appeared, and in the following year a third, *Fettered*, featured in four successive issues. This meant that in an eighteen month period she had three successive serials published in *Weird Tales*, and each of them characteristically provided inventive variations on standard scenarios. All of these titles worked well in their serialised format; without reverting to cliff-hanger endings to each instalment, La Spina had the ability to draw her readers into the narrative and make them eager to know how the plot was going to develop. Nor did the finales disappoint; they were not always wholly conventional but they were always satisfying.

The Gargoyle is a tale of devil worship in which Luke Porter finds himself a prisoner at Fanewold, a replica of a moated, medieval castle built deep in the secluded Pennsylvania woods. He is being manipulated by the deformed and evil Guy Fane, who intends to change bodies with him, achieving this by supplicating the Devil through worship and blood sacrifice. The victim is to be Sybil Fane, his beautiful and chaste half-sister, who has never been outside the castle grounds in her entire life and whose innocence is a key factor in Guy's plans.

THE GARGOYLE by Greye La Spina
A TALE OF DEVIL WORSHIP

Inevitably, Sybil and Luke fall in love, and Luke's apparently archetypal role as the fearless hero leads the reader to assume that he will be the driving force in rescuing Sybil from the fate that awaits her at her brother's hands. There is, however, a twist to the fast moving plot, and things do not develop as anticipated: Guy's mystical powers are far too strong, and ultimately Luke is easily defeated and left immobilised and completely unable to act. Salvation for the two young lovers instead comes from unexpected sources, although in ways that are completely acceptable in the context of the tale.

The story works well, and there is again the underlying theme of occult conflict which appears in much of the longer fiction. In a 1942 letter to *Weird Tales*, La Spina said: "I steadfastly believe that Light will always conquer Darkness ... that in the lowest of creatures there frequently is a responsive chord to what is highest in human beings. That note runs through all I've ever written".

This philosophy is certainly evident in *The Gargoyle*, where the triumph of good over evil is brought about with selfless sacrifices by lesser characters.

The tale does in fact seem to be an extended reworking of "The Ultimate Ingredient", which had appeared some six years earlier in *The Thrill Book*. Even though the basic premise is quite different, the plot does utilise many features from that earlier story; there is an isolated family home, a beautiful woman in mortal peril from an evil sibling, the influential impact of an outsider who is in love with the heroine, a weak character who unpredictably saves the day, and a literally explosive conclusion. Such similarities are unusual in the La Spina canon, and there do not seem to be any other instances of such close parallels between two of her published works.

In 1926 came *Fettered*, with a vampire called Gretel Armitage secluded and semi-imprisoned in the remote woods north of Amity Dam by her husband Dale in an attempt to protect innocents from her bloodlust. But his efforts are in vain, and the arrival of Ewan Gillespie and his twin sister Bessie is the harbinger of events that are to change all of their lives. Ewan is soon a victim of Gretel's seductive wiles, and Bessie finds herself strongly attracted to Dale, who is far from being the villain that he initially seems. All of the characters are "fettered", but in different ways – Gretel by her vampirism, Dale by the guilt he feels, Bessie by her morality and Ewan by his scepticism – with the troubled interaction between the four of them fascinatingly well handled.

The setting of the Northern Woods has dark conviction, and the scenario is capably established in the opening paragraphs, with Bessie and Ewan canoeing upriver as night starts to draw in. Without the need to introduce any specific horror, which is to come later, the author evokes a subtle and unsettling aura of foreboding. The ensuing meeting with Dale and Gretel at dusk reinforces the mood and adds an element of mystery by making it clear that there are depths to the strange couple's enigmatic relationship that it would be better not to plumb.

Characterisation is strong, and the story moves quickly and forcefully towards an engrossing conclusion. There are intriguing developments, and it is a mark of the author's skill that the reader cannot be sure who is going to survive in what is an unpredictable and compelling plot. The tale ends where it began, in a canoe on the river, with all of the fetters having been broken in decisive fashion.

Fettered is possibly the most atmospheric of all La Spina's tales, and also has some of her most potent and memorable scenes. The confrontation between Bessie and Gretel in the aftermath of a far from normal storm has a gripping and palpable tension, while Dale's recounting of the transformation of a supposedly dead corpse is frighteningly effective. The story is enthralling and exciting, ably demonstrating the author's skilled tale-telling and perhaps representing the best of all of her longer fiction.

After *Fettered* came the novelette "A Suitor from the Shades", a fine work relating how Margaret Sloane's impending marriage is threatened by a ghost. As a young girl she had jokingly promised herself to Clifford Bentley, who then died saving her life; but now his spirit is determined to see that Margaret remains true to her word. Her vulnerable sister Clare is the vessel for Clifford's psychic vampirism, enabling him to materialise from the spirit world at her physical expense, until matters are resolved in an unexpectedly poignant manner during a climactic séance. This neatly-crafted tale is unusual and powerful, further emphasising that La Spina's writing was far from formulaic, and ably demonstrating her creative abilities.

"The Dead-Wagon", from later in 1927, is another excellent piece, depicting a curse on the Melverson family, dating from the Plague years, and of the doom that befalls the first born of each generation. The scenes describing the midnight appearances of the death-cart are chillingly powerful, and the ending is dramatic and moving; the story has an evocative authority that lingers in the memory, and it ranks amongst the author's very best fiction.

LA SPINA HAD by this point appeared in sixteen separate issues of *Weird Tales*, making her the most prolific of its relatively few female contributors; her closest rival was Eli (Elizabeth) Colter who featured in twelve issues. "The Dead-Wagon" did, however, mark the start of a hiatus lasting several years before 1930/31 saw the appearance of a new serial, *The Portal to Power*, which was followed by a novelette entitled "The Devil's Pool" in 1932.

In *The Portal to Power*, the "portal" is the Philosopher's Stone, entrusted to Dr John Peabody by the dying witch Hannah Wake as a desperate act of contrition. But the sinister Rex Quint wishes to secure the talisman, and Peabody takes flight for California meaning to deliver it to the safe haven of the Circle of Light. Quint engineers the forcing down of the plane in the Rocky Mountains, and the doctor and a disparate group of individuals are stranded, finding themselves in a hidden valley populated by initiates seeking to summon "Higher Powers" for the good of mankind. Their intentions are wholly altruistic, but Quint has a quite different agenda and intends to use the powers for his own base ends.

The novella is readable enough, but does not have the same impact as its predecessors. After an absorbing and atmospheric opening scene with Peabody and Hannah, culminating in the appearance of the malevolent Quint, the story subsequently loses much of its momentum. More characters are introduced than the story warrants, and it is hampered by implausible romantic sub-plots that have only a peripheral bearing on the narrative. The one "Power" that appears is Pan, although his presence is unconvincing and hardly relevant, and, unusually for La Spina, the ending does leave unanswered questions.

A superior work was "The Devil's Pool"; the pool of the title has the capacity to transform innocent people into werewolves, who then find themselves in thrall to the satanically evil Lem Schwarz. It falls to Mason Hardy to attempt to save his friends from their fate. Although there is more than a touch of a *deus ex machina* ending, with a Holy Wafer solving all the problems, the story is energetically told and is imaginative in its plotting. If it lacks the authoritative strength of such tales as "A Suitor from the Shades" or "The Dead-Wagon", it is still a good story well told.

It is also an example of one of the defining characteristics of most of La Spina's best fiction, that of the remoteness of the locale in which the action occurs. As with both *Fettered* and *The Gargoyle,* the setting of "The Devil's Pool" is not only a major buttress for the development of the story but also adds significantly to the overall effect. Placing the characters in what is basically an inaccessible place sets them apart in more than simply a physical way. The sense of isolation assists the author in creating an underlying atmosphere in which the supernatural can plausibly thrive. Secluded and out-of-the-way locations also feature in "Wolf of the Steppes", "The Haunted Landscape", "The Wax Doll" and "The Ultimate Ingredient", and would also to be used in such powerful later tales as "The Rat Master", "The Deadly Theory" and "The Antimacassar". And while *Invaders from the Dark* may be set in Brooklyn, it is a semi-rural Brooklyn that is far removed from the New York of today.

"The Devil's Pool" also features an archetypal villain in the form of Lem Schwartz, whose leeringly malicious nature has no redeeming features at all. He is therefore similar to Paul Starr in "The Ultimate Ingredient", Guy Fane in *The Gargoyle* and Rex Quint in *The Portal to Power* – although this does not mean that all of La Spina's evil characters were one-dimensional. The malevolence of Clifford Bentley in "A Suitor from the Shades", for example, is eventually shown to be a misunderstood product of desperation, while Dale Armitage's initially sinister presence in *Fettered* is not at all what it appears to be.

LA SPINA APPEARED only once more in the pages of *Weird Tales* during the next decade, with a short story called "The Sinister Painting" in 1934. She did feature in such periodicals as *Bull's Eye Detective*, which featured her short story "Vampire Bite" in 1939, but her writing career had been restricted because she and her husband Robert had bought a farm, Windy Knoll, in Pennsylvania in 1926, and she became fully involved in its running from the mid to late 1930s after Robert's health began to fail.

She returned to *Weird Tales* with "The Rat Master" in March 1942. This insidious and disquieting story sets its scene right from the opening lines, with two desperate people fleeing through dark and windswept woods pursued by unseen and inhuman enemies. It soon becomes apparent that the couple are trying to escape from Dwight Harkness, a black magician who has set an army of rats on their trail. On seeking refuge in an apparently abandoned hovel they find themselves in the company of a baleful individual who is clearly much more than he – or *it* – seems. The tale generates a high level of suspense and the climax, with its deadly confrontation between Harkness and the Rat Master, is forceful and persuasive.

Interestingly, the genesis of "The Rat Master" lies in personal experience. In the previously mentioned letter to *Weird Tales* introducing the story, La Spina said that it:

...was suggested by something ominous about the bold rats we have at Windy Knoll... One of them sat on its haunches on my barn floor, in a beam of light from an electric torch, and bared its teeth at me with such menace that I couldn't get the red, glittering eyes out of my mind until I'd put something on paper that had to do with rats and – yet –

something more *than rats.*

"The Rat Master" was followed by "The Deadly Theory", which is a splendid *conte cruel,* with palingenesis as its premise. When Julian Crosse's beloved Marzha is murdered by her jealous sister Idell, he is persuaded by their uncle to attempt to revive the corpse by occult means. The ritual is successful, but it has consequences that are unexpected and horrific, with Marzha returned to life as she was at the moment of her death, and her soulless revenant sustained by the appalled Julian's blood. Idell's resentful intervention brings further macabre incident until finally the dead are laid to rest, although the final paragraphs cleverly reveal that the attempts at palingenesis did not end where the reader had supposed.

The subsequent tales from the early 1940s were "Death has Red Hair", dealing with a deadly will-o'-the-wisp, and "Great Pan is Here", a fable of sylvan possession. Although pleasing, and serving to demonstrate that La Spina's literary abilities remained nicely honed, these were comparatively lesser works, coming in the wake of the two such exceptional pieces "The Rat Master" and "The Deadly Theory".

Her last two stories for *Weird Tales* also appear to be her last two published works, "The Antimacassar" in 1949 and "Old Mr Wiley" in 1951. The latter is an agreeable if slight tale of a benign spectre, but "The Antimacassar" is outstanding – it combines a sympathetic portrayal of a young girl who is a vampire with a ghost story, as one of the dead victims seeks to warn a friend of her impending fate. It has a haunting atmosphere and forcefulness, with the image of Kathy ("I'm hungry!") lingeringly and plaintively vivid. The vampire here is not an evil character but an innocent victim, knowing nothing different and incapable of changing her nature. And as in *Fettered*, the curse of vampirism is seen to have no cure but death.

GREYE LA SPINA died in her ninetieth year, on 17 September 1969. Despite her many appearances in a variety of different magazines, only one of her works was published in book form during her lifetime, *Invaders from the Dark* in 1960, some thirty-five years after its initial appearance in *Weird Tales*. This Arkham House title was reprinted in paperback by Popular Library as *Shadow of Evil* in 1966 and in France as *Les Envahisseurs De La Nuit* by Galliera in 1973. The only other volume that has appeared under her name to date is *The Gargoyle and One Other*, which included both the title story and "The Devil's Pool", published by Robert Weinberg in 1975. Although her work has been featured in a number of anthologies, many of her stories have never appeared anywhere but in pulp magazines, with the result that some of her best tales are now difficult to find.

It would appear that at least some of La Spina's fiction may be reprinted shortly – at the time of writing, Arkham House has announced the forthcoming publication of *The Gargoyle and Others: A Quarto of Horror*, which will include *Invaders from the Dark*, *The Gargoyle*, *Fettered*, and *The Portal to Power*. Depending on readers' response, this could be followed by a second collection.

Although virtually forgotten, Greye La Spina made lasting contributions to the annals of weird fiction, and her status in the field has been underestimated and overlooked for many years. Her work may today be considered passé and overdramatic, but seeking out her long neglected fiction is a rewarding exercise. The discovery of such stories as *Fettered*, "A Suitor from the Shades", "The Rat Master" and "The Deadly Theory" in the fragile pages of old copies of *Weird Tales* is a pleasure that may be reserved for the few, but which nonetheless will bring much satisfaction to those who make the effort.

SELECTED BIBLIOGRAPHY

Appearances in *The Thrill Book*

"Wolf of the Steppes" – 1 March 1919

"The Broken Idol" – as Isra Putnam, 15 March 1919

"The Miser's Stratagem" – as Isra Putnam, 15 March 1919

"The Inefficient Ghost" – as Isra Putnam, 1 May 1919

"From Over the Border" – 15 May 1919

"The Haunted Landscape" – 1 June 1919

"The Wax Doll" – as Ezra Putnam, 1 August 1919

"The Ultimate Ingredient" – 15 October 1919

Appearances in *Weird Tales*

"The Tortoise-Shell Cat" – November 1924

"The Remorse of Professor Panebianco" – January 1925

"The Scarf of the Beloved" – February 1925

"The Last Cigarette" – March 1925

Invaders from the Dark – serial, April/May/June 1925

The Gargoyle – serial, September/October/November 1925

Fettered – serial, July/August/September/October 1926

"A Suitor from the Shades" – June 1927

"The Dead-Wagon" – September 1927

The Portal to Power – serial, October/ November/ December 1930/ January 1931

"The Devil's Pool" – June 1932

"The Sinister Painting" – September 1934

"The Rat Master" – March 1942

"The Deadly Theory" – May 1942

"Death has Red Hair" – September 1942

"Great Pan is Here" – November 1943

"The Antimacassar" – May 1949

"Old Mr Wiley" – March 1951

NARRATIVES OUT OF NIGHTMARE
EDWARD LUCAS WHITE

AS IN ALL forms of literature, several works of weird fiction have been based on the dreams that their writers experienced. Perhaps the most notable of these are Mary Shelley's *Frankenstein* (1818) and Robert Louis Stevenson's *The Strange Case of Dr Jekyll and Mr Hyde* (1886), and there is the unsubstantiated assertion that scenes in Bram Stoker's *Dracula* (1897) had a similar basis. HP Lovecraft's prose-poem "Nyarlothotep" (1920) was definitely inspired by a dream, with its first paragraph written while the author was still half-asleep. Lovecraft's detailed account of another of his dreams was incorporated in Frank Belknap Long's novel *The Horror from the Hills* (1931). In more recent times, Stephen King's *Misery* (1987) had its origins in a dream, as do several of his other works, while some of the ideas in the fiction of both Thomas Ligotti and Anne Rice also have such a source.

But Edward Lucas White has a niche uniquely his own in that virtually *all* of his short fiction in the genre was based on some of the many dreams and nightmares he experienced. Speaking of this in the Preface to his 1919 collection *The Song of the Sirens and Other Stories*, he wrote that "…a majority of these dreams have been such as come to most sleepers, but a minority have been such as visit few dreamers…" further commenting that they represented "…imaginations beyond my power to banish and seldom entirely within my power to alter, modify or control".

They certainly helped to produce some memorable works of fiction, replete with strong storylines and vivid imagery, and their strength is such as to elevate White to the first rank of weird fiction writers.

In his study *Supernatural Horror in Literature*, HP Lovecraft perceptively commented that "Mr. White imparts a very peculiar quality to his tales – an oblique sort of glamour which has its own distinctive type of convincingness", singling out "The Song of the Sirens", "Lukundoo" and "The Snout" as prime examples. His "small but potent body of weird short fiction", ST Joshi observed in *The Evolution of the Weird Tale* in 2004, "has waited too long to find a new generation of appreciative readers", although the two recent collections *The House of the Nightmare* (1998) and *Sesta & Other Strange Stories* (2000) may have gone some way towards ending that wait.

White's most well known work is certainly the much anthologised "Lukundoo", the chilling account of a horrific and inescapable curse that afflicts an African explorer. Many of his other tales match this for atmosphere and effect, and are works that are deserving of far more recognition than they have achieved. Not only do they succeed as forceful works of horror, but also in the way they so capably transmit a sense of unnerving helplessness in the face of inescapable events. The majority of them evoke an aura of disturbing menace with a lingering aftermath of disquiet that stubbornly stays with the reader; in short, they are skilled recreations of the night terrors that initially spawned them.

WHITE WAS BORN in New Jersey on 11 May 1866, and spent his early years in New York; the family moved to Baltimore when he was eleven. After receiving a BA at John Hopkins University in that city in 1888, he studied for a doctorate in Romance Languages but left before completing it, evidently because of ill health allied with financial difficulties. He subsequently embarked on a career of teaching classics, employed by four schools in Baltimore from 1892 until his death in 1934. Writing was a part-time occupation for him, and although verse was the format that he preferred, and in which he felt he produced his best work, he turned more and more to prose and was to attain literary fame during his lifetime principally through his historical novels.

He had four such novels published, all of which went though multiple printings and which were highly regarded by critics and readers alike. These were *El Supremo* (1916), about the Great Dictator of Paraguay; two books set in Ancient Rome, *The Unwilling Vestal* (1918) and *Andivius Hedulio* (1921); and finally *Helen* (1926), a retelling of the Troy legend. His interest in Rome prompted a non-fiction volume entitled *Why Rome Fell* (1927), which explored the reasons behind the downfall of the Roman Empire. There was also an autobiographical work, *Matrimony*, published in 1932. The novels are all accessible and enjoyable, with the best of them, *Andivius Hedulio*, an exciting tale of the fall and rise of a Roman nobleman.

His first published works were poems, which appeared in such periodicals as *Atlantic Monthly;* his debut, "The Last Bowstrings", appeared in May 1891. The twenty-one stanzas of this poem are made up of rhyming triplets, an unorthodox structure bearing in mind its length, but it is very efficiently done, and demonstrated the author's ability to successfully tell an intriguing tale in verse. The scene is a doomed castle under siege by an irresistible enemy, with the story told from the point of view of one of the women stringing bows for the beleaguered defenders. The final canto brings an expected but well-wrought conclusion showing that White was not committed to happy endings; the poem was a precursor to much of his later fiction with its oblique suggestions of hidden depths.

In 1908 GP Putnam's Sons published his first book, a volume of poetry entitled *Narrative Lyrics*. An impressive collection, it included several pieces with an ethereal flavour, including "Rhampsinitos" and its sequel "Talith", as well as the pleasing "Vertumna"; the most notable is perhaps "The Ghoula" – the theme of which was re-used in the short story "Amina", although the latter has a very different ending. As the title of the collection suggests, the contents concentrate on storytelling, and very successfully so. "The Retribution" is a grim and bloody account of vengeance, with a driving rhythm that is as remorseless as it is compelling; the theme of revenge is also the subject of both "The Measure of the Sword" and the bleak "Benaiah". But not all of the poems take the form of tragic drama – the author convincingly depicts romantic fulfilment in "Marcabrun" and "Kranae", while the short "Deioces" is both action-packed and provocative with its meaningful final line.

WHITE HAD EXPERIENCED vivid dreams and nightmares since his youth, but it was some time before he began to turn these experiences into works of fiction. His earliest efforts were written in the 1890s although his first published short story was "The House of the Nightmare", which appeared in the September 1906 issue of *Smith's Magazine*. The tale is short but effective, and what seems to be an orthodox ghost story takes a dramatic detour with the dream appearance of a "thing" that is graphically and disquietingly portrayed. There are no explanations for the frightening nightmares of the storyteller, but none are needed – the inexplicability of the horror heightens the unsettling atmosphere that is created and gives the tale a lasting impact. Commenting on this tale in his Afterword to *Lukundoo and Other Stories* in 1927, White said that it was "written just as I dreamed it, word for word", regarding it as one of his "paragon nightmares".

Already written by this time were the powerful stories "The Flambeau Bracket", "Gertrude", and "Mandola", but the next story to appear in print was "Amina" in the June 1907 edition of *The Bellman*.

This again evokes a convincing atmosphere of the unearthly, and Waldo's detached reaction to the quite literally ghoulish horror that he encounters in the Persian desert heightens the mood of reverie that is so subtly created. The source of the narrative was again a paragon nightmare, and White said that its climax came as a complete shock to him, as was the case with several of his other tales.

Works that also appeared during this early period, between 1908 and 1910, include "The Buzzards" and "The Death Rattle", both of which are relatively slight tales in comparison to the outstanding "The House of the Nightmare" and "Amina", or indeed with what was yet to come. "The Whirlpool Gorge" is a more interesting example of these early published stories, which with its exotic setting, vivid imagery and outlandish plot, is reminiscent of later pieces such as "The Song of the Sirens" and "Sesta".

It was after White's first two historical novels had met with popular and critical success that he sought to collect his short fiction, and the first compilation was *The Song of the Sirens and Other Stories* published by EP Dutton & Company in 1919. The bulk of these stories had their origin in dreams, as previously mentioned, with most of them set in Ancient Rome, ever a popular period with White. The only piece with a specifically supernatural theme is the title story, "The Song of the Sirens", which had been previously published in *Sunset Magazine* in 1909, as "The Man Who Had Seen Them". It tells of a deaf man's encounter with the legendary Sirens, the uniquely bizarre strangeness of these creatures based on a 1906 dream of the author. This is an instance of White utilising a vivid dream image and weaving a tale around it whilst the other macabre pieces in the collection – "Disvola" and "The Flambeau Bracket" – are tales where the entire plots were derived from nightmares.

"Disvola" is based on a recurrent dream that White experienced between 1899 and 1911. This is the excellent account of an awful act of revenge that is years in the making and which is as bitter as it can possibly be for its victim. "The Flambeau Bracket" similarly deals with revenge, but with its root rather than its execution. It has a genuinely startling final line, and in his Preface to the collection, White says of this dream-inspired tale: "I woke shuddering, tingling with the horror of the revelation at the end … with the last three sentences of it, word for word as they stand in the story, branded on my sight".

Certainly the last sentence is one that will remain in the reader's memory for a long time, and despite its unexpectedness it fully and properly explains the reason for the events leading up to the narrator's tale. In this respect it is structurally similar to the author's earlier poem "The Measure of the Sword", with retribution already meted out and the storyteller now making clear the reasons why; and in both instances those reasons are sufficient to fully justify the act.

THE SECOND VOLUME of short fiction to appear was *Lukundoo and Other Stories*, published by George H Doran Company in 1927, and this is a particularly powerful collection. It not only includes much of the best of White's weird fiction but also ranks alongside the finest collections of horror writing that had been produced up until that time.

Only three of the tales had previously appeared in print, although the majority had been produced prior to 1910, with just "Sorcery Island" and "Floki's Blade" written significantly later, in 1922 and 1924 respectively. With two exceptions the stories derived wholly from the author's dreams, and in his Afterword to the book White said: "Eight of the stories in this book I did not compose. I dreamed them, and in each the dream or nightmare needed little or no modification to make a story of it".

Even the two exceptions are not far removed, with the ending of "Alfandega 49A" taken from a dream and "Floki's Blade" based on a nightmare related by an acquaintance.

The eponymous opening story is rightly regarded as a near classic of the weird genre. It is a memorable tale of African sorcery, recounting the effect of a baleful curse that causes homunculi to sprout from the victim's torso, and the more he excises them, the more they appear. The nightmarish scenario has added effectiveness by virtue of its sparse descriptive prose, and the final conversation between the cursed explorer and the minikin growing from his body provides an intriguing insight into what prompted the curse, its origin seemingly not what was originally inferred.

"The Snout" generates a particularly convincing dream-like quality as intruders make their way through the rooms of Hengist Eversleigh's strange mansion, encountering much that is peculiar and disquieting, although nothing prepares them for their confrontation with Eversleigh himself. In "Alfandega 49A", the idyllic setting of The Alders, with its happy atmosphere and pleasant people, is shattered by events a thousand miles away, a tragedy that is dourly inevitable; that same inevitability is present in the calamitous final revelation of "The Message on the Slate".

Not all of these tales lead to misfortune and dire conclusions. "The Picture Puzzle" starts with inconsolable despair but pleasing and unexpected deliverance is found, while in "The Pig-Skin Belt" what appears to be inexplicably obsessive behaviour on the part of Cassius

Case is shown to be wholly rational when the climax arrives. The narrator's uneasy experiences of the witchery of "Sorcery Island" culminate not in the disaster that he had anticipated but in unfettered escape. The individuals around whom these particular stories revolve are not of course unaffected by their experiences, and living through them instils resolve and strength, quite literally so in the atypical "Floki's Blade". Set in Iceland in Viking times, it is a tale of betrayal and revenge, with the magic sword of the title playing a major part; the most orthodox of all the tales in *Lukundoo*, it still introduces an unexpected plot development after the action is supposedly over, with the Blade of the title proving its worth in an unforeseen manner.

Lukundoo is a fine volume of varied stories. The explicit horrors of "Amina", "The House of the Nightmare", "The Snout" and the title story are deftly balanced by the atmospherically implicit promises of dread in "The Message on the Slate", "Alfandega 49A" and "The Pig-Skin Belt", while the strangeness of such tales as "Sorcery Island" and "The Picture Puzzle" are neatly offset by the more straightforward and conventional "Floki's Blade". If a full explanation of all of the weird events is not forthcoming, as in "The House of the Nightmare" and "Sorcery Island", this amplifies the dream-like effect and adds a thought-provoking aspect. The collection is a splendid example of White's abilities, demonstrating his very real penchant for absorbing, out-of-the-ordinary fiction.

AFTER HIS LAST works of the macabre were written, in the early to mid-1920s, White published little apart from the scholarly *When Rome Fell* and the autobiographical *Matrimony*. However, he did spend much time on what he considered would be his magnum opus, an epic novel set in the year 50,000 called *Plus Ultra;* but sadly this work never saw print, although extracts did appear in *Fantasy Commentator* in 1980.

He committed suicide by gassing himself on 30 March 1934, the seventh anniversary of his much-loved wife's death, and it was over seventy years before anything new was to appear under his name. This was in 2005 when Midnight House published *Sesta & Other Strange Stories*, a collection which included ten previously unpublished stories, all complete and generally polished, which had been gathered from papers that had been left with the John Hopkins University. Many are retellings of nightmares, and the quality of several is such that it is surprising that the author never sold them during his lifetime. Some *were* submitted for publication but failed to sell, and it had been White's intention for them all to be included in what he envisaged as a quartet of volumes of his collected short stories, a project that never reached fruition.

Of the previously unpublished work in *Sesta*, "Gertrude" and "Mandola" are especially powerful, and would not have been at all out of place within the pages of *Lukundoo*, ranking alongside White's best macabre fiction. "Gertrude" may be one of the earliest of the author's tales (the date of composition is unknown but it does seem to come from the 1890s), and is the hauntingly powerful narrative of a post-mortem return during the height of a colossal storm on an isolated island. In "Mandola", another early tale, nightmare literally becomes awful reality as a creature hundreds of thousands of years old gains physical presence and destroys all that the narrator holds dear.

There is another isolated island in "Sesta", but this time in the South Seas, where a naturalist is marooned and left to die. His survival, his meeting with the beautiful Sesta of the title, and his acquiring of a huge hoard of gold, all suggest a traditional adventure story but the plot develops into something far more sinister, with a horrific if abrupt climax. Other noteworthy tales in the collection include "The Voices", a short but intriguing piece dealing with obsession, where the lack of specific explanation markedly intensifies the effect, and "Canea" which tells of a woman's personality being drained from her and trapped in the body of a grey rat.

There are some admittedly minor efforts in *Sesta*, such as "The Serge Coat", which has a fascinating premise but which simply peters out without fulfilling its potential, and "The Startling Blonde", which the author himself referred to as "a trifle". These are outweighed by the strength of the better pieces, and even White's lesser work remains engrossing and readable.

Also included in *Sesta* is the story "The Stirrup Iron", an early version of "The Flambeau Bracket", and it is interesting to see how White changed the tale over a period of what seems to be some ten years or more. The later story is more forceful, with a quite different structure; the first version starts with the duel rather than its aftermath, and its ending leaves much to be inferred, with the final revelation being made far clearer in the later tale. "The Flambeau Bracket" is of course one of the major works that derived from a nightmare, and White's comment mentioned earlier, that he awoke with the last three sentences "branded on my sight", presumably refers to "The Stirrup Iron", where those three sentences differ significantly from the later version.

Sesta is something of a potpourri, but nevertheless a welcome addition to the White canon. The "new" stories apparently represent all of the author's remaining unpublished short fiction in the field, and there is no more to come. The epic *Plus Ultra* may one day appear in its complete form, but there is no indication that this is even a remote possibility at present.

DURING HIS LIFETIME, Edward Lucas White found a degree of success and fame as a writer of popular historical novels, despite his own view that it was in the medium of verse that his best efforts were to be found. His shorter imaginative fiction seems to have been of secondary importance to him, although ironically it is the latter for which he is more remembered today, if only by virtue of a relatively small number of tales.

The dreams that inspired those tales must have been somewhat disconcerting, and in White's own words "anyone dreaming such narratives just had to write them into stories to get them out of his system". We should be thankful that he did seek such literary catharsis for it generated many fine works, a significant number of which rank highly amongst the very best of weird fiction.

SELECTED BIBLIOGRAPHY

The weird fiction
(in reported order of writing along with first publication dates)

"Gertrude" – *Sesta*, 2005

"Mandola" – *Sesta*, 2005

"The Serge Coat" – *Sesta*, 2005

"The Stirrup Iron" – *Sesta*, 2005

"The Voices" – *Sesta*, 2005

"The Message on the Slate" – *Lukundoo and Other Stories*, 1927

"The House of the Nightmare" – *Smith's Magazine*, September 1906

"Amina" – *The Bellman*, June 1 1907

"The Pig-Skin Belt" – *Lukundoo and Other Stories*, 1927

"Lukundoo" – *Weird Tales*, November 1925

"The Turning Point" – *Sesta*, 2005

"The Buzzards" – *The Bellman*, March 1908

"The Tooth" – *Sesta*, 2005

"The Picture Puzzle" – *Lukundoo and Other Stories*, 1927

"The Snout" – *Lukundoo and Other Stories*, 1927

"The Death Rattle" – *The Bohemian*, September 1909

"Canea" – *Sesta*, 2005

"The Whirlpool Gorge" – *Sunset Magazine*, August 1910

"The Flambeau Bracket" – *Young's Magazine*, December 1910

"Alfandega 49A" – *Lukundoo and Other Stories*, 1927

"Disvola" – *The Song of the Sirens*, 1919

"Sesta" – *Sesta*, 2005

"The Startling Blonde" – *Sesta*, 2005

"The Song of the Sirens" – *The Song of the Sirens*, 1919

"Sorcery Island" – *Lukundoo and Other Stories*, 1927

"Floki's Blade" – *Lukundoo and Other Stories*, 1927

FROM SIMORGYA TO STARDOCK
FRITZ LEIBER

UNKNOWN WAS A magazine with a justified reputation for the high standard of the fantasy that appeared in its pages, and the August 1939 issue was no exception. It featured a 15,000 word novelette entitled "Two Sought Adventure", the first published story by Fritz Leiber (1910-1992). Good though the story certainly was, both its writer and readers would have scoffed in disbelief had anyone then predicted that this was to be the start of a series that would endure, still attracting enthusiastic new readers well into the new millennium.

"Two Sought Adventure" introduced into the developing sword & sorcery genre Fafhrd and the Gray Mouser, in a tale about the search for the treasure of Urgaan of Angarngi. Amid much swordplay against rivals for the treasure, and the revelation that it is the treasure house itself that is the sentient and deadly guardian of the riches, the scene is very ably set for future adventures of the duo. Interestingly, this story (later re-titled "The Jewels in the Forest") was not the first Fafhrd/Mouser tale written; that honour goes to "Adept's Gambit", a novella from 1936. Despite being submitted to many publishers and editors, this work did not appear in print until more than a decade later, when a revised version was included in Leiber's first collection, *Night's Black Agents* (1947), making it chronologically the sixth in the series to be published.

The stories of Fafhrd and the Gray Mouser are distinctive in the literature of sword & sorcery, primarily for their novel blend of humour and action. They also distinguish themselves with regard to the attitude and philosophy of the main characters: their heroics are tempered with a degree of human fallibility and a more realistic reaction to, and interpretation of, given sets of circumstances. The two will much prefer to avoid battling against the odds, but are prepared to do so if necessary, and will probably triumph, but perhaps with a little luck and certainly a lot of effort. Rather than embark on valiant quests – unless remunerative or forced upon them – they are more likely to be found in Dim Lane, drinking at the Silver Eel, or pursuing some beautiful Lankhmarese lady.

The pair may seem to be an unlikely partnership. Fafhrd is tall and hugely muscled, with copper-coloured hair and beard, a green-eyed barbarian highly skilled with his longsword, Graywand, and his dagger, Heartseeker; the Mouser, by comparison, is small, nimble, dark-complexioned and black-eyed, as equally skilled in weaponry as his companion but favouring his rapier and dirk, Scalpel and Cat's Claw respectively.

Opposites they may appear, but they have common points of reference – important ones too! – in their wit, their morality, their idealism, their mutual loyalty, and the way in which they embrace life to its fullest extent, characterised by their lust for adventure, women and drinking – although not necessarily in that order. As Leiber said in the Author's Foreword to *The Swords of Lankhmar* (1968): "One of the original motives for conceiving Fafhrd and the Mouser was to have a couple of fantasy heroes closer to true human stature than supermen like Conan and Tarzan and many another…" And in a 1972 article, "Lankhmar and Lands Around", he further elaborates:

A reader first encountering the tales may expect the stereotype of Fafhrd being the brawny but somewhat stupid barbarian and the Mouser the clever, comic rogue, but it soon becomes apparent (I trust), that both are equally clever, rather profound scholars and linguists, Fafhrd veering sometimes towards the romantic, the Mouser somewhat more cynical and Machiavellian, without making them in any way a Don Quixote and Sancho Panza.

THE SETTING FOR the tales is the world of Nehwon (it is surely unnecessary to point out what this spells backwards?), a fascinating realm of such splendid cities as Ool Hrusp, Ilthmar, Illik Ving, Sarheenmar, Horborixen, Gnapf Nar, and of course mighty Lankhmar, City of Sevenscore Thousand Smokes. To the extreme north lies sunless Shadowland, the dread realm where Death resides, and at its antipodes is Godsland ("overcrowded, a veritable slum"), housing all of the gods who have ever been worshipped in Nehwon. Savage Mingols range the Northern Steppes; there is a City of Ghouls by the shores of the Sea of Monsters; Ice Gnomes are to be found north of No-Ombrulsk; hordes of intelligent rats throng Lankhmar Below; an invisible mountain king rules in the Trollsteps; and the sunken city of Simorgya is the grim abode of vengeful sea creatures. *Known* Nehwon holds an abundance of wonders, and who knows what further marvels may be found beyond the Outer Sea and the Sea of Stars?

Certain philosophers maintain that Nehwon is one of many bubbles rising through a universe of water, a concept that the Mouser felt had provided ample justification for the peculiar happenings in "Trapped in the Sea of Stars". Fafhrd, however, was in complete disagreement, and whether those philosophers are right or wrong has yet to be firmly established. Bubble or not, Nehwon is a world of strange places and stranger doings, a world of sorcerers, thieves, assassins, sensual women and supernatural beings, a world of intrigue, wealth and wizardry; just the place in fact for two adventurers such as Fafhrd and the Mouser.

FAFHRD DERIVES FROM Cold Corner in the northern Cold Waste, between the gigantic mountain ranges the Trollsteps and The Bones of the Old Ones. A trained skald-singer, he escaped the domination of his mother and a life of tedium by absconding with an actress from a travelling show, crossing Trollstep Canyon via a rocket-powered ski-jump.

The Mouser's origins are more obscure, although he believes that he was born in the beggar city of Tovilyis. An apprentice to the wizard Glavas Rho, he avenged his master's death at the hands of Duke Janarrl and fled with the Duke's daughter to Lankhmar, where he proceeded to earn a fine living for himself and his mistress by perpetrating a series of brilliant thefts, earning such sobriquets as the Rug Robber, the Carpet Crimp and the Candle Corsair.

The very first meeting of the two was a fleeting one on the shores of the Outer Sea, by the Mountains of Hunger, when a young Fafhrd was a pirate's ship-boy and Mouse (as he was then known) still served Glavas Rho. The definitive encounter comes some years later in Lankhmar the Imperishable, City of the Black Toga, when they each independently decide to rob the thieves who have just relieved Jengao the Gem Merchant of his treasures. Face to face over the jewels, they take a liking to each other and agree to split the proceeds (*sixty-sixty!*); this initial conversation does incidentally clear up any doubts as to the pronunciation of Fafhrd's name: he informs the Mouser that it is "Faf-erd". Tragedy follows; the Thieves Guild of Lankhmar takes exception to actions by non-Guild members, and it is the adventurers' women – Vlana and Ivrian – who die unpleasantly as a result. They are bloodily avenged, but their memories haunt Fafhrd and the Mouser until finally purged by the theft of the Mask of Death from Shadowland itself, and an agreement to respectively serve the magicians Ningauble of the Seven Eyes and Sheelba of the Eyeless Face.

Ningauble and Sheelba are powerful mages, highly-skilled in the sorcerous arts. Sheelba appears to be particularly adept, for after being referred to as "he" and "him" throughout the previous tales, we are told in "The Curse of the Smalls and the Stars" that Sheelba is a *sorceress*. Clearly in the world of Nehwon anything is possible – as Fafhrd says in the same story, not concerning Sheelba but nevertheless appropriately, "…a mere change of sex should not surprise us at all". The two sorcerers are arch-rivals who will only co-operate with one another in the most extreme of circumstances. Sheelba lives in a hut on stilts which wanders around the Great Salt Marsh and the Sinking Land at random, protected by spells and distinguished by an eerie blue glow from within, while Ningauble practices his unearthly arts from a desert cave in the mountains near Ilthmar.

Both are heavily cowled and robed, evidently with good reason – Sheelba's cowl seems to hold nothing but an absolute and impenetrable blackness, while Ningauble's dimly reveals seven pale green eyes, restlessly and constantly shifting position; these eyes are set at the ends of serpentine stalks which occasionally emerge from their concealment with no apparent limit to their extent. As to what manner of bodies the cloaks conceal, nothing is known; and their respective origins can equally only be guessed at. They are treated with a grudging respect by the Mouser and Fafhrd, who are certainly not overawed by them and who at times have been known to risk the wizards' wrath by both their actions and their attitude. Subservience is not a concept that sits comfortably with the pair.

NEHWON MAINTAINED AN impressive consistency in both geography and characteristics throughout the series to the final book, *The Knight and Knave of Swords,* in 1988. Additionally, key events may not have been elaborated on until years later, but tended to slot in effortlessly and complement whatever had gone before; this is emphasised by the fact that the entire saga was published in 2001 as two volumes, and it reads well as a continuous sequence of events. The various individual episodes bear vague but defined links even though there is a wide disparity in the dates of first publication for each story. This is in no small part due to several astute linking portions written by Leiber for the five books published by Ace between 1968 and 1970, which collected together all of the stories published up to and including the latter date. One does get the impression from the ease with which the continuity is achieved that broad details of the full saga may well have been in the author's mind when he first put pen to paper.

THERE IS MUCH that is original and memorable in the Fafhrd/Mouser tales. The standard of writing is consistently high, and the stories are each distinct and fresh with no signs of stagnation; inspiration never seems to be lacking. Leiber had a subtle way with his writing, sometimes light and sometimes complex, but always marvellously appropriate to whichever of the various aspects of plot he was dealing with. Although humour is present in many of the stories, it is generally in the background, supplementing rather than overshadowing the thrust of the narrative, but of equal effect are those stories in which humour plays no part at all, such as "The Unholy Grail". And in many of the tales Leiber's literary artistry is emphasised in the smooth, sure transition from light-hearted verbal banter to a sudden confrontation with something chilling – a cleverly worked switch that invariably succeeds.

Perhaps the best example of what the saga of Fafhrd and the Mouser represents is found in *The Swords of Lankhmar:* an extended and revised 1968 version of the novelette "Scylla's Daughter", which originally appeared in 1961. Very briefly, the plot revolves around an invasion of Lankhmar by intelligent rats, and of the efforts of Fafhrd and the Mouser to defeat them. In this outstanding novel, we find all of the elements that have made the series so popular – an intriguing and well-developed storyline, the superb interaction of the protagonists, excellent characterisation, a well-paced narrative, and a stirring climax. There are many memorable scenes, and humour subtly underscores much of the plot such as when the Mouser, drastically reduced in size by magic, is disguised as a rat to spy in the rat-city of Lankhmar Below. Trying to act the part, he wanders around muttering oaths like "All rat-catchers fry!" and "By God's hairless tail!" and at one stage "...he found himself trying so hard to be a convincing rat that without volition his eyes now followed with leering interest, a small, mincing she-rat". At the same time, Fafhrd is speeding to Lankhmar, and dallies awhile with a female Ghoul, whose skin and internal organs are transparent and who therefore appears visually to be a skeleton: "It was a moderately strange sight," (Fafhrd and the girl, having made love, are now in each other's arms) "yet one to touch the hearts of imaginative lovers and enemies of racial discrimination in all the many universes".

The book is full of amusement and excitement – add Karl Treuherz the German time-traveller appearing intermittently in his search for monsters; the antics of Glipkerion Kistomerces, the mad ruler of Lankhmar; the plotting of the arch-villain rats Lord Null and Skwee; the cryptic machinations of Sheelba and Ningauble; the sensual wiles of Hisvet; the reluctant heroics of Fafhrd and the Mouser – and you have one of the most entertaining sword & sorcery stories ever written.

HEROICS ON THE part of the duo, whether reluctant or not, may give a slightly misleading impression. Leiber had likened them to Corund and Gro in ER Eddison's *The Worm Ouroboros*, although this seems a strange comparison when one considers that these two characters do not seem remotely similar to Fafhrd and the Mouser, except in physical appearance. The author did, however, qualify his comments by continuing "...yet I don't think they're touched with evil as those two, rather they're rogues in a decadent world where you have to be a rogue to survive".

Certainly, neither of them has any qualms when it comes to relieving a wealthy jeweller of his riches, eagerly participating in a drunken brawl, or departing the City with a mound of unpaid bills left behind. But this apparent lack of morality, which is merely a survival trait in a basically amoral society such as Lankhmar, is counteracted by an inherent sense of rightness when it comes to the resistance of evil or oppression, as well as a keen loyalty both to one another and to their beliefs of good and bad. Admittedly their worthy intentions may often fade rather too quickly, and their resolutions to lead a "proper life" may waver within hours of being made, but such a roguish addiction to wine, women and song cannot be that easily overcome.

The relationship between Fafhrd and the Mouser is one involving great friendship and great trust, but also great rivalry. Whenever danger threatens, each is ready to automatically lay down his life for the other, but should they both be interested in the same woman then it is a case of Fafhrd trying to do the Mouser down and vice versa, the Mouser with perhaps a reference to certain dull-witted barbarians and Fafhrd with an equally disparaging remark concerning people of diminutive stature. They are not very often rivals for the favours of the same female, their respective tastes tending to differ considerably; at the end of "The Price of Pain Ease" for instance,

...the Mouser began the hottest sort of love affair with a slightly underage and most winsome niece of Karstak Ovarmortes, while Fafhrd took on the identical twin daughters, most beauteous and wealthy and yet on the verge of turning to prostitution for the excitement it promised, of Duke Danius.

Notable exceptions to the rule have been Hisvet (*The Swords of Lankhmar*) and Anra Devadoris ("Adept's Gambit"), neither of whom turned out to be quite what she seemed. Perhaps in both cases it was the unattainability of the women concerned that led to such a passion for possession.

The two are not always lucky in love. Apart from the tragic affairs with Vlana and Ivrian ("Ill Met in Lankhmar"), they have for instance been brilliantly double-crossed by Nemia and the Eyes of Ogo ("The Two Best Thieves in Lankhmar"), almost destroyed lusting for sea-queens ("When the Sea King's Away") and for a Simorgyan demoness ("Sea Magic" and "The Mer She"), and had an extremely unpleasant experience with Atya in "Claws from the Night". And in "Adept's Gambit" Fafhrd has the disconcerting experience of finding that every girl to whom he makes advances turns into a pig, which prompts the Mouser to think up an ingenious scheme

...to engage an amiable girl, have Fafhrd turn her into a pig, immediately sell her to a butcher, next sell her to an amorous

merchant when she has escaped the bewildered butcher as a furious girl, have Fafhrd sneak after the merchant and turn her back into a pig ... then sell her to another butcher and begin all over again. Low prices, quick profits.

The Mouser soon discovers that every girl *he* attempts to have his way with turns into a giant snail; all that is except the cross-eyed Chloe – much to Fafhrd's chagrin...

Burly barbarian though he certainly is, Fafhrd can be the equal of the silver-tongued Mouser when it comes to dealing with the gentler sex. But successful as they often may be, there does seem to be a problem with overconfidence, in that each of them sincerely believes that he is the ultimate gift to womankind. Failures (not too uncommon) are never dwelt upon, but are generally quickly forgotten in a deluge of cheap beer or wine at the Silver Eel or the Golden Lamprey, until such time as another shapely figure appears or the prospect of obtaining gold is brought to their attention.

THE PAIR ARE an inseparable team – or *nearly* inseparable. The one time that their partnership was broken resulted in the most outrageously funny of all the stories in the saga, "Lean Times in Lankhmar". This tale gives an interesting insight into the gods in Lankhmar (the gods *in* Lankhmar being very different to the gods *of* Lankhmar), detailing the trials and tribulations of Fafhrd as an acolyte of Issek the Jug, and the traverse of the latter up the Street of the Gods (the further a god gets up the Street, the more successful that god is). We are told that Issek the Jug is

...not to be confused with Issek the Armless, Issek of the Burnt Legs, Flayed Issek or any of the other numerous and colourfully mutilated deities of that name ... a few scholars have confused him with Jugged

Issek, an entirely different saintlet whose claim to immortality lay in his confinement for seventeen years in a not overly roomy earthenware jar...

The intricate story of the parting of the ways of Fafhrd and the Mouser, of how Fafhrd is deified as the resurrection of Issek the Jug, of the conversion of Pulg the racketeer, of the problems which confront the blasphemous Quatch and Wiggin, of the Mouser's innovative role as god-maker, and of the heroes' eventual reconciliation and departure with a cask of brandy (not the loot that they had anticipated) is the closest to slapstick comedy that the series ever comes, and it succeeds brilliantly as quite one of the most amusing fantasy stories ever written.

Other adventures have seen them range over virtually the whole of known Nehwon, from claustrophobic subterranean kingdoms ("The Lords of Quarmall") to places so remote as to be near mythical ("Rime Isle"), from submarine cities ("The Sunken Land") to cities in our own universe ("Adept's Gambit"); they have scaled unscalable mountains ("Stardock") and escaped the inescapable ("Trapped in the Shadowland"). Their adversaries have ranged from ghostly hounds ("The Howling Tower") to murderous houses ("The Jewels in the Forest"); from talking killer birds ("Claws from the Night") to giant spiders ("Bazaar of the Bizarre"); and even a deadly skull ("Thieves' House"). And there has of course also been a wonderful variety of relatively mundane mortal foes such as Kranarch and Gnarfi, the hunchbacked Hristomilo, Laras Laerk, Anra Devadoris, Gwaay and Hasjarl – evocative names and memorable characters.

AS ALREADY INDICATED, all of the various facets of the series came together perfectly in *The Swords of Lankhmar*, and if this book represented a level of achievement that could not be surpassed, it was hardly surprising. With *The Swords of Lankhmar*, Leiber had scaled Stardock; there was nowhere higher to go. He never attempted to reprise the narrative length that had been so effective in the novel, nor the consistently light-hearted touch that had characterised it. Instead, he chose to write episodically and in a more brooding and melancholy style, and while the stories still retained their wit, they had bleaker overtones. However, later offerings do still have much to commend them, and are important milestones in the ongoing shaping of the Mouser and Fafhrd, for Leiber was looking to do more than have them stagnate in adventure after adventure, and had something more realistic in mind for them.

The penultimate book in the series, *Swords and Ice Magic*, published in 1977, comprises short and long pieces from the mid-1970s. Collected in a single volume, the vignettes – which had seemed frankly rather frivolous in isolation – now took their place as scene-setting forerunners to the main action embodied in the longer works "The Frost Monstreme" and "Rime Isle". Rime Isle is one of the northernmost outposts of Nehwon, isolated and regarded as mythical, a place which the Mouser muses seems to be "...on the edge of the other worlds ... a sort of rim". This conjecture is borne out by the appearance of the gods Odin and Loki, who have apparently been ejected from our own universe due to a lack of worshippers, and whose motives are not as selfless and pure as they may appear.

Fafhrd and the Mouser are lured north to thwart an invasion (the luring being fairly easily achieved on behalf of Odin and Loki, by two attractive women whose charms are heightened by the gold that they are offering). The invasion is mounted by the Sunwise Mingols and the Widdershin Mingols, and is engineered by Khahkht the Ice Wizard, in preparation for the bloody conquest of the whole of Nehwon. Khahkht spends his (or more appropriately *its*) time in a sphere of black ice, and is aided and abetted by Faroomfar, an old enemy of Fafhrd and the Mouser (the first encounter with this irascible and invisible being occurred during the "Stardock" adventure). Fafhrd and the Mouser each hire a dozen men – berserkers and thieves respectively – to assist in the struggle, the Mouser being careful to find twelve who are smaller than he. After a struggle with the Frost Monstreme, they reach Rime Isle and manage to save the situation. In a climax that is as dramatic as it is unexpected, Fafhrd is left with a permanent reminder of events that serves to reinforce the fact that these tales are very different to standard sword & sorcery fare, in that the heroes do not always come through unscathed.

However, such adventuring does take its toll in more ways than the physical, and here again Leiber departs from "normal" heroic fiction. The passing of the years has instilled a growing sense of dissatisfaction in both Fafhrd and the Mouser, and as they consider their transitory existence they come to question their ongoing roles, seeking a more purposeful future for themselves. The lifestyle that has served them adequately for so long has begun to pall. In the aftermath of the Rime Isle adventure, this spiritual malaise crystallises into the thought of finally settling down, an idea fostered by the fact that for perhaps the first time they are aware of responsibilities, and reinforced at having found the right women with whom to forge a meaningful relationship – another reflection of their developing sense of maturity. Since the loss of Vlana and Ivrian, their

...erotic solacing had mostly come from a very odd lot of hard-bitten if beauteous slave-girls, vagabond hoydens, and demonic princesses, folk easily come by if at all and even more easily lost, accidents rather than goals of their weird adventurings.

Neither stunningly beautiful nor particularly young, Afreyt and Cil do suit Fafhrd and the Mouser, and seem to be the complementary partner that each needs.

But withdrawal from the designated role of hero is not straightforward in Nehwon. The Rime Isle episode ended unsatisfactorily from the point of view that significantly more is demanded of any *final* adventure to end such a career as that of Fafhrd and the Mouser:

...their noisiest partisans and most ardent adherents alike will be demanding that it end at the very least in spectacular death and doom, endured while battling insurmountable odds and enjoying the enmity of the evilest archgods.

Nor is the news well received in other quarters – Sheelba and Ningauble are dismayed at the prospect of losing the pair's services; certain enemies decide to make their retirement permanent; and even the gods who claim Fafhrd and the Mouser as their "chiefest lapsed worshippers" are perturbed. These gods, who are of course gods *in* Lankhmar (and, as already mentioned, very different to gods *of* Lankhmar), are "spiderish Mog, limp-wristed Issek, and lousy Kos," who in Godsland sit "somewhat apart from the mass of the more couth and civilised Nehwonian deities". But deities they still are, capable of delivering damnation when it suits them. They do, however, need to be a little careful in this respect, as none of them can really afford to lose any of the few remaining worshippers that they have, even lapsed ones like Fafhrd and the Mouser – a lesson they do seem to learn in "The Curse of the Smalls and the Stars", in which not only are curses thwarted but also assassins outwitted.

THERE IS NATURALLY one last adventure and this is related in "The Mouser Goes Below". This imaginative tale, with the Mouser in the bowels of the earth and Fafhrd high in the sky, is a fitting climax to the series and is almost a retrospective of what has gone before, with many characters reappearing and many places re-visited, both in actuality and in memory. References are made to incidents from such stories as "The Bleak Shore", "Bazaar of the Bizarre", "Stardock", "The Price of Pain Ease", "Trapped in the Sea of Stars", "The Lords of Quarmall", "The Mer She", "Thieves' House" and *The Swords of Lankhmar*; and there are appearances by such old acquaintances as Ississi, Hisvet, Odin, Quarmal of Quarmall, and Frix (now once more Queen Frixifrax of Arilia), as well as cameos by the gods Mog, Issek and Kos, together with Death and Sister Pain (Death's sibling, who more than lives up to her name). Two other minor characters who appear offstage, but who are now revealed to be of considerable significance in the lives of Fafhrd and the Mouser, are Friska and Freg, who provide the duo with particularly pleasant surprises.

One intriguing omission is that only a single passing reference is made to Sheelba and Ningauble in "The Mouser Goes Below", despite the fact that when last we heard they were "devising new stratagems to procure the return of their favourite errand boys and living touchstones". We must assume that those stratagems failed, for there is an undeniable finality to the last tale that makes it clear that the saga is complete. Rime Isle now a permanent home, our heroes are settled, and although there is talk of the possibility of "an interesting field assignment or two from time to time", this may well be wishful thinking on the part of these newly married men (in the last chapter,

Cif talks to Afreyt of their *husbands).*

With the conclusion of the series, Leiber achieved something rather special – he had provided his readers with a full history of Fafhrd and the Mouser, with every important element duly detailed from start to finish. We are left convinced that any un-chronicled adventures between "Ill Met in Lankhmar" and "The Mouser Goes Below" could only have been minor, hardly worth the telling, for otherwise we would know about them – our confidence in the writer is such that we are certain that he can have left no significant episodes untold. This is one reason why a new Nehwon novel by Robin Wayne Bailey (*Swords Against the Shadowland*, 1998) failed to convince. Anyone having read the whole series by Leiber is well aware of the fact that there is no room for anything more to be added. Bailey's book is inventive, well-written and well-plotted, an entertaining novel in its own right, but it cannot surmount the fact that it is an intrusion into the saga; nor can it surmount the fact that it is simply impossible to consistently emulate Leiber's unique style of writing, which is such an integral element in the enjoyment of the original tales.

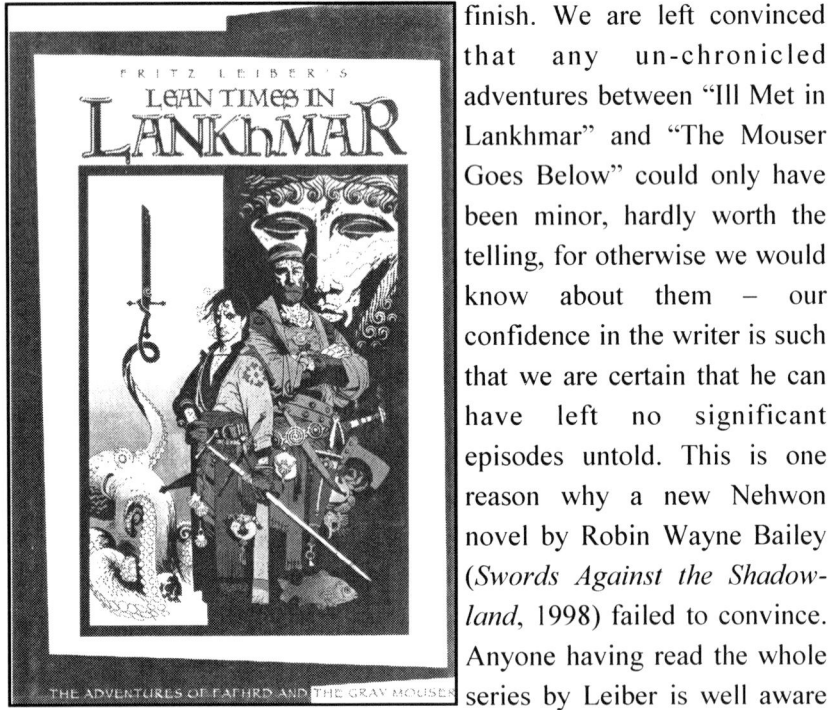

The ending of the Nehwon chronicles means that we will now never learn what lies in Horborixen, the citadel-city of the King of Kings,

beyond a single tantalising glimpse in "The Sadness of the Executioner"; nor will we visit the Sea of Monsters, the Mountains of the Elder Ones or Dragon Rocks, or learn what lies south of Klesh or on the far side of the Outer Sea. And of the east, far beyond Tislinilit, little is known of what is actually there beyond passing references to "the skeletally shrunken empire of Eevamarensee" and to "lands that were legends in Lankhmar and even Horborixen".

We can alas only conjecture about these exotic locations, as well as the adventures that might have transpired there. However, we have had the undoubted privilege of sharing in the unfailing originality and peerless style of perhaps the most literate, colourful and enjoyable series of stories in the entire fantasy genre, remarkable creations that really do stand in a class entirely of their own. For that privilege, grateful thanks are certainly due to the gods *of* Lankhmar, but primarily of course those thanks are due to the inspired imagination of the late, great Fritz Leiber.

BIBLIOGRAPHY

The Fafhrd and the Gray Mouser stories

"The Jewels in the Forest" – *Unknown*, August 1939, as "Two Sought Adventure"

"The Bleak Shore" – *Unknown*, November 1940

"The Howling Tower" – *Unknown*, June 1941

"The Sunken Land" – *Unknown Worlds*, February 1942

"Thieves' House" – *Unknown Worlds*, February 1943

"Adept's Gambit" – *Night's Black Agents*, December 1947

"Claws from the Night" – *Suspense*, Fall 1951, as "Dark Vengeance"

"The Seven Black Priests" – *Other Worlds*, May 1953

Two Sought Adventure May, 1957

"Induction" – *Two Sought Adventure*, May 1957

"Lean Times in Lankhmar" – *Fantastic*, November 1959

"When the Sea-King's Away" – *Fantastic*, May 1960

"Scylla's Daughter" – *Fantastic*, May 1961

"The Unholy Grail" – *Fantastic*, October 1962

"The Cloud of Hate" – *Fantastic*, May 1963

"Bazaar of the Bizarre" – *Fantastic*, August 1963

"The Lords of Quarmall" – *Fantastic*, January and February 1964 (with Harry Fischer)

"Stardock" – *Fantastic*, September 1965

The Swords of Lankhmar – January 1968

"The Two Best Thieves in Lankhmar" – *Fantastic*, August 1968

Swords Against Wizardry, July 1968

"In the Witch's Tent" – *Swords Against Wizardry*, July 1968

Swords in the Mist – September 1968

"Their Mistress, the Sea" – *Swords in the Mist,* September 1968

"The Wrong Branch" – *Swords in the Mist,* September 1968

"The Snow Women" – *Fantastic*, April 1970

"Ill Met in Lankhmar" – *Magazine of Fantasy & Science Fiction*, April 1970

Swords and Deviltry – May 1970

Swords Against Death – August 1970

"The Circle Curse" – *Swords Against Death*, August 1970

"The Price of Pain-Ease" – *Swords Against Death*, August 1970

"The Sadness of the Executioner" – *Flashing Swords!* #1, April 1973

"Trapped in the Shadowland" – *Fantastic*, November 1973

"The Bait" – *Whispers*, December 1973

"Beauty and the Beasts" – *The Book of Fritz Leiber*, January 1974

"Under the Thumbs of the Gods" – *Fantastic*, April 1975

"Trapped in the Sea of Stars" – *The Second Book of Fritz Leiber*, September 1975

"The Frost Monstreme" – *Flashing Swords!* #3, August 1976

"Rime Isle" – *Cosmos SF&F Magazine*, May and July 1977

Swords and Ice Magic – July 1977

"Sea Magic" – *The Dragon Magazine*, December 1977

"The Mer She" – *Heroes and Horrors*, December 1978

"The Curse of the Smalls and the Stars" – *Heroic Visions*, March 1983

"The Mouser Goes Below" – *Whispers*, October 1987

"Slack Lankhmar Afternoon Featuring Hisvet" – *Terry's Universe*, June 1988

The Knight and Knave of Swords – December 1988

OTHERWORLDLY PRESENCES
MARY E WILKINS FREEMAN

MARY ELEANOR WILKINS Freeman (1852–1930) was the prolific author of nineteen novels and nearly 250 short stories, as well as an extensive amount of verse. Her fiction was set primarily in New England, and as an early regional and feminist writer, she dealt regularly with the role of women in a society that was reluctant to accept independent thought and action in the female gender.

She is largely forgotten today but was very successful and respected in her time, her reputation initially founded on two notable collections, *A Humble Romance* (1887) and *A New England Nun* (1891), and she maintained a consistent and popularly acclaimed standard of writing for many years. In 1926 she became the first recipient of the William Dean Howells Medal for Distinction in Fiction from the American Academy of Arts and Letters, and in the same year she was one of the first women to be elected to that Institution. A mark of her achievement is that the bronze doors of the Academy in Manhattan are "dedicated to the memory of Mary E Wilkins Freeman and the women writers of America".

Although renowned for the realistic approach of her work, she also wrote some two dozen supernatural and related tales in her fifty-year literary career, and the general excellence of this relatively modest output places Freeman high in the ranks of the field's gifted storytellers.

Her talents were not unrecognised by other renowned authors – she was evidently the one American writer of such fiction whom MR James "appreciated unreservedly"; and HP Lovecraft wrote that "material of authentic force" was to be found in her works. He also commented that her 1903 collection *The Wind in the Rose-Bush and Other Stories of the Supernatural* contained "a number of noteworthy achievements", while August Derleth openly acknowledged her influence on his own writing, stating that he regarded her as being among the genre's "absolute formative masters" and that she had written "some of the most perfect ghost stories in the language".

Freeman's stories of the uncanny were just as regional as her other writing – she used many of the same themes and characterizations, and her adroit combination of the commonplace and the mystical was particularly effective. Her characters are rooted in the everyday world with concerns that may be mundane to others but which to them are all-important. When they find themselves unexpectedly confronted with extraordinary events their reactions range from strong denial to wholehearted acceptance, but ultimately their experiences fundamentally affect both their own lives and the lives of those around them.

There is an inventive array of unusual occurrences throughout the narratives. There are wraiths seeking justice and lost spirits searching for succour; there is a woman who lives her life by feeding on the essence of others, another who can physically regress to her long lost youth, and yet another who sees glimpses of the future but then loses her grasp of the present; there is a room which is a gateway to a strange and disturbing place; and there is an evil bracelet that irretrievably dooms its wearer to nightmarish visions. Although there are scenes of horror, Freeman generally preferred to achieve her effect by use of atmosphere rather than graphic description, and more of her ghosts are portrayed with sympathy than with dread.

HER FIRST PROFESSIONALLY published work was the poem "The Beggar King" in the March 1881 edition of the children's magazine

Wide Awake, which featured many more of her contributions in the ensuing ten years, some 60 poems and 25 works of prose. She also became a regular contributor to another periodical for children, *St Nicholas Magazine*, and her total contributions to both of these titles numbered to around a hundred. While continuing to write for *Wide Awake* and *St. Nicholas Magazine*, she also began to produce adult fiction, and her first such story was "The Shadow Family" in 1882, for which she won a $50 prize from the *Boston Sunday Budget*.

It was not until the following year that her adult writing career began to blossom, starting with "Two Old Lovers" in *Harper's Bazaar* for March 1883. This was followed by a further six tales by the end of the year; 1883 also saw her first published book, a collection of poems entitled *Decorative Plaques*, all of which were reprinted from *Wide Awake*. Subsequently, her work began to appear frequently, mainly in the pages of *Harper's Bazaar*, other *Harper's* titles, and in such periodicals as *The Ladies' Home Journal*, *Everybody's Magazine* and *Woman's Home Companion*. Her collections and novels were published regularly from 1886 onwards.

Freeman demonstrated early on that she had a notable talent for recounting the imaginative and the out-of-the-ordinary, producing some eerily atmospheric tales during 1883. The first of these was "The Bar Light-House", which tells of how the unlit lamp in a deserted lighthouse mysteriously starts working during a fierce storm and how a white rose blooms where no roses have bloomed before, leading an old woman to regain her faith in God. This was followed by "The Story of Little Mary Whitlow", the affecting and poignant account of a humble dying girl whose only wish is to see Portland.

Her first two patently supernatural tales, "A Symphony in Lavender" and "A Far-Away Melody", appeared later in that same year. Both are bitter-sweet reflections on life and living, with the unearthly element augmenting the narratives. In "A Symphony in

Lavender" a strange dream portends evil consequences for a potential romantic relationship. It is a tale of regret for what might have been, tempered with the knowledge that the dream may well have been a true harbinger of what the future could have held. In "A Far-Away Melody" the sound of distant music heralds death for the middle-aged woman who is the only person who can hear it, leaving her twin sister waiting for her own end and listening for that same melody herself.

"A Village Lear" (1888) also deals with the approach of death: a dying old man seeing what he most wants as his life expires. But none of Freeman's work to this point had been specifically ghostly. She did, however, embrace that theme with "A Gentle Ghost" in 1889, which features an apparently haunted bedroom and a lonely little girl who sees the spirits of dead people. There is ultimately a rational if far-fetched explanation for the former, but the spectres are real enough and only recede when the child finds the companionship that she has been craving from the living rather than the dead. In that same year "The Twelfth Guest" appeared, about an unknown waif who appears mysteriously, insinuates herself into the heart of a family, and who just as mysteriously disappears when her altruistic work as a guardian angel is done.

"The Little Maid at the Door", Freeman's strongest story to date, was published in 1892. Set in the 1700s, it is an indictment of the witch-hunting purges of the time of Cotton Mather (who makes an appearance at the end of the tale), and also touches upon the hysteria which affected ordinary people during that period. The "little maid" of the title is the young child Abigail Proctor whose whole family is arrested on trumped-up charges; she is then pitilessly left alone on their remote farm to fend for herself, with inevitable consequences. Her end is movingly portrayed as is her final post-mortem appearance at the door, an appearance which lifts the bleakness of the narrative without detracting from the cruel reality that lies at its heart.

Another interesting story is "Silence" from 1893, again set in Colonial times and revolving around the bloody French and Indian raid on the isolated town of Deerfield in 1704. Silence Hoit provides an intriguing air of mystery to what is outwardly a straightforward historical romance. She has premonitions of the impending disaster, seeing blood in the snow as well as a red glare in the sky that no-one else can see, and her reaction to the carnage is to close her mind to all but the immediate present. She casts herself mentally adrift from reality, even unable to recognise her lover on his return from captivity, and it is only the "witch-work" of Goody Crane that eventually restores her.

There was a gap of some years before Freeman turned again to the weird tale, although she had produced several peripheral pieces. These included "The Lost Book" (1899), a very short metaphorical vignette about the placing of too much reliance on material things; "The Christmas Ghost" (1900), an apparent ghost story which eventually has a logical explanation; and two agreeable light fantasies: "Arethusa" (1901), about a rare, delicate orchid and its human counterpart; and "The Prism" (1901), about a girl who sees magical things though a glass crystal.

However, these last few were simply precursors to what was to be an exceptionally fruitful fifteen month period spanning 1902 and 1903, which saw the publication of seven supernatural tales, including most of her best work. All but one of them were included in the single volume of her genre work published during her lifetime: *The Wind in the Rose-Bush and Other Stories of the Supernatural* (1903). The excluded piece was "The Hall Bedroom", which appeared in *Collier's*; the other six had originally featured in *Everybody's Magazine*. This suggests that Freeman may have been writing "to order", perhaps having been asked by *Everybody's* to produce just such a series; if so, then she certainly demonstrated a remarkable talent for a type of tale that she had only touched upon before then. That these pieces were quickly assembled into book form might indicate that such publication was the original intention, although the inconsistent appearance of "The Hall Bedroom" in *Collier's* and its exclusion from the collection are puzzling.

The first of the 1902 stories was "The Wind in the Rose-Bush", and it ably set the scene for what was to be a succession of memorable narratives. It tells of Rebecca Flint, who has not seen her niece Agnes for several years and goes to collect her from Emeline Dent, the stepmother with whom she has been living. The exact whereabouts of Agnes presents a bizarre problem, for she seems to be both present and absent, and there are strange happenings in the house where she supposedly lives. What turns out to be a gentle haunting is skilfully portrayed, and while the ending comes as no great surprise it remains quietly potent.

"The Wind in the Rose-Bush" was followed by "The Vacant Lot", the tale of a family who moves into a house which has an adjacent empty lot that is the source of a variety of ghostly occurrences. The story is perhaps not entirely successful at generating a convincing aura of the uncanny, with the actions and reactions on the parts of the protagonists rather stilted and implausible, but the parade of ghosts that move in indifferent ways through the tale are depicted with dexterity and a keen sense of subliminal menace. The ending, with its emphasis on historical synchronicity, is an unusual but inventive coda.

Next came the superior "Luella Miller", a vampire tale but not in the conventional sense. The beautiful Luella drains not blood but the life-force of those around her, sustaining her own vitality at the cost of theirs. Luella is not a conscious predator – she seems to be naively unaware of her deadly personality, with her selfishness blinding her to the destruction that she wreaks. Her demise is grimly dealt with, although the implication is that even after death Luella still retains her alluring power. The premise of the story may be more outré than its predecessors but paradoxically it is far more believable by virtue of its characterisation and its simpler storytelling structure.

"The Shadows on the Wall" is another good tale, dealing with the ghostly appearance on a wall of the shadow of a murdered man. Much of the authority of the simply told narrative lies in the author's flair for seamlessly melding the everyday behaviour of the characters with the strange manifestation in the Glynns' study. The tale has a forceful conclusion which not only confirms the reader's suspicions regarding the original death but also provides an assurance that justice has finally been done.

This very impressive sequence of short fiction was maintained with "The Hall Bedroom", the compelling and atmospheric narrative of a boarding house bedroom that at night becomes a **portal** to somewhere completely different. Whether that place is good or evil is a question that remains tantalisingly unresolved, and George Wheatcroft's uncertainties are subtly handled and depicted with considerable skill, as is the covert menace inherent in the utter darkness of that other location (the concept of an entrance to elsewhere was later utilised in Freeman's 1910 story "The Green Door" in which the door of the title opens into the past, with no immediately apparent way of returning).

Similarly set in a boarding house is "The Southwest Chamber", in which a bedroom is haunted by a mean spirit whose malice affects different people in different ways. Each person who sleeps in the room has a different experience, all disturbing and unsettling. In an ending that echoes that of "The Vacant Lot" and "The Hall Bedroom", there is no combating the room's evil inhabitant and instead a practical course of action is adopted, that of conceding defeat to the otherworldly power and escaping its influence by moving away.

"The Lost Ghost" was the last of this outstanding group of seven tales, and is a superior ghost story about the spectre of a little dead girl who is unable to understand her condition. She is seeking comfort that is not forthcoming and is unable to move on, remaining earthbound until she can come to terms with the fact of her death. The ending of this satisfying piece is reminiscent of "The Little Maid at the Door" and the later "School-Teacher's Story" with its emphasis on the peace and happiness that accompany the transition of a lost spirit to higher realms, and its final lines are just as gratifying as they are in those other stories.

All of Freeman's works up until 1902 had been published as by Mary E Wilkins (or Mary Wilkins or ME Wilkins), but following her marriage to Dr Charles Freeman she began to use the by-line Mary E Wilkins Freeman. Although she had been engaged to Dr Freeman for five years her marriage was not a happy one, culminating in her husband's committal for alcoholism and drug abuse in 1920 and his death three years later after unsuccessfully attempting to disinherit her.

She wrote only a few supernatural stories after her marriage, with perhaps real life having become depressing enough without her wishing to indulge in otherworldly problems. However, some of her tales from this period were particularly fine, positive pieces. In "Sweet-Flowering Perennial" (1915), a middle-aged woman stays with an old school acquaintance and is puzzled by the strange periodic appearance of a young girl who resembles her friend. It is actually the woman herself who physically regains her lost youth for a few hours at a time, possessing "the power of perennial bloom". A theme similar to this was also used in the earlier tale "The Travelling Sister" (1909), in which a woman relives happier times in "the lost land of youth" and is convinced that she really has moved backward to those days when her lover was still alive and her own life held a promise which never materialised.

"The School-Teacher's Story" (1917) tells of the ghost of a long dead child who is longingly haunting an old school room and who is eventually laid to rest thanks to the pragmatism of an aging schoolteacher using an old primer and a rag doll. This, together with "The Lost Ghost", is a primary example of one of Freeman's major strengths: relating the meeting of the ordinary and the extraordinary and the uplifting results of compassionate communication with beings not entirely of this world.

Two other stories from this stage of her career were "The Witch's Daughter" (1910), a short romantic tale of the supposed witch Elma Franklin attempting to magically ensure true love for her ostracised daughter, and "The Jade Bracelet" (1918), which tells of a wristlet infused with vicious evil. This latter story is very unusual for Freeman in that the major characters are both male, as is the malevolent villain, and with the exception of the brief appearance of a maid, not a single woman appears. While it is not one of her very best pieces, it does represent an interesting departure from her normal type of fiction and is the closest that she came to writing a pure horror story.

The last of her spectral tales to be published was "The White Shawl", an undated manuscript – possibly a draft – found amongst her papers and included in *The Uncollected Stories of Mary Wilkins Freeman* in 1992. It has two separate (but not very different) endings, and tells of a railway crossing which needs to be manned during a storm, with its operative near to death and no-one seemingly able to prevent a potential disaster – but the crossing lights *do* mysteriously operate. This engaging story has similarities to "The Bar Light-

House", although it does differ considerably from that story in the same way that "Sweet-Flowering Perennial" and "The Travelling Sister" share a common theme but remain individual and diverse pieces.

A number of the other stories mentioned do have common features, not in their plots but in their central characteristics. The principal players are often unmarried middle-aged women, usually schoolteachers. There is a strong suggestion that the lack of marital status is a mark of their independence, coming from choice as opposed to the need to fulfil others' expectations. Several of the tales are set in boarding houses, locations that not only have a subtly emphasised sense of isolation, with the tenants away from their own homes and living amongst strangers, but also locations that can have their own unknown and unhallowed histories. Some of the family units depicted are far from idyllic, with hostility maintained even beyond the grave, but some of the most memorable and touching fiction is that dealing with the death of the very young. Freeman's portrayals of forlorn dead children and their benign hauntings are consistently well wrought and are emotive without being maudlin.

In certain of the narratives there is an underlying symbolism. "The Prism", for example, is an allegory of the setting aside of childhood, the tale demonstrating what must be sacrificed in the rites of passage into adulthood. There are also rites of passage that the dead must experience if they are attain their rest and not remain as troubled and troubling spectres – as in "The Lost Ghost" and "The Schoolteacher's Story". Each of these two tales ends on a pleasing note of finality; the spirits and their hauntings are stopped, but with empathy and understanding rather than any ritualistic exorcism.

Although the ghosts of the latter two stories are not at all daunting, seeking peace above all else, the dead are neither gentle nor sad in such tales as "The Southwest Chamber" and "The Vacant Lot", and they actively seek justice in "The Wind in the Rose-Bush" and "The Shadows on the Wall". Freeman's darker creations were, however, more wide-ranging: "The Jade Bracelet" is an object instilled with the essence of an Oriental malice that entraps the unwary, while "Luella Miller" is herself a conduit for another kind of evil, just as pervasive if less deliberately malignant. And if the ultimate fate of the occupants of "The Hall Bedroom" is admittedly unknown, it does not seem likely that it will have been at all beneficial.

If placid ghosts are helped in their search for solace, those of a less temperate variety are in effect left to their own devices. In "The Vacant Lot" and "The Southwest Chamber" there is no attempt to banish the spirits responsible for the bizarre events and the protagonists simply leave, as is also the case in "The Hall Bedroom". Such tacit acceptance of the futility of combating otherworldly presences highlights the unpretentious approach that Freeman's characters exhibit throughout much of her fiction; there are some things that cannot be changed, and it is pointless to make the attempt. Thus these characters move on physically in the same way that the dead in the other tales move on spiritually.

Apart from the six-story 1903 collection *The Wind in the Rose-Bush and Other Stories of the Supernatural*, Freeman's weird tales were interspersed amongst a number of different volumes of her work. A compilation of all of them was long overdue but it was not until 1974 that her *Collected Ghost Stories* appeared from the publisher Arkham House. This volume, despite the title, was not devoted exclusively to ghost stories, and was credited to "Mary E Wilkins-Freeman" although she had rarely been published with her name hyphenated. The book purported to be "the first complete edition" of her tales; however, this was not the case at all for only eleven stories were included. Such fine pieces **as** "The Little Maid at the Door", "Silence", "The School-Teacher's Story" and "Sweet-Flowering Perennial" were omitted.

In his Introduction to the volume, Edward Wagenknecht seemed to have some doubts as to the validity of the claim to completeness, saying of the contents: "I cannot of my own knowledge swear that there is nothing of a supernatural character elsewhere ... which has not been caught between these covers".

It does seem odd that the publisher missed out so many titles, particularly ones of such quality, and the fact remains that a full edition of Wilkins Freeman's eerie tales has yet to appear. If and when it ever does, that edition will be properly representative of a writer whose predominantly down-to-earth and regional fiction included a number of supernatural stories that really do highlight her understated capabilities in the field.

SELECTED BIBLIOGRAPHY

"The Bar Light-House" – *Harper's Bazaar*, April 1883

"The Story of Little Mary Whitlow" – *Lippincott's Magazine*, May 1883

"A Symphony in Lavender" – *Harper's Bazaar*, August 1883

"A Far-Away Melody" – *Harper's Bazaar*, September 1883

"A Village Lear" – *Harper's Bazaar*, November 1888

"A Gentle Ghost" – *Harper's Monthly*, August 1889

"The Twelfth Guest" – *Harper's Monthly*, December 1889

"The Little Maid at the Door" – *Harper's Magazine*, February 1892

"Silence"– *Harper's Monthly*, July 1893

"The Lost Book"– *Book Culture*, September 1899

"Arethusa"– *Harper's Bazaar*, November 1900

"The Christmas Ghost"– *Everybody's Magazine*, December 1900

"The Prism"– *The Century*, July 1901

"The Wind in the Rose-Bush"– *Everybody's Magazine*, February 1902

"The Vacant Lot"– *Everybody's Magazine*, September 1902

"Luella Miller"– *Everybody's Magazine*, December 1902

"The Shadows on the Wall"– *Everybody's Magazine*, March 1903

"The Hall Bedroom"– *Collier's*, March 1903

"The Southwest Chamber"– *Everybody's Magazine*, April 1903

"The Lost Ghost"– *Everybody's Magazine*, May 1903

"The Travelling Sister"– *Harper's Monthly,* December 1909

"The Green Door"– *The Green Door*, 1910

"The Witch's Daughter"– *Harper's Weekly*, December 1910

"Sweet-Flowering Perennial"– *Harper's Monthly*, July 1915

"The School-Teacher's Story"– *The American Woman*, June 1917

"The Jade Bracelet"– *The Forum*, April 1918

"The White Shawl"– *The Uncollected Stories of Mary Wilkins Freeman*, 1992

SCREAMING SKULLS AND DEAD SMILES
F MARION CRAWFORD

FRANCIS MARION CRAWFORD (1854-1909) wrote something like forty-four novels in a career that spanned three decades, and was enormously successful from the publication of his very first book, *Mr Isaacs*, in 1882. The vast majority of his works were historical romances; amongst the most well-known were *Saracinesca* (1887) and its two sequels *Sant' Ilario* (1889) and *Don Orsino* (1892), all of which went through multiple printings and sold well over a million copies. Crawford was *the* fashionable author of his time, to the extent that when he was ill and nearing death *The New York Times* felt it necessary to include regular bulletins about his health on their front page. And yet all of his novels are now virtually forgotten, with little likelihood of there being any literary renaissance for them; such fame as may be the author's today instead rests on a handful of superior weird tales that were not collected together in book form during his lifetime.

Crawford's distinction of having written many volumes of extremely popular fiction that are now almost completely overlooked is shared with such authors as Robert W Chambers and Lord Dunsany. Chambers produced a limited number of influential stories of considerable macabre power and Dunsany is acknowledged as *the* master of evocative fantasy, but like Crawford they were writers who devoted only a small part of their impressive literary talents to such works. However, what may have seemed to be their lesser efforts are now those that are their most renowned; for all three, an ephemeral prominence has been replaced by a lasting reputation in a quite different area of literature.

Crawford wrote three genre novels: *Zoroaster* (1885), a story of magic and mysticism; *The Witch of Prague* (1891), with its wizardry and horror; and his own personal favourite, the Arabian Nights-type fantasy *Khaled* (also 1891). There were several others that had peripheral supernatural elements, including *Mr Isaacs*, with its astral projection; *With the Immortals* (1888), which tells of the resurrection of the spirits of long dead famous people; while *Cecilia* (1902) and *The Heart of Rome* (1903) deal with re-incarnation. These are not books that are readily available, and nor do they rank amongst the higher annals of imaginative fiction, but all are reasonably enjoyable if somewhat dated.

However, the author's eight tales of the extraordinary, most of which were featured in various contemporary periodicals, do remain in print. Three of these appeared in two slim volumes, *The Upper Berth* (1894) and *Man Overboard* (1903), but the bulk of them were not collected in book form until the posthumous publication of *Uncanny Tales* in March 1911 – renamed *Wandering Ghosts* for its American printing later that same year. The seven stories contained within this volume (the eighth was unaccountably omitted) each demonstrate a rare facility for this type of fiction, with not a single one being less than exceptional and several attaining the standard of classics of the field.

CRAWFORD WAS BORN in Italy of American parents, and was educated in a variety of places around the world. He is said to have mastered an astonishing eighteen different languages, but had originally set his sights on becoming a professional singer. It was only when he realised that this was not going to happen that he turned to writing, and *Mr Isaacs*, based on a story he had heard in India, was published to immediate acclaim. After this, his literary future was assured and he produced well-received and popular novels on a regular basis for the rest of his life.

His first genre effort was "The Upper Berth" (1886) and is perhaps his best known work, one which HP Lovecraft described as "one of the most tremendous horror stories in all literature". It is certainly a chilling tale, one that lingers in the memory long after it is finished. It details the events that occur in a particular cabin on an ocean liner, events that have previously led to madness and suicide. The narrator, stubbornly level-headed, chooses to stay in the cabin despite its ominous reputation and the inexplicable happenings that he himself begins to experience. The smell of stagnant sea-water and a porthole that will not remain closed take on an ill-omened significance in the context of what is to occur on the third night, with events then coming to a head. When the occupant of the upper berth is finally clearly seen, Crawford's descriptive powers do not fail him as he fully and graphically details the horror of what appears.

There is no specific explanation given for the haunting, but none is needed. The fact that the manifestation is dreadfully real is all that is relevant in the context of this story, and the gradual building of tension leading up to the eventual confrontation is conveyed in a manner that skilfully evokes a mounting apprehension. "The Upper Berth" is a particularly fine tale, eloquently impressive, and it fully justifies the praise it has earned.

In the following year, 1887, "By the Waters of Paradise" appeared.

This atmospheric and forceful story is essentially a romance, telling of a young man dogged by bad luck who falls in love with someone who he thinks is a ghost but whom he then discovers is a flesh and blood beautiful woman. His luck runs true to form and the spirit of his family home – the Woman of the Waters – seems to take the life of his fiancé, but he saves her and thereby vanquishes the curse that has so persistently plagued him. It is descriptively excellent – Crawford paints an indelible image of the brooding Cairngorm Castle with well-chosen words that emphasise its austere nature and infuse a sense of doom-laden melancholy into the plot. The lifting of the curse is mirrored in the lifting of the depressed tone of the narrative, a distinct shift from darkness into light which works well without being at all heavy-handed.

These first two of the author's eerie stories were published together in 1894 as *The Upper Berth* under the imprint T Fisher Unwin in London (as by Marion Crawford, without the opening initial) and GP Putnam's Sons in New York, but it was to be some years before Crawford returned to the realm of the outré, with "The Dead Smile" in 1899.

"The Dead Smile" is a first-rate work with elements of the Gothic. There is a gloomy mansion, a sepulchre where the bodies are laid out on top of their tombs rather than being interred (with one particular corpse that persistently and disconcertingly changes position), and a spiteful old man who takes dire knowledge to his grave knowing that it will destroy his son if it becomes known. Sir Hugh Ockram refuses to the very end to divulge the secret, and his dying words are "They know it in Hell".

The "secret" is very clearly telegraphed from the opening pages, but this was almost certainly a deliberate device used by the author to heighten the suspense of the story. The reader is well aware of a specific relationship that is unknown to the two characters involved, and watches its development with foreboding. This is a rather clever ploy, and one which takes skill to successfully bring off, but Crawford manages it very well, leaving us with a splendid final line. This compelling story generates bleak anticipation as the seeming inevitability of what would be an awful revelation for Gabriel and Evelyn is deftly brought to the forefront of the narrative and resolved with skilled facility. "The Dead Smile" may not quite reach the heights of Crawford's *very* best works, but is far superior to the vast majority of fiction of its type.

"Man Overboard!" appeared as a hardcover book in 1903 (lacking the exclamation mark), and is a potent story of post-mortem revenge. Constructed as the reminiscence of a sailor telling a long-time friend of the incident, the prose is straightforward as it relates its tale simply and without embellishment. After the loss of a man overboard, one of identical twin crew members, strange things begin to happen on the ship; initially, there is nothing that can be construed as out-rightly alarming, but a combination of minor things suggest that the dead man remains aboard, unseen and persistent. The feelings of unease escalate, with everyone affected; trepidation suffuses the ship, all the more disquieting for the fact that there is nothing genuinely frightening happening. Even so, the haunting is insidious and unsettling, with the ghost persistently emphasising his existence and driving the crew close to mutiny with his ubiquitous presence, until finally the ship reaches the comparative safety of land.

But things are far from over. The surviving twin brother never returns to the sea, and several years later he marries the woman to whom he has been engaged since before the fateful voyage. It is after the ceremony that suspicions are finally confirmed, the truth uncovered, and justice meted out in chilling fashion. There is memorable imagery in the closing scenes, when the latent sense of menace so capably instilled becomes unadulterated horror.

"For the Blood is the Life" (1905), another classic from Crawford's pen, is an excellent vampire story set in southern Italy. The vampire is a young woman driven obsessively by her love of the victim; no explanation is given for her vampirism except that she was violently killed and buried in unhallowed ground. After the traditional despatch with a stake – related at second hand but none the less powerfully depicted – all that remains is her revenant that haunts the place of her death, incapable of doing anything other than to appear by moonlight.

Crawford thus creates something different – the ghost of a vampire. Despite the terror of the vampire's predations, there is a sadness about the girl's condition that is portrayed with a subtle poignancy. This combination of dread and pity works well; the fact that the horror is now nullified and the vampire powerless does not detract from the impact. There is also an inference that perhaps she *can* still have a physical effect if given the opportunity, and this adds a further unsettling dimension to what is a superior tale.

As mentioned above, the bulk of Crawford's short weird fiction was posthumously collected as *Uncanny Tales* in 1911, but there was one story which was puzzlingly missing from that volume, "The King's Messenger", which had been published in 1907. Its omission must have been an oversight, for it is a very good story, one that fittingly evokes a dream-like atmosphere as it describes an unusual dinner party and its late-coming thirteenth guest. The true identity of that enigmatic guest is never in any real doubt, and nor is the fate of the beautiful Lorna, but the narrative remains persuasively interesting. And when all is revealed there is an unforeseen development right at the end which rounds out the tale, giving it a satisfyingly complete conclusion.

Next came "The Screaming Skull" in 1908, another of Crawford's primary works. The author acknowledged in an Afterword that this intriguing and unnerving story was based on the existence of a supposed screaming skull at Bettiscombe Manor, in Bettiscombe,

Dorset, which is apparently still there to this day. Legend has it that the skull cannot be removed from the house without causing the phenomenon that gives it its name, and Crawford utilised the myth well. The tale is told as one side of a conversation between two old friends, one visiting the other and hearing a strange noise, then being informed of the story behind it. The narrator is living in a lonely isolated house that previously belonged to his late cousin, and one of the things he inherited was a skull that could be that of his cousin's wife, whom he may have inadvertently caused to be killed by suggesting a fool-proof method of murder to her husband.

Crawford establishes a powerful aura of the supernatural, and although the teller of the story persistently attempts to rationalise the strange events that occur, those attempts become more and more feeble. "The Screaming Skull" is a very strong tale; its unusual construction works well and instils tense foreboding. The ending is a sombre confirmation of all that had previously been supposed, as the narrator ultimately faces the truth of things in the most awful of ways.

"The Doll's Ghost" has an unknown provenance, having first appeared in *Uncanny Tales,* and is the only one of Crawford's supernatural stories that does not involve an element of menace. It is the gentle and pleasing story of a broken doll, the man whose task it is to repair it, and his missing daughter. The characters are well drawn and even in its short length "The Doll's Ghost" vividly brings Bernard Puckler and Else to life, as well as their relationship to the doll of the title. Supposedly written as an expression of regret for the breaking of a doll belonging to a young girl (possibly his sister) in his youth, it is the most straightforward of all Crawford's stories and has a warmth that underlines the author's literary diversity, making it an interesting contrast to the almost unrelenting grimness of his other tales.

That grimness was certainly a hallmark of the bulk of Crawford's genre fiction; his major attribute in the writing of these eerie works was the ability to create a sense of the ominous in a subtle and understated way. He was adept at delicately but fully drawing his reader into the uneasy ambiance of his narratives, gradually infusing an awareness of the forbidding and pervasive powers that dominate his fiction. His writing style was fluid and straightforward, directly approaching his subject with little or no circumlocution – here for example is how he starts "The Screaming Skull": "I have often heard it scream. No, I am not nervous, I am not imaginative, and I never believed in ghosts, unless that thing is one. Whatever it is, it hates me almost as much as it hated Luke Pratt, and it screams at me".

This technique of immediately seizing the reader's interest is not difficult, but Crawford succeeded in the far harder task of effortlessly *sustaining* that interest.

The eight stories that comprise his contribution to weird literature are each notable, with no repetition in theme or setting, although a love of the sea and sailing is readily apparent. The plots are original and absorbing, and each work has its own unique piquancy, with their re-reading providing as much pleasure as that experienced on first encountering them. Many an observer has rightly commented that the only criticism one can make is that there are just too few of these remarkable tales.

Crawford lived most of his life in Italy, and he died of a heart attack in Sorrento on Good Friday, 9 April 1909 at the age of only fifty-four. Although his overall contribution to the field was modest in quantity, its quality was such that he will be long remembered; if *Saracinesca*, *Sant' Ilario* and *Don Orsino* are now forgotten novels, "The Upper Berth", "Man Overboard!", "For the Blood is the Life" and "The Screaming Skull" are unlikely ever to be forgotten short stories.

SELECTED BIBLIOGRAPHY

Short stories

"The Upper Berth" – *The Broken Shaft: Unwin's Annual*, 1886

"By the Waters of Paradise" – *The Witching Time: Unwin's Annual*, 1887

"The Dead Smile" – *Ainslee's Magazine*, August 1899

"Man Overboard!" – *Man Overboard*, 1903

"For the Blood is the Life" – *Collier's Magazine*, December 1905

"The King's Messenger" – *The Cosmopolitan*, November 1907

"The Screaming Skull" – *Collier's Magazine*, July 1908

"The Doll's Ghost" – *Uncanny Tales*, 1911

DARK AND SINISTER SHADES
MARJORIE BOWEN

MARJORIE BOWEN (1885-1952), a British writer, was principally an author of historical fiction, and a very prolific and successful one. She is credited with some 170 books, and in one remarkable four-year period starting in 1932 she published no less than thirty-six titles, with a total of 75 books through the whole of the 1930s. Although her output was mainly historical novels, there were additionally various biographical works, several plays, some non-fiction, a number of collections, and an autobiography. She also found time to edit two anthologies of horror stories, translating several of them from French. Bowen used the pseudonyms George R Preedy and Joseph Shearing for many titles, with the names Robert Paye and John Winch employed on a few occasions as well, while her autobiography appeared under the by-line of Margaret Campbell, which was actually a shortened version of her real name.

Born Gabrielle Margaret Vere Campbell, Bowen's early years were not happy, to the extent that she admitted "I would have destroyed myself had I known how". She indicated that she began to write "not only to express my own ideas, and to exercise the technique I was trying to acquire, but to escape from the world in which I lived". Her inclination towards historical fiction was the result of having no desire to "depict the life about me, it was too stale and wearisome. I tried to escape from it as best I could".

She displayed much stoicism in the face of what was considerable adversity, supporting the profligacy of an unkind and ungrateful mother and sister for many years. Tragedy was also present – she lost her first child before its first birthday and her husband died a few years later, as did his doctor, a man with whom Bowen had fallen deeply in love. Her subsequent marriage to Arthur Long was one which she stated was "a singular and pleasing union" but there seem to be indications to the contrary. Even so, she did appear to ultimately find gratification in her family and her writing, and with commendable inner strength she was able to pragmatically accept her earlier unhappiness as a part of what she considered to be an overall learning experience.

Although she said that most of her tales were "often full of dark and sinister shades", supernatural and macabre fiction comprised only a relatively minor part of her overall output, totalling some fifty short stories and a number of novels; nevertheless, her writing has prompted comparisons with the likes of MR James, Arthur Machen and Walter de la Mare. That such comparisons are not at all exaggerated is amply demonstrated in three excellent collections published during her lifetime, *Seeing Life* (1923), *The Last Bouquet* (1933) and *The Bishop of Hell* (1949); all display the author's impressive penchant for dark fiction. Such pieces as "Kecksies", "Florence Flannery", "The Avenging of Ann Leete", "The Crown Derby Plate" and "Ann Mellor's Lover" are particularly memorable exercises in chilling storytelling. There are also a number of outstanding contributions that are not featured in the three volumes mentioned, but are interspersed throughout the author's other collections.

Posthumously, *Kecksies and Other Twilight Tales* (1976) included many of the most significant Bowen stories, and *Twilight and Other Supernatural Romances* (1998) was a completely different selection, including two previously unpublished pieces. This latter title is evidently the first of two volumes that, together with *Kecksies,* are intended to encompass the whole of Bowen's genre writing.

Within Bowen's *oeuvre*, there are stories involving various types of haunting, benign as well as horrific, and accounts of revenge taken in wide-ranging macabre and ghostly ways; spectres seeking to right their own past wrongs, and others that are interested only in maintaining their evil natures; tales evoking a poignant and gentle post-mortem atmosphere and others instilling a sense of utter horror. Although the author's average length for her short fiction was around five thousand words, there are also narratives of less than two hundred that carry an authority disproportionate to their brevity.

Bowen's stories very capably sustained a powerful effect regardless of their word count. They were consistently interesting and it was only the rare exception that fell short of the high standards that she established for herself from her earliest prose. She could write in a deceptively light and beguiling manner that drew the reader gently into uncanny events or establish an overtly sharp edge of terror from her opening lines. She did not see the need for happy endings, although some do occur, and she decried stories of false or comic ghosts – her horrors tend to be real and disturbingly close, and are never to be underestimated.

THE BULK OF Bowen's fiction is set in the eighteenth century, while several of the contemporary pieces involve a retreat to the past, with old portraits bringing that past to convincing life for the characters who become obsessed by them. Dilapidated buildings and desolate landscapes play a part in many of the stories, with the depiction of a lingering aura of decay commandingly forceful, both physical and moral decay. Antagonistic relationships are also portrayed with particular strength, as are doomed love affairs and unhappy memories, emotional areas that one suspects the author could write about with a rueful wealth of experience.

Bowen's literary fame was achieved and then sustained despite the domestic unhappiness that dogged her, and while her abilities may have been unappreciated by most of those around her, publishers and readers had no doubts at all as to her talents, and her many books were highly successful. Her writing career began when she wrote the novel *The Viper of Milan*, reportedly at the age of sixteen. The book was eventually published several years later in 1906, having been rejected by many publishers who did not consider it proper for a young girl to have written such an ominous and violent story. The book was very successful and went though many printings; a succession of well received historical novels followed, including the unusual *Black Magic* in 1909. Subtitled "A Tale of the Rise and Fall of the Antichrist", the book was a departure from the author's previous five novels in that it dealt specifically with the occult with an entertaining interpretation of the apocryphal tale of Pope Joan.

Other mystical novels appeared from Bowen, but bearing in mind her large overall output they were relatively few, and included such works as *The Haunted Vintage* (1921), *I Dwelt in High Places* (1923), *The Presence and the Power* (1924), *Five Winds* (1927), *The Shadow on Mockways* (1932) and the posthumously published *The Man With the Scales* (1954). These were narratives in which the unearthly elements were often secondary to the plot and lacked the immediacy and impact of the short stories, although they remain worthy books. There were also many popular Gothic novels published under the Joseph Shearing pseudonym.

Bowen moved into the arena of shorter fiction early in her career, and within a few years of the appearance of *The Viper of Milan* she had a number of tales published, primarily in the pages of *Harper's Monthly*, starting with "A Princess of Kent" in the April 1908 issue. Her first collection was *God's Playthings* in 1912, which comprised sixteen original stories, all of which remained within the confines of the past eras that typified her writing, but which were of a uniformly bleak aspect. They were cheerless tales, reflecting the unforgiving times in which they were set, each of them revolving around the deaths of historical characters.

The supernatural plays a part in several of the narratives. The first of these, "A Poor Spanish Lodging", has a mysterious woman visiting the dying Duke of Wharton and leading him through reminiscences of his past by becoming each of the women he has carelessly betrayed and cast aside. One of them – whom he remembers with genuine fondness and guilty regret – finally draws him to a forlorn death. "Twilight" powerfully tells of the aftermath of the death of Lucrezia Borgia, with her ghost appearing lasciviously and horrifically to a young courtier at the Ducal Palace. "The Burning of the Vanities" is the story of Girolamo Savonarola, the priest who established the republic of Florence in 1497 and became its leader. Confronted by a mysterious stranger, he has an unsought vision of his own grisly demise; the paranormal aspect lies in the fact that his death did occur a year later in *exactly* the same terrible way.

Although such stories as "The Polander" and "The Extraordinary Adventure of Grace Endicott" have hints of haunting and witchcraft respectively, they are essentially non-genre, unlike the penultimate tale, "The Prisoner". This concerns the Princess Sophia of Zell who was imprisoned in a remote castle in Hanover after being discovered with her lover, whom her husband then had killed and burned in an oven. Thirty-two lonely years later, her lady-in-waiting finds her mistress strangely rejuvenated, looking as she had done all those years earlier, and then the maid hears phantom oven doors closing… The Princess is of course dead, having finally escaped her unhappy captivity. This is a well told story which impressively generates an atmosphere of mortality and unwelcome remembrance, and is a very good example of Bowen's interweaving of the factual with the mystical. It also incorporates a further feature that distinguished much of her writing: the depiction of a well-drawn female character at the forefront of the plot.

A further macabre historical tale appeared late in 1912: "The Folding Doors", set in the aftermath of the French Revolution, is a potent account of jealousy and revenge. There is no weird element, but the story is instilled with an insidious menace, compellingly drawing the reader towards a final line that is memorably shocking in its suggestiveness. Another story dating from this period was "The Recluse and Springtime", written around 1915 but evidently not published until 1998 in the *Twilight* collection; it is an interesting piece set in a dilapidated palazzo where spring can never flourish and where the dead are stranded in an awful ghostly limbo.

Bowen's 1916 collection *Shadows of Yesterday* included several strong stories. "The Fair Hair of Ambrosine", set in eighteenth century France just after the Revolution, is a compelling and eerie tale of murder and a premonition which turns into frightful reality in what was becoming a customary downbeat ending for the author's forays into the realm of the weird. Similarly, "Giudetta's Wedding Night" ends darkly, this time on a note of unadulterated horror with a terrible revenge being taken in plague-ridden Venice. In contrast, "Petronilla of the Laurel Trees" is a gentle, moving account of a woman loved by two men but possessed by neither, with an expressive final paragraph demonstrating that her warm presence has outlasted her short life. Another exceptional story in the book is "The Scarlet Rose", which has a remarkable twist in the tail, one that the lead character can only cope with by retreating totally into insanity.

Curious Happenings was another collection of short stories, appearing in 1917, and again included some notable tales of the uncanny. "The Sign Painter and the Crystal Fishes" is a strange but very effective piece. Little is revealed and much is left to be surmised, but there is undeniable power in the imagery of the dead returning to either exact or receive justice. There is an eerie ambiance pervading the two-part narrative, with the second half in particular evoking a strong dream-like quality, amply demonstrating both Bowen's descriptive skills and her ability to smoothly impart unsettling notions. "The Scoured Silk" is also forceful: it is another eighteenth century tale, one in which a man keeps his unfaithful wife locked up in a small room for twenty years until she finally takes a bloody revenge on him. The book additionally includes powerful stories of murderous resentment ("The Pond"), lethal tragedy ("The Umbrella Mender") and doomed relationships ("A Venetian Evening").

Crimes of Old London (1919) reprinted "The Scoured Silk" and also included a further three weird tales. Of these, "The Housekeeper" is a strong ghost story set in 1710, in which a man is driven to confess to his wife's murder because of her continuing haunting of him, a haunting that, far from being terrifying, is persistently and devastatingly *kind*. "Brent's Folly" is a minor and frankly rather puzzling tale about the Philosopher's Stone, while "The Extraordinary Adventure of Mr John Proudie" (also known as "The Mystery of Dr. Francis Valletort") is a tale of revenge set in 1690. Two lovers meet a dire fate with the eponymous Mr Proudie unwillingly drawn into a baleful scenario of jealousy and brutal retribution.

The title tale of *The Pleasant Husband and Other Stories* (1921) has the same theme as "Folding Doors" from 1912 – bitterness and revenge are the props for a similar grim denouement, although the structure is quite different. The "pleasant husband" is seemingly just that, as opposed to conveying the aura of charged malevolence that surrounds the character of Durosoy in the earlier tale; but the endings are equally macabre, and a mark of their strength is that only later will the reader ponder on what subsequently happened to the wife's lover in each case. This collection also includes "The Blue Glove", a sad and ghostly story that is surely based on the loss of Bowen's first child.

Seeing Life (1923) comprised predominantly supernatural tales, several of which rank amongst the most notable in the Bowen canon. "The Avenging of Ann Leete" is a first-class story about a man fascinated by a painting of a beautiful woman and determined to find out who the subject was; he learns the truth about her death and the way in which her lover brought the murderer to his end by seeing the events projected from the past. Superficially similar is "Ann Mellor's Lover", although it is completely different in its execution – a man in 1920 is captivated by a pencil sketch of a young woman and finds himself remembering the tragedy that led to her death in 1750. Bowen deals very capably with post-mortem revenge in "An Appointment with Stiffkey", and the same theme is present in "Kecksies", one of the grimmest of all her stories. It is the powerful and disquieting tale of a man's lust for another's wife outliving his death, with a drunken practical joke backfiring horrifically and setting ghastly events in motion. "Decay" is a short piece telling of a "perfect" marriage, but which is so perfect that it stifles both partners and literally taints their lives. Other stories including minor occult inferences are "The Tarnished Mirror", "The Proud Pomfret" and "Cabriolet".

Between *Seeing Life* and her next collection, four years later, Bowen had a number of weird tales published in various magazines. Some of these were reprints – "The Avenging of Ann Leete" and "Kecksies" appeared in 1925 and 1926 respectively – but there were also a number of original stories that featured in publications. "The Incantation" appeared in *The Queen* for 6 September 1923 (it is also known as "The Necromancers", under which title it surprisingly appeared in *Girls Own Paper* in September 1939). Minor but quite enjoyable, it tells of how a false magician agrees to sorcerously bring about the death of a nobleman, well aware that he will be unable to do so. He then finds to his dismay that his spell seems to be working, and that the victim is dying as intended. All is not as it seems, but the sorcerer and his assistants acquire a life-long belief in the power of the dark arts.

"I Will Never Leave You" featured in *TP's and Cassell's Weekly* on 8 December 1923. Very short at 475 words, it is the story of the captain of a slave ship who kills a member of his crew who then haunts the ship and kills his murderer. A distinctly mediocre tale, it was very soon followed by one that was even shorter but which conversely is quite excellent. "The Accident" was first published in the *Mathematical Gazette* in December 1923, and in a mere 171 words presents a perfect example of the art of writing a vignette. The later "A Persistent Woman" is even shorter at 143 words, and the two pieces taken together demonstrate that even in such an abbreviated format, Bowen could produce a memorably chilling final paragraph. "Vigil", unpublished until the appearance of *Twilight* in 1998 is another vignette, three pages long, and might also have been written in the 1920s if this was perhaps a period during which the author was experimenting with shorter lengths. It is quietly forceful, telling of a dying old man who is a heretic and whose death summons a ghost of the Inquisition to draw him away for a final reckoning.

ONE OF BOWEN'S best-known stories, and one much anthologised, is "Florence Flannery", which appeared in the *Regent Magazine* in December 1924. It is set in 1800, when a 300 year old curse finally reaches fruition in a rundown and isolated old house, with the spiteful and mutually destructive relationship of the main characters as fragile and mouldering as the property itself. Their barely suppressed mutual malevolence becomes an almost tangible force that provides a gateway for an inexorable and terrible doom, and the story ends in horror as a creature from the year 1500 takes a savage retribution on the ancestor of the one who caused his death.

Another fragmented and bitter marriage is central to "Cambric Tea" (*Hutchinson's Magazine*, July 1925), the tale of a bizarre revenge plot that has an untypically happy ending. "Marwood's Ghost Story" (*John o' London's Weekly*, 6 December 1925) is a light but capable story about a man who wants to write the best ghost story ever written but instead discovers the meaning of fear. "The Murder of Squire Langtree" (*Sovereign Magazine*, January 1926) is a superior effort that starts with the hanging of two innocent men and ends with the figurative haunting of the narrator by the real killer.

Dark Ann and Other Stories was published in 1927, and included the two excellent vignettes "The Accident" and "A Persistent Woman" as well as a further notable weird tale, "Dark Ann". This is the story of a man who inherits an old and remote house, and finds himself intrigued by Dark Ann, a much earlier mistress of the house who died in 1648. The ensuing occurrences may be ghostly or may be hallucination, but they haunt the man for the rest of his life.

Old Patch's Medley appeared in the following year, 1928, and featured two re-titled stories, "The Confession of Beau Sekforde" (originally published as "The Housekeeper") and "The Orford Mystery" (previously "The Scoured Silk").

A 1929 appearance in the *London Magazine,* "The Prescription" was an old fashioned ghost story that works well. It is the simply recounted tale of a doctor who is confronted with the inexplicable: a phantom from a hundred years earlier who is seeking to atone for his misdeeds but who can never put things right. Together with "An Appointment with Stiffkey" it was included later that same year in

Sheep's Head and Babylon; the title story of this collection tells of a Scottish minister who successfully strives to resist diabolic temptation, but who is drawn to his death by evil forces all the same. The tale is somewhat marred by its dialogue, which is in a broad Highland brogue that is difficult to make sense of, with the result that reading the story is something of an effort. It is otherwise well written and skilfully evokes the intensity of the storm that persists throughout the narrative. The impact of adverse weather was something that Bowen was able to use to great effect, interacting with her strong plotting and underlining the sense of foreboding with which she adroitly suffused her fiction.

The Gorgeous Lovers and Other Tales also appeared in 1929, marking the first appearance of "Florence Flannery" in book format; in addition it included "The Bishop of Hell". This is a bleak fable concerning the price to be paid for evil, with a voluptuary being deservedly condemned to the nether regions and then dreadfully reappearing to the man who he promised "If I go to Hell tomorrow, I'll pay you a visit to let you know what 'tis like". This story gave its name to the notable 1949 volume that was the author's final collection of the macabre before her death.

Grace Latouche and the Warringtons (1931) reprinted two of Bowen's best tales, "Kecksies" and "The Avenging of Ann Leete", and also featured "The Crown Derby Plate". This is another exceptional work, about a strange survival beyond the grave. Its ending comes as no surprise at all, but it is quite *deliberately* telegraphed to enable the reader to understand the truth of a situation that the lead character does not appreciate. The book also included "Raw Material", a lightweight piece about an elderly woman who is murdered for her money and who then proceeds to make the most of her newly-acquired ghostly status by joining her killers on their spending sprees in a haunting that is mutually beneficial.

The Devil Snar'd, as by George R Preedy, appeared in 1932. In a lonely and desolate part of Northern England, a man and woman rent a rambling old house with the reputation of being haunted. The wife becomes convinced that her husband is trying to kill her so that he will be free to marry another, and is persuaded to take matters into her own hands. The only ghosts are almost certainly those in the imaginations of the two main characters, but the novelette sustains a well-constructed brooding mood and is very readable. The book was published with a second short novel, *Dr Chaos*, which, a little like "The Incantation" nine years earlier, concerns itself mainly with bogus sorcery.

The Last Bouquet: Some Twilight Tales was published in 1933 and amongst some superior stories that had appeared in previous collections there were several others of particularly high quality. "The Last Bouquet" has twin sisters meeting for the first time in nearly thirty years, each harbouring a strong resentment against the other although for very different reasons. Parting with ill feeling, Martha promises Kezia her last bouquet and after her violent end she returns to deliver bloody roses, and death, to her sibling. In "The Hidden Ape" a drunken revelation leads to a frighteningly taken vengeance, with a final paragraph notable for its unsettling and lingering imagery. "Madam Spitfire" is the excellent tale of a spiteful woman who becomes obsessed with a younger man and who will stop at nothing in her attempts to win him. Ultimately it is her dead husband whose ghostly return brings about her downfall in a story that is cleverly constructed, the ruins of the house many years later descriptively framing the narrative in a very capable manner. "The Lady Clodagh" is about another woman obsessed by a man, but she is quite the opposite of Madam Spitfire – ruined and driven to despair and then to death by her new husband, her gratitude for the joy she once experienced with him leads to an unexpected and poignant denouement. "Elsie's Lonely Afternoon" is a story told from the point of view of a friendless and neglected six-year old girl whose life is full of gloom and who unknowingly assists in the undoing of her own future prospects; this arresting but cheerless little tale may well have been based on Bowen's own childhood memories, reflecting the fact that her formative years were far from joyful.

Julia Roseingrave is a 1933 novelette that bore the by-line Robert Paye. Impressively written with some fine descriptive passages, it is only a very marginal genre tale. It has suggestions of witchcraft, but the only spell that Julia casts does seem to be that of her own sensual allure, an earthly enchantment which captivates William Notley to the extent that he will do anything – including murder – to possess her.

The Knot Garden: Some Old Fancies Reset was published under the pseudonym George R Preedy in 1933. It was a mixed collection which included two very good weird efforts. The first of these is "Red Champagne", a short but incisive historical tale of how a man and woman pledge themselves to each other "till death and past death"; the woman dies, and the man's later marriage to another culminates in a wedding night that is grimly fatal. In "Graf Maarten and the Idiot" a man kills his rival and frames someone who is then hanged. However, that person's dead face then haunts the killer, as does the presence of his simpleton sister whose eyes are a constant reminder of her dead brother; eventually remorse drives the murderer to pay the ultimate price for his crime.

1933 ALSO MARKED the author's debut as an editor, with the appearance of the anthology *Great Tales of Horror*, an admirable collection containing some lesser known but outstanding pieces. As well as her own "The Murder of Squire Langton" (previously published as "The Murder of Squire Langtree"), Bowen included three anonymous tales that she had translated from French: "The Grey Chamber" (also included in her later collection *The Bishop of Hell*),

"The Dead Bride", and "The Skull". No less than eleven of the twenty stories included had appeared in *The Great Weird Stories*, published in 1929 and edited by Arthur Neale. Some sources suggest this to be yet another of the author's pen names, but her son Hilary has categorically stated that Arthur Neale was *not* a pseudonym of his mother.

More Great Tales of Horror followed in 1935, which included two further Bowen translations, "The Fatal Hour" and "The Accursed Portrait". Again the contents included some lesser known works as well as multiple offerings from J Sheridan Le Fanu (four stories), WW Fenn (three), A Cunningham (three) and Mrs Catherine Crowe (two).

An anthology edited by Cecil Madden and entitled *My Grimmest Nightmare* was published in 1935, comprising stories that had originally been broadcast in a BBC Radio series called *Nightmares*. Included in this volume was Bowen's "Incubus" (also known as "Nightmare", under which title it was reprinted in 1947 in *The Night Side*, edited by August Derleth). This is an absorbing story about a woman visiting a deserted monastery she has long dreamed about, a monastery built in the grounds of a heathen temple and hemmed in by dark, forbidding woods: "I had heard tales of what used to try to come in from the woods, and the prayers the monks put up to keep them out".

There is a tomb in the monastery that she is drawn to and whose occupant's identity is just out of reach, his name effaced but his memory tantalisingly close. The ending is intriguing, bringing a different perspective to a narrative which generates an enigmatic aura of ambiguity.

"One Remained Behind" appeared in the *Help Yourself Annual* in 1936. In this story, a man obtains a grimoire that enables him to summon Lucifer and arrange for his life's aspirations to be wholly fulfilled. But there is a price to be paid and his happiness is short lived. More overtly supernatural than most of Bowen's other work, it is not entirely successful, being a competently told tale but with little of the atmosphere of the mysterious and the ill-omened that singles out the bulk of the author's weird fiction, and lacking the subtlety of her better efforts.

Orange Blossoms was a 1938 collection published as by Joseph Shearing, and included the notable "They Found My Grave", about the dangers inherent in offending a spirit, something that Ada Trimble discovers to her cost. Discovering the truth about a boastful presence at a séance, she reveals the fabrications that he has been telling about his life and in particular his grave, but is ill-prepared for the violent consequences.

BOWEN PUBLISHED HER autobiography, *The Debate Continues,* in 1939. This has an interesting account of her own experiences in what was purportedly a haunted house in St John's Wood, a district in west London, where she lived with her dysfunctional family early in her career. There were unexplained occurrences, and an investigation by the Society for Psychical Research concluded that the haunting was real. Despite having herself seen some strange things, Bowen did not accept the existence of ghosts in the house, maintaining: "I believe that all this so-called haunting was produced by those who lived in it. They, out of their frustration and unhappiness, were giving forth evil phantasms and sinister hallucinations".

What seems to be a somewhat fictionalised version of events appeared in *Twilight* as an "Author's Afterword", and perhaps it was her intention to transform these experiences into a short story that was never finalised.

The 1940s saw few books published in Bowen's own name, but no less than nineteen under the pseudonyms of George R Preedy and Joseph Shearing. Two significant shorter pieces appeared with the Shearing by-line towards the end of 1948, "The Chinese Apple" and

"A Stranger Knocked". The first tells of a woman returning from abroad to the dark unwelcoming home of her childhood and finding her youthful resentment of that earlier life to be fully founded, as unwanted memories resurface. The components of her unlikeable niece and a brutal murder in the house opposite meld together and lead to a disturbing ending in a very compelling narrative. By comparison, "A Stranger Knocked" is a genuinely heart-warming Christmas story, a story in which the weird element *charms* rather than unsettles.

The Bishop of Hell and Other Stories (1949) was the last Bowen collection to appear before her death in 1952, and although all of the twelve stories were reprints (six had appeared in *The Last Bouquet*) it was an excellent selection. It included such classics as "Kecksies", "The Crown Derby Plate", "Florence Flannery" and "The Avenging of Ann Leete", and one must assume that it could only have been lack of available space that meant the omission of such tales as "Incubus", "Giudetta's Wedding Night", "The Hidden Ape", "The Last Bouquet" and "An Appointment with Stiffkey". Such exclusions serve to emphasise the strength in depth of the author's fiction, for all of those missing pieces are first-class examples of her ability to produce chilling fiction.

Bowen's last genre piece appears to be "The Tallow Candle" under the Joseph Shearing pseudonym, published in the 1950 anthology *The Uncertain Element*, edited by Dick Kay. It is a fictionalised account of the famous 1762 "Cock Lane Ghost" mystery in London; this was revealed as a hoax, but in Bowen's version the ghosts are ultimately very real and drive the central character of "Kempe" (his actual name was Kent) to an early and wretched death. This last story thus reverts to the theme of several of those included in *God's Playthings* from nearly forty years earlier, presenting a historical event in the form of an imaginative and sinister supernatural tale.

DURING HER LIFETIME, Bowen produced some twenty volumes of short stories, and many of her weird pieces were reprinted in these several times. Three of them, "The Scoured Silk", "The Avenging of Ann Leete" and "Kecksies", appeared in four separate collections, while "The Fair Hair of Ambrosine", "The Housekeeper", "The Crown Derby Plate" and "Florence Flannery" featured in three. Two of her books, *The Seven Deadly Sins* and *Exits and Farewells,* were essentially reprints of earlier titles, *Crimes of Old London* and *God's Playthings.* 1933's *The Last Bouquet* included four stories that had appeared only two years earlier in *Grace Latouche and the Warringtons*, emphasising that the author was never averse to reusing good fiction.

For the last fifteen years of her life, Bowen produced few weird stories, although eleven Gothic novels were written under the Joseph Shearing pseudonym, four of which were made into films. She also produced a number of historical books, her autobiography and a book on Art. A total of fifty-five books appeared in those fifteen years but only sixteen of them in her last decade, which by her own productive standards represented a significant lessening in output. Her writing career stretched from 1906 to 1952 and her average throughout that period was four books per year. There was only one year – 1946 – when no new title appeared. The peak was 1932 and 1933, when eleven books were published in each of those two years.

Marjorie Bowen died in 1952 following a fall at her London home, and it was almost a quarter of a century before a further collection of her stories would appear. This was *Kecksies and Other Twilight Tales* in 1976, which included many of the author's superior works including "The Hidden Ape", "Kecksies", "The Avenging of Anne Leete", "The Crown Derby Plate", "Florence Flannery" and "Half Past Two" (originally published as "An Appointment with Stiffkey"); it also featured two previously uncollected pieces. The first of these was "The Breakdown", a good ghost story with a pleasing twist at the end, about an old drawing that captivates the main character, as was the case with "The Avenging of Anne Leete" and "Ann Mellor's Lover", although the treatment of the theme is markedly dissimilar. A quite different story is "The House by the Poppy Field", an atmospheric and powerful account of a man moving into a property that had been left to him. This is shown to be symbolic of a change in his mortal state, the progression from life to death, and is something that he comes to passively accept and then ultimately embrace.

Over twenty years later, in 1998, *Twilight and Other Supernatural Romances* appeared, with an interesting Preface by the author's youngest son, Hilary Long, and a detailed Introduction by the editor Jessica Amanda Salmonson. There is the promise of a further volume appearing from the same publisher, Ash-Tree Press, which will supplement both *Twilight* and *Kecksies* by publishing all of the remaining weird fiction not included in the latter two volumes.

Marjorie Bowen's works rank alongside the very best in the field. They consistently entertain, which is precisely the purpose for which they were written – as the dust-wrapper of *The Bishop of Hell* says of the stories in that collection: "…various critics have found various meanings in them, but the writer knows of none save that which appears on the surface, the fascination of terror set remote in time and place".

That fascination led to the production of a significant number of excellent weird tales, tales that have easily withstood the test of time and which will undoubtedly continue to occupy what is an eminently secure place high in the field.

SELECTED BIBLIOGRAPHY

Black Magic – 1909

"A Poor Spanish Lodging" – 1912

"Twilight" – 1912

"The Burning of the Vanities" – 1912

"The Polander" – 1912

"The Extraordinary Adventure of Grace Endicott" – 1912

"The Prisoner" – 1912

"The Folding Doors" – 1912

"The Fair Hair of Ambrosine" – 1916

"Giudetta's Wedding Night" – 1916

"Petronilla and the Laurel Trees" – 1916

"The Scarlet Rose" – 1916

"The Sign Painter and the Crystal Fishes" – 1917

"The Scoured Silk" aka "The Orford Mystery" – 1917

"The Pond" – 1917

"The Umbrella Mender" – 1917

"A Venetian Evening" – 1917

"The Housekeeper" aka "The Confession of Beau Sekforde" – 1919

"Brent's Folly" – 1919

"The Extraordinary Adventure of Mr John Proudie" aka "The Mystery of Dr. Francis Valletort" – 1919

"The Pleasant Husband" – 1921

The Haunted Vintage – 1921

"The Blue Glove" – 1921

"The Avenging of Ann Leete" – 1923

"Ann Mellor's Lover" – 1923

"An Appointment with Stiffkey" aka "Half-Past Two" – 1923

"Kecksies" – 1923

"Decay" – 1923

"The Tarnished Mirror" – 1923

"The Proud Pomfret" – 1923

"Cabriolet" – 1923

"The Incantation" aka "The Necromancers" – 1923

"I Will Never Leave You" – 1923

"The Accident" – 1923

I Dwelt in High Places – 1923

"Florence Flannery" – 1924

The Presence and the Power – 1924

"Cambric Tea" – 1925

"Marwood's Ghost Story" – 1925

"The Murder of Squire Langtree" aka "The Murder of Squire Langton" – 1926

"A Persistent Woman" – 1927

"Dark Ann" – 1927

Five Winds – 1927

"The Prescription" – 1929

"The Bishop of Hell" – 1929

"Sheep's-head and Babylon" – 1929

"The Crown Derby Plate" – 1931

"Raw Material" – 1931

The Shadow on Mockways – 1932

Dr. Chaos – 1932 (as by George R Preedy)

The Devil Snar'd – 1932 (as by George R Preedy)

"The Last Bouquet" – 1933

"Madam Spitfire" – 1933

"The Hidden Ape" – 1933

"The Lady Clodagh" – 1933

"Elsie's Lonely Afternoon" – 1933

Julia Roseingrave – 1933 (as by Robert Paye)

"Red Champagne"– 1933 (as by George R Preedy)

"Graf Maarten and the Idiot"– 1933 (as by George R Preedy)

"The Grey Chamber"– 1933 (translation)

"The Dead Bride"– 1933 (translation)

"The Skull"– 1933 (translation)

"The Fatal Hour" – 1935 (translation)

"The Accursed Portrait"– 1935 (translation)

"Incubus" aka "Nightmare" – 1935

"One Remained Behind" – 1936

"They Found My Grave"– 1938 (as by Joseph Shearing)

"The Chinese Apple"– 1948 (as by Joseph Shearing)

"A Stranger Knocked"– 1948 (as by Joseph Shearing)

"The Tallow Candle" – 1950

The Man with the Scales – 1954

"The Breakdown" – unknown, first collected 1976

"The House by the Poppy Field" – unknown, first collected 1976

"The Recluse and Springtime" – 1988

"Vigil" – 1988

Key Collections

Seeing Life – 1923

The Last Bouquet: Some Twilight Tales – 1933

The Bishop of Hell and Other Stories – 1949

Kecksies and Other Twilight Tales – 1976

Twilight and Other Supernatural Romances – 1998

MOSTLY IN SHADOW
MARY ELIZABETH COUNSELMAN

MARY ELIZABETH COUNSELMAN was a regular contributor to *Weird Tales* for a considerable period of time. There was a remarkable fifty-eight years from her debut in 1932 to her final appearance in 1990, a feat matched by few if any other authors, although the bulk of her work appeared from the 1930s to the 1950s. In addition, her fiction and poetry also appeared in various other periodicals, both in her own name and under several pseudonyms.

While many of her stories were anthologised only two collections have appeared, both of which were titled *Half in Shadow* even though their respective contents differed significantly. Her other publications included a volume of fantasy verse, other poetry titles, a compilation of jungle tales, and two non-fiction books.

Her best work was particularly good and she was always popular with the readers. Although her work encompasses no unqualified classics, for the most part it is effective and agreeable, leaving the lasting impression of well-told stories.

Counselman was born in Birmingham, Alabama, on 19 November 1911 and was educated at Alabama College and the University of Montevallo before beginning her career as a reporter for *The Birmingham News*. She appeared in print several times with early poetry such "The Fay-Child" in *The Delineator* (1926, but written when she was only six years old!) and "Swamp Cypress" in *The Alabamian* (1930); her *Weird Tales* debut was the poem "Madman's Song" in the April 1932 issue. This was followed later that year by a further verse contribution, "Echidna", before her first short story, "The House of Shadows", featured in the April 1933 edition.

"The House of Shadows" tells of the narrator's visit to the family home of an old school friend she has not been in contact with for some years. It is a gentle and convincing ghost story that is not overly original but which is competently written and pleasing. The ending will hardly come as a surprise to any reader, but the tale succeeds by virtue of its atmospheric narrative. The simplicity of approach and the elegance of the prose were to be hallmarks of all Counselman's subsequent fiction, setting the scene for what was to be a productive and long-lasting career.

Farnsworth Wright, the editor of *Weird Tales*, was plainly impressed by this new author; three more stories appeared during 1933: "The Girl with the Green Eyes", "The Cat-Woman", and "The Accursed Isle", as well as two further poems, "Voodoo Song" and "Nostalgia". Of this early work, "The Accursed Isle" is notable for showing that Counselman could write a very efficient horror story. It tells of seven shipwrecked sailors who one by one fall prey to a monstrous entity that strikes at night – the survivors realise that with no-one else on the islet where they are marooned the killer must be one of their own number, and that he probably does not know of the murderous transformation that overtakes him when darkness falls. Soon there are only two men left alive and the story concludes on a note of bleakness and despair, demonstrating that Counselman was not an author who was dedicated to orthodox plot resolution.

Her most admired story – and evidently one of the most well-liked pieces ever published in *Weird Tales* (in August 1934) – was "The

Three Marked Pennies", which has been anthologised many times. Forceful and imaginative, it tells of three pennies that are put into circulation, each having a distinctive mark, and at the end of a week each person who has one of these coins will win one of three prizes: immense wealth, world travel, or death. The coins pass through various hands, and ultimately their possessors get their respective rewards, although there is neither joy nor fulfilment for the recipients. An allegory accentuating that what you most want is not always what you get, and that what is extremely desirable to one person is quite the opposite to another, this tale is written with vigour and style, and the praise it received was fully justified.

Thematically similar is "The Devil's Lottery" from 1948, this time telling of three questions that are posed to townsfolk by a mysterious stranger. The people with the correct responses are rewarded in ways that reflect their answers but which are far from what they might expect. An interesting parallel to "The Three Marked Pennies", the story uses the same basic premise, but in a more sardonic way with its emphasis on "the power of evil and the futility of good". The setting for "The Devil's Lottery" is the town of "Blankville", although why it should be granted anonymity is a minor mystery in itself – one of the characters is the town's newspaper editor, Jeff Haverty, who was the editor of the same paper in "The Three Marked Pennies", and in that story the town is named as "Branton".

That same locality was used in "The Web of Silence" a decade earlier, which again featured newsman Jeff Haverty, although the later stories were in no way sequels to the first one. All three of the Haverty stories invoke a sense of ineffectiveness in combating unknown forces, although "The Web of Silence" deals with its subject in a lighter manner than the others, but a manner that is fully appropriate to its denouement.

Counselman was primarily a writer of ghost stories, and she

produced much of her most memorable fiction in that arena. She was not overly concerned with shambling extra-dimensional horrors, and in her introduction to the Arkham House edition of *Half in Shadow*, she says:

The Hallowe'en scariness of the bumbling-but-kindly Wizard of Oz has always appealed to me more than the gruesome, morbid fiction of HP Lovecraft, Clark Ashton Smith, and those later authors who were influenced by their doom philosophies. In that same introduction, she adds: *Fearsome only in that they are not like us, my supernatural beings are helpful to the well intentioned but ruthless to the predatory.*

Her "supernatural beings" do vary considerably in their character and attitude, from the loving protectiveness shown in "The Tree's Wife" to the random viciousness of "Something Old". But even the callous evil of the latter fits in with the writer's expressed philosophy of these things being "not like us"; and in a lighter way so does "A Death Crown for Mr Hapworthy", but from a quite different angle with its moral that salvation is for all those who are deserving of it, whether they realise it or not.

Counselman adroitly covered many of the "standard" themes of weird fiction as well as some that were uniquely her own. There are post-mortem returns in "Night Court", with the dead questioning the reason why their lives should have been taken from them; there is shape-shifting in "The Cat-Woman"; telepathy in "Rapport"; and a poltergeist terrorising generations of a Southern family in "Parasite Mansion".

Her writing also displayed ideas that were distinctly original, such as the long-dead town held "in a terrible bondage of dread" in "Twister"; the future deaths that are shown through the panes of "The Green Window"; the musical instrument that provides the means for deadly revenge in "The Bonan of Baledewa"; and the artist who literally petrifies his subjects in "The Black Stone Statue". The ghosts of "The Unwanted" are amongst the most unusual in all weird fiction: spirits of the unborn and the discarded that are brought into being and sustained by the love and the need of a backwoods woman.

Misunderstandings lead to consequences quite the opposite of what is intended in "The Smiling Face" and in the poignant "Seventh Sister". The unnecessary tragedies that unfold in these tales arise from the isolation of the lead characters – "Seventh Sister" is isolated because she is shunned and feared, a young and lonely albino Negro girl with supernatural powers; while Cedric in "The Smiling Face" is also isolated, but this time by injury and by a language barrier, and it is this that instigates the horrific events that are to come. Conversely, there is the completely inescapable nemesis of "Monkey Spoons", where the curse is undirected and lies on the spoons themselves. Whoever comes into possession of them unavoidably suffers harrowing consequences. The innocent become victims, with their innocence of no account at all as far as the malevolent evil of the spoons is concerned.

A number of the stories take the form of first-person narratives. This is particularly successful in such tales as "The Breeze and I", in which a young woman discovers incantations that can summon and manipulate the wind. Her ultimate loss of control and the lethal consequences that follow are depicted well, with the final lines expressing the storyteller's fear at what she has done – and her horror at what she might yet do – with impressive strength. The forces of Nature are also meddled with in "Drifting Atoms", at a ruinous cost that involves insanity and death. Such stories as "The Prism", "The Lens" and "Kellerman's Eyepiece" deal with various devices that allow the viewer to see far more than is apparent to normal vision, but at an inevitably high price.

Counselman could if necessary rely on a dramatic finale to impart shock, and does so particularly successfully in "The Green Window", where the reader is very much caught out by the last line – but such literary artifice tends to be uncommon in her prose. An uncomplicated storyteller, she wrote in a clear-cut manner and could convey appropriately atmospheric moods with consummate ease, always in an immensely readable way. While the element of macabre demonstrated in "The Accursed Isle" is also evident in such stories as "Night Court", "The Lamashtu Amulet", "The Huaco of Señor Perez" and "Something Old", the graphic aspect is generally subdued, and there is usually a lightness of touch to the storytelling. This can heighten the effect quite considerably – in "The Shot-Tower Ghost", for instance, the tone is cheery and jocular right up until the final page where an intimidating truth is uncovered. And in "Drifting Atoms" there is a similarly unsettling revelation in the last few lines that transforms a forthright narrative into a harsh fable.

Something of a "regional" writer, much of her fiction is set in the South, in the Blue Ridge Mountains area, where she was born and lived for most of her life. She had a real feel for the idiosyncrasies of the local people, and delineates them with affection and skill, even if her attempts to convey accents and dialect can sometimes seem laboured and unwieldy. There is no interconnection in these regional stories, and the only common factor is in the locale and that all of them are persuasively written and highlight some of her best prose. In particular, such tales as "The Tree's Wife" and "The Unwanted" are infused with an atmosphere that evokes their location in an expert and fluent way.

COUNSELMAN ARGUABLY ATTAINED her artistic peak in 1949-50, with successive issues of *Weird Tales* including the stories "The Shot-Tower Ghost", "The Green Window", "The Smiling Face", "The

Tree's Wife" and "The Monkey Spoons". All five of these stories were outstanding, and for them to appear one after the other was certainly an impressive accomplishment. Further excellent works, such as "Something Old", "The Unwanted" and "Night Court", also appeared within the next few years, but after the publication of "Way Station" in one of the last issues of the original magazine in 1953, she published little fiction, although she was a regular contributor of poetry to *The Saturday Evening Post* and other periodicals.

"Way Station" had shown no lessening in her literary abilities, and was as gentle and pleasing a ghost story as "The House of Shadows" had been two decades earlier. However, her only new tales over the next twenty years were three contributions to anthologies of original fiction, although each of these confirmed that she remained a fine writer with imaginative ideas. The first of them, "Hargrave's Fore-Edge Book", is about a murderous bibliophile who is betrayed by the very object that he loves; "The Huaco of Señor Perez" is a grim account of the consequences of sacrilege where Incan gods are involved; and the classic premise of the Wandering Jew is handled in an absorbing and compassionate manner in "A Handful of Silver".

The anthologies in which these appeared were all edited by August Derleth. Counselman had in fact been in contact with Derleth in the late 1950s regarding the publication of a collection of her stories by Arkham House. The delays that occurred eventually prompted her to sell her own selection of tales to the English publisher Consul Books, and these appeared in paperback form in 1964 under the title *Half in Shadow*, with a striking Josh Kirby cover. Arkham House did eventually publish the agreed collection, also entitled *Half in Shadow*, in 1978 and while each volume included fourteen stories, only seven were common to both, with surprising omissions. Neither includes "The Accursed Isle", "Drifting Atoms", "Way Station" or "The Breeze and I", impressive tales that are superior to several of those that were featured in either of the two books, although overall the contents of both were well above average.

OVER THE FIRST five years of Counselman's *Weird Tales* career there were as many of her poems published as there were of her short stories. Most of these were included in the slim volume *The Face of Fear*, which appeared in a very limited edition in 1984. She had already published other verse collections, including *Move Over – It's Only Me* in 1975 and *The Eye and the Hand* in 1977, but *The Face of Fear* was the first to feature her fantasy work. The thirty-nine poems are notable for their variety and ability to paint vivid word pictures, with the best of them being very good indeed. There is fine imagery in "African Wood-Carving" ("You are a scream frozen in wood"), in "Tupilaq", and in "Famine", while the excellent "Witch-Burning", "Vampyra" and "Blackout" all have strong stories to tell, and do so chillingly well. A much later poem, "The Summons" from 1988, seems to be the author's sole contribution to the Cthulhu Mythos, which impresses in the way it so capably evokes its subject matter despite its brevity.

African Yesterdays, a collection of poems and prose centred on the Dark Continent, was published in 1977. These were stories that had originally appeared in such periodicals as *Jungle Stories* in the 1950s and are enjoyable but generally lightweight. Both the background and the basic ideas are engaging, but in the main the plots tend to be slight and the people depicted are rather one-dimensional. This is not helped by the fact that the tales are all rather short, perhaps due to limitations imposed by the magazines for which they were written, although this does not detract from the excellence of "Blood Brother of the Crocodile", which is a notable highlight of the book. However, as far as the bulk of the contents are concerned, it is the setting and the native folklore that take centre stage, and while there are some interesting concepts they are never quite fully realised.

Apart from the minor "Kellerman's Eyepiece" in 1975, Counselman did not publish any new genre stories for some years prior to the short-lived re-appearance of *Weird Tales* in 1981.This did bring forth two new offerings from her and they were both very good, up-to-date in their settings but still retaining the innate style and appeal of the author's earlier writing. In the first of these, "Healer", the narrator falls in love with a doctor who cures people empathetically, but soon finds that she has been cold-heartedly manipulated by him. The resolution is clever, with the exploitation on the part of the doctor unexpectedly turned into something quite different, an unsought revenge that is fittingly ironic.

The second story was "The Lamashtu Amulet", set in Iraq, which has the feel of the earlier "Something Old" with its cruel and pitiless deity seeking innocent lives. The ending of the tale is again well handled, and also brings a satisfying element of humanity to the unprepossessing lead character, who learns that the things he thought he no longer needed are actually the most important things of all. A third story was also written for the new *Weird Tales* but never appeared there, published instead several years later in an anthology. This was "My Cup of Tea", an undemanding account of an aunt's ability to deal death through reading tea leaves, and telling of how she uses her powers to ensure the steadfast and unwilling devotion of her favourite niece.

Counselman's fiction subsequent to 1981 appeared in small-press publications, but she did not reproduce the volume or the superiority of her earlier years. Not that she had retired, for she gave many lectures and attended writers' workshops. In 1976 she founded Verity Publishing Company in Gadsden, Alabama, for which she was both publisher and editor, producing a regular periodical called *Year at the Spring*, which specialised in poetry. She also taught creative writing classes at Gadsden State Junior College and at the University of Alabama, and published two works of non-fiction, *Everything You Always Wanted to Know About the Supernatural – but are Afraid to Believe* in 1976, and *SPQR: The Poetry and Life of Catullus* in 1977.

She made one last return to the pages of *Weird Tales* with the poem "Ani-Yunwiga" in the Fall 1990 issue, fifty-eight years after her debut with "Madman's Song". But even that notable record of longevity loses some of its lustre when one considers the period between her first and last published works elsewhere – a 1926 poem and a 1994 short story – which represents a writing lifetime of an astonishing *sixty-eight years*!

COUNSELMAN WAS EVIDENTLY a bright, witty and attractive woman, but was reportedly unhappily married for a number of years. Perhaps writing became a form of escape for her, and it may be significant that many of the relationships depicted in her fiction are ill-starred in one way or another, with the most caring of them depicted in "The Tree's Wife" and "Mommy". In both of these tales it is the presence of a loving but unearthly spirit that establishes the sort of bond that Counselman may have seen as being unattainable in real life.

Not a particularly prolific author (she had something like fifty stories to her credit in her long career), one does get the distinct impression that she pored over every paragraph, reworking her fiction until it was precisely as she wanted it to be. Her writing is carefully textured with barely a word out of place, and the end result is consistently interesting and enjoyable to read. However, the tales that appeared in the last dozen years of Counselman's life were variable in quality; her final few offerings were very minor pieces. The last story that she published was "Two Demons – or Three?" in 1994, which is an uncharacteristically poor effort, but it was apparently extracted from a letter and never intended for publication – in any event, it is hardly a fitting epitaph, and is frankly best forgotten.

Her last published poem, "Ani-Yunwiga" in 1990, is far better and reverts back to the author's fascination with native cultures. Aniyunwiga is the Cherokees' original name for themselves, and the eponymous verse is atmospheric and subtle, dealing with the forbearance of ancient powers not from timidity or apathy but from a cosmic viewpoint, in which time and space are intermingled and transient ("Since Yesterday is Now ... and There is Here"). It also presents an interesting counterpoint to her first *Weird Tales* poem, "Madman's Song", which had appeared nearly six decades earlier, the solipsistic theme of the earlier piece contrasting with the outreaching spirituality inherent in "Ani-Yunwiga".

Mary Elizabeth Counselman died on 13 November 1995, a few days short of her 84th birthday. Her lasting contribution to the genre is generally considered to be "The Three Marked Pennies". This tale, good though it certainly is, does not represent the high-water mark of her output of creative fiction but was simply characteristic of several surges in an ongoing and gentle tide of worthy tales, a tide that only gradually subsided in later years and left much to admire in its wake. Although her weird fiction may not rank with the *very* best, her stories deserve more recognition than they have received.

SELECTIVE BIBLIOGRAPHY

Appearances in *Weird Tales*

"The House of Shadows" – April 1933

"The Girl with the Green Eyes" – May 1933

"The Cat-Woman" – October 1933

"The Accursed Isle" – November 1933

"The Three Marked Pennies" – August 1934

"The Black Stone Statue" – December 1937

"Mommy" – April 1939

"The Web of Silence" – November 1939

"Twister" – January 1940

"Drifting Atoms" – May 1941

"Parasite Mansion" – January 1942

"Seventh Sister" – January 1943

"The Breeze and I" – July 1947

"The Lens" – November 1947

"A Death Crown for Mr Hapworthy" – May 1948

"The Devil's Lottery" – September 1948

"The Bonan of Baladewa" – January 1949

"The Shot-Tower Ghost" – September 1949

"The Green Window" – November 1949

"The Smiling Face" – January 1950

"The Tree's Wife" – March 1950

"The Monkey Spoons" – May 1950

"Cordona's Skull" – July 1950

"Something Old" – November 1950

"The Unwanted" – January 1951

"Chinook" – July 1951

"Rapport" – September 1951

"The Prism" – March 1952

"Night Court" – March 1953

"Way Station" – November 1953

"Healer "– Spring 1981 #1

"The Lamashtu Amulet" – Spring 1981 #2

Other weird fiction

"Hargrave's Fore-Edge Book" – *Dark Mind, Dark Heart*, 1962

"The Huaco of Señor Perez" – *Over the Edge*, 1964

"A Handful of Silver" – *Travellers by Night*, 1967

"Kellerman's Eyepiece" – *Night Chills*, 1975

"Cellini's Pitchfork" – *Fantasy Book*, 1982

"The T'ang Horse" – *Fantasy Book*, 1983

"Pyramid" – *Etchings & Odysseys*, 1983

"Linkage" – *Doppelgangers*, 1984

"Wings" – *Fantasy Book*, 1985

"My Cup of Tea" – *All the Devils are Here*, 1986

"Korowaar" – *Minnesota Fantasy Review*, 1987

"The Curtained Cabinet" – *Crypt of Cthulhu*, 1988

"In Sextuplicate" – *Sterling Web*, 1990

"Flashflood" – *Fantasy Macabre*, 1992

"Two Demons – or Three?" – *Fantasy Macabre*, 1994

OPPORTUNE RECITALS
AT CONVENIENT INTERVALS
ERNEST BRAMAH

GRANT RICHARDS LTD published a book in 1900 entitled *The Wallet of Kai Lung* by an author called Ernest Bramah. It was his first work of fiction and was reasonably well received, although the first printing sold slowly. There were several editions over the next few years, and when Methuen issued a paperback version in 1917, it was reprinted at least seven times over the following decade, and seems to have been in print virtually ever since. A signed, numbered hardcover edition of 200 copies was also produced in 1923, at what must have been a really exorbitant price at the time: two guineas (£2.10).

Although appearing at first sight to be a novel, *The Wallet of Kai Lung* is essentially a volume of short stories set in an imaginary dynastic China. It is a land peopled by magicians, demons, dragons, bandits and beautiful women, a place where people can be divinely struck down for failing to honour their ancestors, where rapacious earth demons vent their spleen on those who disturb their slumbers, and where dark Powers haunt deep forests. Travelling through this landscape is the erudite Kai Lung, an itinerant storyteller who will unroll his mat beneath the shade of a mulberry tree and regale his audience with all manner of narratives in return for a few coins in his bowl, preferably silver taels, although such glittering bounty is rare indeed.

As will be appreciated, Bramah's stylised China is as much China as ER Eddison's Mercury of *The Worm Ouroboros* is really Mercury. Bramah never actually visited the East, never venturing further than

Moscow according to his family, although many critics assumed that he was a well-travelled man. He wrote of the China of his imagination, the China of Willow Plate patterns and mythology, a land that never was but which perhaps should have been, so far as the author was concerned. In any event, it is a superb creation and one that has fascinated and entertained readers for well over a century.

It is not simply the inventive nature of the tales and their setting that captivates but also the way in which they were written. Bramah used a formally elaborate style, one that is in keeping with his invented milieu. All characters speak in the same ornate manner, in "shafts of polished conversation", whether they are peasants, Mandarins or the Sublime Emperor himself, brother of the Sun and Moon, and Upholder of the Four Corners of the World. Politeness and civility are paramount; for example, in "The Story of Wong Pao and the Minstrel" the wealthy merchant annoyed by a singer in the street says to the servant he has summoned: "Bear courteous greetings to the accomplished musician outside our gate ... and convince him – by means of a heavily-weighted club if necessary – that the situation he has taken up is quite unworthy of his incomparable efforts".

The cadence of the language is beguiling, and as well as abounding with elegant prose, the writing is instilled with drollness and irony, delicate and insidious. There have been few writers who have so deftly and entertainingly portrayed a fantasy world as fascinating and appealing as that of Kai Lung's China, and fewer still have succeeded in so completely immersing their readers in its milieu.

ERNEST BRAMAH WAS born Ernest Bramah Smith in 1868 and died in 1942. Despite the fact that his first book was autobiographical (*English Farming and Why I Turned It Up*, in 1894), an aura of mystery surrounded him. Few people ever met him, and photographs are scarce; even his date of birth is debatable. He seems to have shunned the limelight, and was not interested in self-publicity, saying: "I am not fond of writing about myself and only in less degree about my work. My published books are about all that I care to pass on to the reader".

There was a persistent rumour that Ernest Bramah did not exist, a rumour that the author himself covers in some detail in his amusing introduction to the 1924 collection *The Specimen Case*. Having been informed in a letter from his American publisher that he was thought to be a "mythical person", Bramah characteristically comments that "...there is something not unattractive in the idea of being a mythical person ... though from a heroic point of view one might have wished that it could have been *a mythological personage...*"

According to William White in his introduction to *Kai Lung: Six*, Bramah "was as complete a recluse as an author can become", a man who "refused to see almost everyone, who cancelled appointments at the last minute, 'summoned away to the country', fended off interviewers, and naturally eluded literary lion-tamers in London". This "outsider" quality does not seem to have been a pose, and it appears that the writer was a naturally shy and unassuming individual. Kai Lung, with his gregarious nature and uninhibited ability to publicly entertain does therefore represent an intriguing contrast with his creator, an alter ego through whom Bramah perhaps displayed how outgoing his personality might have been in the unrestrictive China of his imagination.

HIS PUBLISHED BOOKS included a novel and several collections about a blind detective called Max Carrados, a futuristic political novel (*The Secret of the League*), a contemporary satire *(The Mirror of Kong Ho)*, a light comedy *(A Little Flutter)*, and a reference work *(A Guide to the Varieties and Rarity of English Regal Copper Coins, Charles II to Victoria, 1671-1860).*

Good though most of these other books are – and Max Carrados in particular remains much admired; the entire writings were republished in *The Max Carrados Portfolio* in 2000 – the most enduring of all are those of the Kai Lung cycle. There were seven books in all: *The Wallet of Kai Lung* (1900), *Kai Lung's Golden Hours* (1922), *Kai Lung Unrolls His Mat* (1928), *The Moon of Much Gladness* (1932), *Kai Lung Beneath the Mulberry Tree* (1940), *Kai Lung: Six* (1974), and *Kai Lung Raises His Voice* (2010). All of these titles uphold a very high standard of writing, and are well worth seeking out.

The Moon of Much Gladness was published in the United States as *The Return of Kai Lung,* while the even less imaginatively titled *Kai Lung: Six* was a slim volume privately printed in 1974 and limited to 250 copies. It comprised the last six tales that were uncollected at the time of the writer's death (all had previously appeared in the British magazine *Punch)* while *Kai Lung Raises His Voice* reprints those same stories and also includes previously unpublished material.

KAI LUNG HIMSELF is an endearing character, silver-tongued and quick-witted, but with a calculated humility. He is armed with a seemingly endless fund of tales, of which one suitable to the occasion will always be available, and of which he will happily provide an "opportune recital at convenient intervals". Some of these – the story of Princess Taik for instance – would take weeks to tell, although: "...there is a much-flattened version which may be compressed within the narrow limits of a single day and night, but even that requires for certain of the more moving passages the accompaniment of a powerful drum or a hollow wooden fish".

The self-effacing modesty he habitually displays is pretence, for he is clearly a clever and talented individual, although it must be said that he does have a singular talent for becoming enmeshed in difficult situations. Admittedly, that talent is outweighed by the facility with which he extracts himself from such situations, and the way in which his wide-ranging adventures invariably conclude with him being completely in control of events and suitably rewarded for his efforts.

The first book in the series, *The Wallet of Kai Lung*, very much sets the scene. Kai Lung is captured by a brigand and has to tell an intriguing story to save himself from the tender mercies of the bandit chief's mercenaries who, in their chief's own words:

...keep an honoured and very venerable rite, which chiefly consists in suspending the offender by the pigtail from a low tree, and placing burning twigs of hemp-palm between his toes ... it seems a foolish and meaningless habit; but it would not be well to interfere with their religious observances, however trivial they may appear.

The story that is told – successfully of course – is "The Transmutation of Ling", in which the studious and initially ingenuous Ling finds himself in command of an Imperial army of bowmen vastly outnumbered by rebels. Although he eventually triumphs, he is betrayed and disgraced, and in trying to kill himself he finds that he has been transmuted into gold. The problem is that although he is now worth a million taels, how can he get his hands on any of this fortune? Cutting his hair yields a regular income, but not enough ... he contemplates cutting off a limb, but then things get *really* complicated...

In "The Story of Yung Chang" (which was the very first Kai Lung story that Bramah wrote, according to Grant Richards), the eponymous hero becomes the first person to discover the concept of multiplication. Unfortunately he does not fully master it, with inevitably disastrous consequences, although all eventually ends well for him and the beautiful Ning. In "The Probation of Sen Heng" we find a typical Brahma character – naive but honourable and honest – who is sarcastically told by his employer *not* to sell certain flawless items, and proceeds to do just that. His exasperated employer then sends him on what is effectively a suicide mission, but Sen's abilities to mimic duck calls and train locusts to do tricks stand him in good stead and lead him to the right hand of the Emperor himself. Bramah did not often indulge in overt slapstick comedy, preferring instead a more subtle brand of humour, but the scene between Sen, the Emperor, and a third individual called the Provider of Diversions and Pleasurable Occupations is *very* funny.

The reader learns something of the narrator's background in "The Confession of Kai Lung", in which Bramah also indulges in Shakespearean parody when dealing with Kai's attempts to discredit a famous writer from hundreds of years earlier. Well-known lines from that writer's work include such famous quotations as that of Emperor Tsing on the battlefield of Shih-ho: "A sedan-chair! A sedan-chair! This person will unhesitatingly exchange his entire and well-regulated Empire for such an article"; and of course the immortal funeral speech which begins:

Friends, Chinamen, labourers who are engaged in agricultural pursuits, entrust to this person your acute and well-educated ears; he has merely come to assist in depositing the body of Ko'ung in the Family Temple, not for the purpose of making remarks about him of a graceful and highly complimentary nature.

In the main, these are light, witty stories, but there is a chilling counterpoint in "The Vengeance of Tung Fel". Much of the effect of this grim tale is in the implication of what will happen after the final lines, as Yang Hu decides on his course of action, a course of action which will clearly involve neither mercy nor forgiveness...

As well as the consistently gracious prose that is maintained throughout the whole book, there are also many memorable aphorisms, all of course absolutely in context, from subtle variations on existing proverbs to such wonderfully droll and sardonic axioms as:

Although there exist many thousands of subjects for elegant conversation, there are persons who cannot meet a cripple without talking about feet.

He is a wise and enlightened suppliant who seeks to discover an honourable Mandarin, but he is a fool who cries out, "I have found one".

Although it is desirable to lose persistently when playing at squares and circles with the broad-minded and sagacious Emperor, it is none the less a fact that the observance of this etiquette deprives the intellectual diversion of much of its interest for both players.

Before hastening to secure a possible reward of five taels by dragging an unobservant person away from a falling building, examine well his features lest you find, when too late, that it is one to whom you are indebted for double that amount.

Such Confucian dictums are never used gratuitously but are always perfectly placed and entirely appropriate to the occasion. If they sometimes seem opaque – such as "Even Yuan Yan once cast a missile at the Tablets" – then the reader can be sure that any ambiguity will be resolved and the saying made clear in the ensuing tale.

It is too much of a temptation not to include one final example of Bramah's way with words. When Yen, the picture maker, visits Peking he finds that despite his attempts at economy "...his taels melted away like the smile of a person of low class when he discovers that the mandarin's stern words were not intended as a jest".

THE SECOND VOLUME, *Kai Lung's Golden Hours*, was published a surprising twenty-two years after its predecessor, and was "immediately successful" according to Grant Richards in his introduction to the 1922 limited edition of *The Wallet* (*Golden Hours* was reprinted twice within three months of its initial appearance). Richards quotes Bramah as saying, "It was not until last year (1921) that I began to see before me something like sufficient material for a second volume". *Golden Hours* is perhaps the best of the six books, with many intriguing stories, and the chapter titles are an entertainment in themselves, including: "The Degraded Persistence of the Effete Ming-Shu"; "The Inopportune Behaviour of the Covetous Li-Loe"; "The Incredible Obtuseness Of Those Who Had Opposed The Virtuous Kai Lung"; and "Of Which it is Written: In Shallow Water Dragons Become the Laughing Stock of Shrimps".

The book is not simply a collection of short stories thrown together on a frail storyline. The connecting link, with Kai Lung continually managing to avoid the deadly intentions of the implacable Ming-Shu, is in itself extremely enjoyable and Bramah's mordant wit is evident on the very first page – when Kai encounters two women in a wood we are told "the elder and less attractive of the maidens fled, uttering loud and continuous cries of apprehension in order to conceal the direction of her flight". The one who remains is the delightful Hwa-Mei, who is instrumental in aiding Kai in his quest for survival, and with whom he ultimately makes his escape.

As with the opening story in *The Wallet*, Bramah is using a device from *The Arabian Nights*, where the princess Scheherazade averts death by telling stories to her would-be executioner, stories that were never finished by the time set for her strangling, so postponing the fatal act over and over again. In *Golden Hours*, it is the villainous Ming-Shu who is continually thwarted in his malicious intentions. These intentions are to ensure that Kai Lung is rendered liable to one or more of the penalties that the Mandarin Shan Tieng describes as "hanging, slicing, pressing, boiling, roasting, grilling, freezing, vatting, racking, twisting, drawing, compressing, inflating, rending, spiking, gouging, limb-tying, piece-meal-pruning and a variety of less tersely describable discomforts".

Ming-Shu is described at various points as "contemptible", "vindictive", "detestable", "insufferable", "base", "reptilian", and "a repulsive featured despot". He is a wonderfully deliberate caricature, and the reader almost feels obliged to boo whenever he appears onstage – his eventual downfall at the hands of Kai Lung is of course inevitable, and brings about a satisfying conclusion with Kai and Hwa-Mei outfoxing their foes and making a dignified exit, appropriately enriched with silver taels.

Entertaining as the ongoing background links are, the stories themselves also enchant and dazzle. The promise of the first book is more than fulfilled in a series of gratifying tales that never fail to captivate with their imagination and charm. The narratives include the tale of a would-be dragon killer who finds that it is easy enough to kill a dragon, but the problem is, it doesn't stay dead, regenerating almost immediately. He still manages to complete his mission and brings back six dragon skins, thus winning the hand of the delightful Wondrous Vision and lives happily ever after ... or does he? The final lines do suggest that perhaps he has certain regrets...

There are also accounts of vengeful demons, benevolent luminous insects, murderous barbers and burial robes. Heroes usually triumph over adversity, winning the beautiful maiden, but evildoers rarely prosper – here is what happens to Tsin Lung, who is forced to flee the city after being outwitted by Hien, and who decides that he will take up piracy:

...he was only able to purchase a small and dilapidated junk and to enlist the services of three thoroughly incompetent mercenaries. The vessels which he endeavoured to pursue stealthily in the hope of restoring his fortunes frequently sailed towards him under the impression that he was sinking and trying to attract their benevolent assistance. When his real intention was at length understood both he and his crew were invariably beaten about the head with clubs.

There is a marked change in mood in "The Story of Weng Cho; or, The One Devoid of Name", in which Weng Cho, faced with an absolutely intolerable choice, is saved at the last by Chance – or perhaps Fate, which is ever a factor in Kai Lung's world. It is not idly warned that "Destiny writes with an iron spear upon a marble stele; how then shall a merely human hand presume to guide her pen?"

The final tale, "The Story of the Loyalty of Ten-teh, the Fisherman", is quite different to what has gone before. It is touching and poignant, a bleak commentary on corruption and its effects, but ultimately uplifting in its depiction of the steadfast fidelity of Ten-teh. As with "The Vengeance of Tung Fel" in *The Wallet*, Bramah ably demonstrates his ability to deal more than capably with darker themes, an ability that was to become more apparent in later collections.

Epigrams are characteristically sprinkled throughout all the tales, again from the relatively mundane such as "Do not seek to escape from a flood by clinging to a tiger's tail" and "The lame duck should avoid the ploughed field" to the amusingly profound, including such gems as these:

There is a time to silence an adversary with the honey of logical persuasion, and there is a time to silence him with the argument of a heavily directed club.

In three moments a labourer will remove an obstructing rock, but three moons will pass without two wise men agreeing on the meaning of a vowel.

Even leprosy may be cured, but the enmity of an official underling can never be dispelled.

From three things cross the road to avoid: a falling tree, your chief and second wives whispering in agreement, and a goat wearing a leopard's tail.

The writing is matchlessly and consistently sublime, not to be read quickly but to be savoured in small quantities, much like an exotic meal of myriad courses. The decorous speech of all the characters is a continual delight, replete as it is with formal ambience and civility: "It is useless to raise a cloud of evasion before the sun of your penetrating intellect" is Kai Lung's response on being asked by the Mandarin Shan

Tieng about an alleged indiscretion; and even the dragon who Chang Tao has tried to kill says in response, "Fortunately it is possible to take a broad-minded view of your un- courteous action".

THE NEXT VOLUME in the series is *Kai Lung Unrolls His Mat*, and the iniquitous Ming-Shu returns, eager for a reckoning with Kai Lung, and more abominable than ever now that he has become a rebel chief of the army of the Avenging Knife. Again Bramah finds a multitude of adjectives to describe his villain, including "contumacious", "offensive", "insufferable", "opprobrious", as well as "notoriously incompetent", "dog faced", "pock-browed", and, really damningly, as having "his usual lack of refinement".

The first chapter, entitled "The Malignity of the Depraved Ming-Shu Rears its Offensive Head", finds the storyteller living happily with the delectable Hwa-Mei until Fate inevitably intervenes. Ming-Shu stumbles by chance upon their location and proceeds to burn the house and kidnap Hwa-Mei, leaving Kai to find and rescue his lady love for the major part of the book.

The format of *Golden Hours* is repeated, with the background story entwining the series of tales being recounted, although the connecting narrative is far longer and more involved; an exceptionally able story in its own right. This time then, the stories buttress the main theme, Kai's quest to liberate Hwa-Mei, rather than the other way around, and the book is far nearer to the accepted concept of a novel than either of its predecessors. Bramah perhaps realised that in Kai Lung he had a character eminently suited to a more starring role, and certainly this book has far more of him in it than any of the others. We also see a different side of Kai, who while preferring as ever to talk his way out of trouble, is quite prepared to take physical action when necessary, bearing in mind that "a literary aphorism makes a poor defence against a suddenly propelled battle-axe".

In his search for Hwa-Mei he comes upon all manner of unusual people and tells an assortment of stories for a variety of reasons. Satire is ever present, as in "The Story of Tong Ho, the Averter of Calamities", wherein Tong comes up with the idea that getting people to pay protection money is far easier and more profitable than robbing them. The protection racket soon develops into formal insurance cover against fire and accident, although Tong's insurance business is not quite above board, for "...if *some* among those who sought Tong's aid *might* occasionally experience fire or fatal injury, *all* of those who stubbornly refused to do so *inevitably* did".

There is also "The Story of Lin Ho and the Treasure of Fang-Tso", in which Lin Ho is killed but changes bodies with his murderer, proceeding to take his place until events conspire to enable him to cleverly switch back again at a most opportune time. The final sentence is one of delightful inference, leaving the reader to conjecture what would be happening to Lam-Kwong in the very near future as Fang-Tso, "comparable with gods in strength and with demons in resentment", returns...

This same story demonstrates that even when Bramah's characters are in urgent need of information, courtesy and graciousness still hold the ascendant; in the words of the lady Kuei, there is:

... a time to speak in the flowery terms of poetical allusion and a time to be distressingly explicit. Descending to the latter plane for one concise moment, O my dragon-hearted, state definitely whether you have or have not at last succeeded in slaying this long-enduring one's offensive and superfluous lord, and in attaching to yourself his personal belongings.

Kai also relates the tale of a sorcerous Mandarin whose daughter is possessed by "the perfidious influence of the spirit of an uprooted banyan tree", and then narrates the chronicle of the scholar Yan, set in a more distant time when dragons, phoenixes and winged snakes were common, as well as such a variety of other malign beings that "the more ordinary manifestations of spectres, ghouls, vampires, demons, voices, presages, and homeless shadows excited no comment". This is an unusually figurative story telling of how the Moon came to have its crescent shape and its phases.

The final tale in the book is "The Story of Ching-Kwei and the Destinies", a relatively straightforward account of a goatherd fulfilling his sorcerously fixed destiny "to end a sovereign's life and by the same act terminate a dynasty". Forming and leading the Army of the Restoring Ying, Ching-Kwei eventually takes the capital with a clever strategy but then finds that what he wants most is that which Fate seems to conclusively deny him. His destiny, however, proves to be more mutable than he had appreciated, and this agreeable story ends on an unusually sentimental note that is pleasing and satisfactory.

Kai Lung's quest also has a happy conclusion for all concerned, except of course for the execrable Ming-Shu. Hwa-Mei's rescue and the cleverly effected victory over the rebels is achieved two thirds of the way through the book, and the remaining third is set some years later, with Kai's adventuring days seemingly behind him and various children now gracing his household.

Again there is a heady variety of clever aphorisms throughout the whole book, such as "Two willing men can cleave a passage through the rock while four pressed slaves are moistening their hands", and "It is one thing to cast a noose about a tiger's neck, but it involves another attitude to conduct it to an awaiting cage". Bramah also offers up some amusing "Chinese" versions of old saws, as with "Refrain from instructing your venerated ancestress in the art of extracting nutrition from a coconut". But the most memorable lines are pure Kai Lung, as in "If two agree not to strive about the price, then before the parcel is made up they will fall out upon the colour of the string", and "It is more profitable to step upon an orange skin before a cloyed official than to offer pearls of wisdom to a company of sages".

By the end of this third volume, Kai is an old man (the defeat of Ming-Shu being "some two-score years" previously), and has to be helped around his orchard grove by his daughters. Readers would almost certainly have got the impression that this was the end of the saga, but presumably Bramah was reluctant to abandon his intriguing world with its distinctive customs and its variety of captivating inhabitants, for it was just a few years before a further book was to appear.

THE WALLET OF *Kai Lung* was a series of short stories with no on-going link. *Kai Lung's Golden Hours* had a continuing narrative thread running through it and *Kai Lung Unrolls His Mat* then took this a step further to provide a plot interlaced with narratives. The logical progression was now a complete novel, and this is precisely what *The Moon of Much Gladness* is. Kai Lung does not appear in this 1932 book at all, and his name is mentioned nowhere in the text; the only evidence of his involvement being the sub title *Related by Kai Lung*.

Having used Kai as a device to introduce readers to the feudal China that he had created, Bramah perhaps felt the need to mention the name of his storyteller for reassurance regarding the setting of this latest book. There is, however, no doubt as to the identity of the narrator and he is at his deferential and self-deprecating best, referring to himself on the first page as "...the obsequious-mannered relater of this depressingly inept chronicle", and his audience as "...those who may have been enticed into purchasing his lamentable effort".

The book takes place in the familiar environment of the earlier volumes, with the action covering a single Moon, a one-month period (hence the title). It is essentially a mystery, a "whodunit", the crime being the theft of the Mandarin T'sin Wong's pigtail, but the plot itself is convoluted and fascinating, the investigation leading to a variety of deeper waters.

The lead character is soon established as the lovely Hwa-Che, who having "incurred the malignity of one of the most powerful dragons frequenting the Middle Spaces" appears throughout most of the book disguised as a man. She has studied literature covering "the hidden wisdom of the West", and in particular the detection of crime, of which the foremost exponent is one who:

... inhales the acrid fumes of smouldering weeds and wraps about his form a flowing robe of talismanic virtues. He it is who also calls up attending Shapes by means of forbidden drugs and restores the harmonious balance of the Spheres with a machine of wood and string that in his hand produces music.

She identifies a suspect early in the book by his footprints, and her comment that she had "made a close study of the eighty-seven distinctive kinds of sandals in use throughout the Empire" cannot fail to raise a smile on the face of any Sherlockian, and nor can her reference to "the significant behaviour of the gold-fish in the ornamental tank".

Hwa-Che, conscientiously and resolutely trusting to the "Barbarian method of crime detection", gets into all sorts of bizarre and outrageous situations but comes through them all with her ardent belief that the system she is using can do nothing else but lead her to success.

Her eventual triumph is inevitable and the happy ending is no less predictable, nicely rounding out an engaging and pleasurable reading experience.

Bramah's wry humour is evident throughout. The customary plethora of proverbs include such gems as "Before adventuring into a neighbour's house it is well to decide within yourself what to explain should he meet you coming out again", and "He who is compelled to share a cavern with a tiger soon learns to stroke fur in the right direction", as well as "The foolhardy puts his head into the indulgent tiger's mouth. When the creature sneezes, presumption is effectively corrected". And when the chief of the Avenging Knife rebels finds his camp surrounded by the War Lord's army, he sees that all of the latter:

...had their weapons accurately fixed so that at a given moment they could discharge their missiles – the javelin men with arms upraised, the slingers gently swinging their thongs, the bowmen crouched with bolts well drawn – so down to the very bandiers of taunts and obscene gibes, whose throats were already cleared for a nerve-destroying volley.

Thoroughly enjoyable though *The Moon of Much Gladness* is, it does lack the advantage of the earlier three collections, which were of course able to present a wider-ranging variety of characters and locales within their pages. With *Moon*, the scenario is necessarily restricted and plot therefore takes precedence; there is consequently a relative lack of diversity, and this could have come close to heavy-handedness in a lesser writer's hands. As it is, the subtly clever unfolding of events and the deft pacing present the reader with a novel that is very agreeable indeed.

The book's reliance on narrative drive was at odds with what had gone before, and may conceivably have been an experiment on the part of its author, who perhaps wanted to establish whether he could sustain the flair and appeal of the shorter fiction throughout a 300 page novel. The answer was most definitely in the affirmative, but it is difficult to imagine what format a second novel could have taken without being disappointing after the remarkable achievement of the first.

Perhaps tellingly, *Moon* seems to have been the least successful of the first five books, with far fewer printings than any of the others. Bramah's own thoughts on the matter are unknown, but interestingly he did not return to this longer format in any of his later Kai Lung writings, which were one more published collection and a further six appearances in magazines.

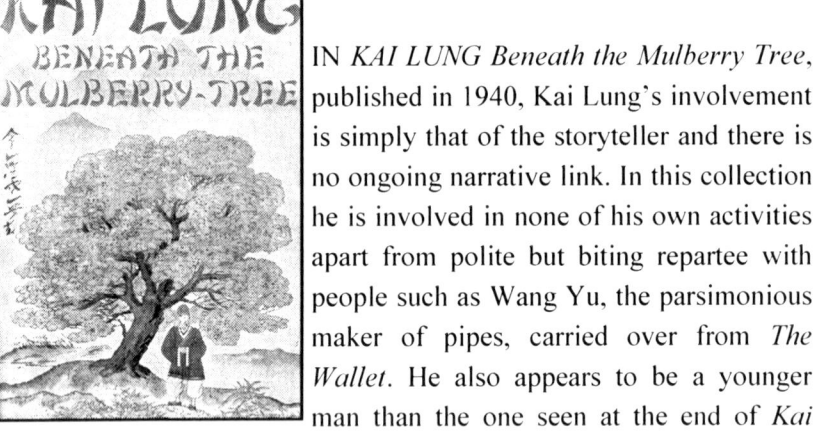

IN *KAI LUNG Beneath the Mulberry Tree*, published in 1940, Kai Lung's involvement is simply that of the storyteller and there is no ongoing narrative link. In this collection he is involved in none of his own activities apart from polite but biting repartee with people such as Wang Yu, the parsimonious maker of pipes, carried over from *The Wallet*. He also appears to be a younger man than the one seen at the end of *Kai Lung Unrolls His Mat* where he had, of course, apparently been "retired".

Some of the tales are of a darker hue than those in the preceding books, and to those used to the consistently intrinsic wit displayed in the bulk of the earlier tales, some of the content of *Mulberry Tree* may seem a little oppressive. A story such as "The Ignoble Alliance of Lin T'sing with the Outlaw Fang Wang, and how it Affected the Destinies", for instance, has an unexpectedly downbeat and cheerless ending, as does the chapter concerning the Judgements of Prince Ying.

These cover "inventions" such as duplication and chess (or "tchess" as it is described), but there is also a salutary lesson, clearly reflecting contemporary concerns, in Ying's attitude to the creation of an awesome weapon of mass destruction. So fearful is its potential that Ying, moral and compassionate as he is, orders not only its creator killed but also his entire family, with his house burned to the ground and the ashes dispersed, "so that neither seed nor root of that pernicious growth should survive ever to flourish".

Conversely though, there is "The Story of the Poet Lao Ping, Chun Shin's Daughter Fa, and the Fighting Crickets", in which Fa cleverly and advantageously persuades the necromancer Sze Chang to transfer his spirit into the body of the champion cricket Valiant Tiger in the upcoming battle with Lao Ping's contender Ancient Bygone. And in "The Story of Yin Ho, Hoa-Mi and the Magician", Yin fortuitously manages to obtain the post of Chief Detector of Hitherto Undetected Crimes despite his inability to pass examinations (when asked to "state as concisely as possible what you know of the Chang-tung theory of the relation of one class of immaterial conceptions to another", Yin's "undisputably laconic statement *Nothing*" fails to impress the examiners...).

Bramah is naturally never short of an incisive saying or a witty anecdote, and so we find that "Springs will dry up with the drought, and even rivers be stilled by the forces of winter, but nothing can ever stop the tongue of an interfering woman", and "If the deities are on your side you can cross the ocean on a single plank; without them you may slip and be drowned in a wayside puddle".

When it comes to the necessities of life, "...a piece of money, a smooth-noosed cord, and a knife of superior keenness... Properly used, as the several emergencies arise, these should be enough to bring a resourceful man through most ordinary difficulties..." while we also learn that:

It is related of a certain music-loving official who was accustomed to play on a vibratory shell fitted with hollow tubes that when a friend demanded of him why he did not marry one whose voice was notorious for its melody, he replied, "Because although Mu's notes are admittedly superior to those of a perforated shell she cannot be put away in a box when the song is finished."

And on the public criticism the Ying's consort Mei, we are told: "This, needless to relate, was in the care-free days before the salutary practice of shortening at either one or both ends those who allowed incautious tongues to outrun the dictates of loyalty had induced a more charitable outlook".

But perhaps more than in any of the other books, there is a variety of pithy one-liners, including:

He who is to be decapitated for a treasonable word may as well throw in an offensive gesture.

The beggar who wears a costly silk robe displays his sores in vain.

Only the foolish pig exults when he finds that he is being taken to the fair.

But although there is much to enjoy in the book, it does in the main seem to be somewhat more laboured and less inspired than its predecessors. Perhaps after four decades of the intermittent chronicling of Kai Lung's narratives Bramah lacked some of the motivation that had stimulated him in earlier years.

IT WOULD APPEAR that *Kai Lung Beneath the Mulberry Tree* was fairly successful – it was reprinted several times within a few years of publication – and Bramah had obviously not completely tired of chronicling the exploits of the array of characters and plots that he had to hand. Six further rather short stories appeared in the British periodical *Punch* in 1940 and 1941, and no doubt there would have been more had the author not died in Somerset in 1942.

It was over thirty years before these last few tales were collected in *Kai Lung: Six*, a very nicely produced fifty-eight page publication from The Non-Profit Press, limited to a mere 250 numbered copies. Its contents are admittedly rather slight, but such tales as "The Story of Sing Tsung and the Exponent of Dark Magic" and "The Story of Chung Pun and the Miraculous Peacocks", if not up to the standards set by *Golden Hours*, are still very enjoyable.

Bramah's customary stylistic smoothness and elegant prose had not deserted him, and nor had his flair for the apposite maxim, although these had acquired a stronger element of cynicism in such lines as "It is as profitable to expect compassion from a disturbed adder as gratitude from one to whom you have lent a bar of silver" and "Give a beggar a joint and he will throw the bone at you when the meat is eaten".

In "The Story of Kwey Chao and the Grateful Song Bird" there is also the wonderful description of the heroine's unbound hair, which "streamed unconfined until it was frequently mistaken for a flock of migratory ravens as she sped with graceful unconcern among the glades of the neighbouring forest". The unconventional Kwey Chao does in fact win the hand of a Mandarin with the help of a bird that teaches her to exactly mimic its song.

It is not only its brevity that separates this volume from *The Golden Hours* or *The Wallet*; the generally light mood of those earlier works is replaced by a more sceptical tone, quite probably reflecting the times in which they were written, the early 1940s, a bleak and depressing time of war. But relatively minor though these stories may be, the fact is that even a lesser Kai Lung volume such as this is very readable and a naturally welcome addition to the chronicles of the master raconteur.

The last published tale, and presumably the last that Bramah ever wrote, was "The Story of Li Pao, Lucky Star and the Intruding Stranger", dating from 17 November 1941, which appeared in *The Punch Almanack for 1942*. Li Pao, totally averse to the fame that he gains, and horrified that his name may be known for generations hence, eventually succeeds in his aim for anonymity, for we are told that "No reference to his work exists in the contemporary record of his day, while ... his name has been equally unknown at any subsequent period". Whether or not the author of the story craved the same obscurity, it was not to be his to achieve, for Kai Lung has secured a literary niche all of his own for over a century, and refuses to be forgotten.

IT WAS SOMETHING of a surprise when *Kai Lung Raises His Voice* appeared in 2010, primarily because it included four previously unpublished stories, all dating from the early 1900s. It also included "Ming Tseuen and the Emergency" from the *Specimen Case* collection, together with all of the stories from *Kai Lung: Six*. One of them, "Yuen Yang and the Empty Lo-Chee Crate", was an earlier version of "Yuen Yang and the Empty Soo-Shong Chest", although apart from its longer beginning it is little changed.

It might be expected from the dates that they were written the unpublished tales would exhibit the flair found in *The Wallet of Kai Lung* and *Kai Lung's Golden Hours*, but unfortunately they do not match the quality of those early volumes. They are much more ornate in their style but less flowing in their prose, and are consequently far less accessible than the author's other works, and one can understand why Bramah discarded them.

They are not without some infrequent but noteworthy axioms. In

"The Subtlety of Kang Chieng" it is advised "do not dispute with a scorpion concerning the length of its tail, but rather let the argument turn upon the weight of your own heavily-shod staff", while in "The Destiny of Cheng, the Son of Sha-Kien" we find that

the snail may travel a thousand li by sitting on the camel's tail, but the ill-witted outcast who attempts to press in between the deities and one of their authentically-inspired soothsayers will find himself in the unenviable position of the person who remained beneath the avalanche in order to protect his chrysanthemums.

Overall, however, these previously unpublished works are for completests only.

AMONGST BRAMAH'S OTHER fiction are the stories of the blind detective Max Carrados. He featured in three collections, *Max Carrados* (1914), *The Eyes of Max Carrados* (1923), and *Max Carrados Mysteries* (1927), as well as the novel *The Bravo of London* (1934). One story also appeared in *A Specimen Case* in 1924.

These tales are regarded as landmarks of early twentieth century detective fiction, although they admittedly do not stand the test of time in the same way that the Sherlock Holmes canon does. Even so, they are fascinating period pieces that remain very agreeable, written in a quite different style to that of the Kai Lung saga, with unembellished but polished prose. To today's taste the style of writing may seem stilted and passé but, even so, Bramah's ability with words is clearly apparent, as is his imaginative prowess.

Max Carrados himself is an endearing character with a touch of mystery about him (as of course was the case with his creator), and his winning personality is developed as the series progresses. He is an amateur detective, dealing with those baffling cases that his old friend the enquiry agent Louis Carlyle consults him about. Other regular characters include the stolid but exceptionally observant attendant Parkinson, the faithful secretary Greatorex, and Scotland Yard's Inspector Beedel.

Carrados is far more perceptive than any sighted person, using all of his other senses to a remarkable degree. He can read newspapers by feeling the imprint of the type, can make Sherlockian deductions about people by smell and touch, and can learn all sorts of things by simply listening. "My ears are my eyes" he says in "The Tragedy at Brookbend Cottage", although it is actually all of his remaining sensory organs that serve to not only replace his sight but to augment his talents such that his disability is hardly more than a slight inconvenience. In "The Secret of Dunstan's Tower", when night has fallen and he is sitting by an open window, Max says,

There are a thousand sounds that you in your arrogance of sight ignore, a thousand individual scents of hedge and orchard that come up to me here. I suppose it is quite dark to you now, Jim? What a lot you seeing people must miss!

The detective's blindness works very much to his benefit in some situations, as is demonstrated in "The Game Played in the Dark" and "The Ingenious Mr Spinola", while it is the enhancement of his other senses that gives him the advantage in such tales as "The Coin of Dionysius" and "The Missing Witness Sensation". However, it is usually his instinctive deductive abilities that solve the mysteries that he is confronted with, and some of that deductive reasoning is impressive indeed, if occasionally a little problematical as far as the intuitive leaps are concerned.

For although the idea of the intellectual superiority of a blind man is readily acceptable, some of the detective's achievements are barely credible and indeed at times come close to complete implausibility. But disbelief is happily suspended when it involves such an agreeable and clever individual as Max Carrados in such pleasing accounts as these.

Not all of the stories constitute the sort of detective fiction that would be regarded as the norm for the time in which they were written. While Carrados was certainly not a "psychic sleuth" along the lines of Hodgson's Carnacki or Blackwood's John Silence, he was one of the first to become involved in supernatural themes. There are tales of the apparently paranormal which eventually have a rational explanation, as with "The Secret of Dunstan's Tower" and "The Ghost at Massingham Mansions", but there are also certain of the stories that do involve outré situations and which are genuine weird tales.

In "The Eastern Mystery", for instance, an amulet that is reputed to be the tooth of the ape god Hanuman is revealed to be a holy relic – a nail from the True Cross – and its powers are remarkable indeed. This is a particularly powerful narrative, and its conclusion is forceful and satisfying. In "The Strange Case of Cyril Bycourt", the spirits of plague victims are brought into the mortal world by means of electric current – the power house is built on a charnel pit, and is found to "have stirred up the buried corruption of that dreadful place".

BRAMAH WAS RATHER adept at conveying chilling effects; nor did he shy away from the unconventional. Although he concentrated on his two major characters, his fiction covered a wide variety of areas, as is demonstrated by the 1924 collection *A Specimen Case*. Not only do we have the worlds of Kai Lung and Max Carrados within these pages, but also "The Dead March", in which the discovery of an old Roman coin at the time of the Battle of Mons summons the Emperor Vespasian from the distant past; and "Hautepierre's Star", where a dying man's miraculous recovery is clearly the result of far from natural causes. Then there is a phantom coalman (!) in "A Very Black Business", and an unpleasant doom in the short but effective "From a London Balcony". There are also romances, satires, historical pieces and science-fiction.

It must be said that many of the tales within the collection are inconsequential at best, but what is almost casually demonstrated is a remarkable and wide-ranging versatility. Bramah seemed to be at ease with just about any type of story, and the fact that he concentrated on writing imaginative fantasy and intelligent crime fiction, rather than specialising in other areas, was perhaps simply because it was those fields that appealed to him most. He was plainly his own man, and seems to have been in a position whereby he was able to write what he wished when he wished. As a consequence his entire output reflects a partiality for its subject matter, diverse as it may be. There is nothing forced or hackneyed in any of the work, all of it having presumably been what he wanted to write.

This extensive range of subject matter does bring its own problems, and *A Specimen Case* is ultimately dissatisfying. Bramah was not a master in all areas of fiction and, to be blunt, there are as many mediocre stories as there are good ones. Although "Once in a Blue Moon", "The Heart of the Pagan" and "The Marquise Ring" are undeniably excellent, other promising concepts ("The War Hawks" for example) never really gain momentum, while others are far too contrived ("Revolution" and "Fate and a Family Council") and some are simply ineffectual ("The Making of Marianna" and "The Delicate Case of Mlle. Celestine Bon").

ERNEST BRAMAH IS steadfastly remembered by both lovers of literate fantasy and aficionados of the detective story. His contributions to these distinct genres are significant, and his creation of a unique and charismatic character in each domain make him an important literary figure. The depiction of Kai Lung and his stylised version of China are in particular lasting and unique gifts to the connoisseur of imaginative fiction.

Lin Carter, in his introduction to the Ballantine edition of *Kai Lung's Golden Hours* (1972), expresses his hope that "a readership can still be found, even in this benighted age, for polished irony and lapidary prose, for sharp-edged wit and jewelled satire ... books as good as this deserve long lives". Bramah's work may no longer be to popular taste, but his writings have endured for many years, and to those who savour his ornate style he is an incomparable master.

There is no question that his books will always be sought out by lovers of fine prose, and that they will still be read and enjoyed well after the latest best seller has been long forgotten. "It suffices," as Kai Lung himself might have said, "for the most fragrant and pleasing of the lotus blossoms are rarely perceived by the flower gatherers who frequent the well-trodden paths".

SELECTED BIBLIOGRAPHY

The Kai Lung books

The Wallet of Kai Lung – Grant Richards, 1900

Kai Lung's Golden Hours – Grant Richards, 1922

Kai Lung Unrolls His Mat – Richards Press, 1928

The Moon of Much Gladness – Cassell, 1932

Kai Lung Beneath the Mulberry Tree – Richards Press, 1940

Kai Lung: Six – Non-Profit Press, 1974

Kai Lung Raises His Voice – Durrant, 2010

WEST INDIAN FRIGHTS
HENRY S WHITEHEAD

THE REVEREND HENRY St Clair Whitehead was born in New Jersey in 1882. In his younger years he was a reporter, a newspaper editor, and the holder of various political offices. The major part of his adult life was spent in the Episcopal Church, into which he was ordained in 1912. He held a PhD degree, and had several books published including *The Invitations of Our Lord*, *Neighbours of the Early Church* and *Good Manners in Church*. He had various postings during his religious career, including one in the Virgin Islands; he eventually became a rector in Dunedin, Florida, where he died in 1932.

Such a basic biography gives no clue at all to the fact that Whitehead was also a fine writer of macabre fiction. He was a major contributor to *Weird Tales* from the mid-1920s to the early 1930s, during which time twenty-five of his stories were published, and he was regarded as one of the magazine's foremost writers. Like his *Weird Tales* contemporaries HP Lovecraft, Clark Ashton Smith and Robert E Howard, Whitehead was a writer of superior and enduring fiction, the quality of which rose well above its limiting pulp source. However, in sharp contrast to those other luminaries little of his work is presently available.

The key aspect of the broad biographical information provided above is the period spent in the Virgin Islands; it was here that Whitehead became intrigued by Caribbean culture. Although he initially spent a limited time in the Islands, he returned each year as Acting Archdeacon until his health prevented him from doing so. The fictitious writer Gerald Canevin, who appears in many of the stories, is clearly an alter ego of the author and it was primarily through the Canevin tales that Whitehead produced his most impressive work. This dealt with the rich vein of dark folklore revolving around the traditions of Obeah and Voodoo, the magic of the West Indies, and its traditional multi-faceted manifestation, the Jumbee.

A short factual article by Whitehead, "Obi in the Caribbean", was published in the Catholic journal *The Commonweal* in 1927, which is fascinating background to his stories, encompassing the magic beliefs of the region. These are covered in a forthright manner, with a cautious respect, and the writer's philosophy on the subject appears to be summed up in the story "The Shut Room", when a character says "the Church has always recognised the existence of the invisible creation... And – this invisible creation; it doesn't mean merely angels!"

The Jumbee does feature in Whitehead's tales in a variety of guises: there is the mummified hand seeking vengeance in "Black Tancrede"; the fish-god zombie in "The Shadows"; the obi-doll in "Sweet Grass"; and the "canicanthrope" in "Jumbee". Admittedly, equally strange happenings do occur that are not Voodoo-related, with a monstrous spider dealing death in "The Left Eye"; revenge from beyond the grave in "The Fireplace"; an intriguing variation of déjà-vu in "The Sea-Tiger"; and a malevolent mirror in "The Trap". But it is the Jumbee tales that tend to have the most impact. From the grisly Voodoo curse in "The Lips" to the particularly ill-fated shape-shifting in "The Black Beast", these are narratives that consistently captivate and enthral.

The very first story that Whitehead published in *Weird Tales* was "Tea Leaves" in the combined May, June and July issue of 1924. It did not provide any hint at all as to what was to come, but was a nicely crafted tale of a young woman finding a near priceless necklace given by Walter Raleigh to Queen Elizabeth. The main settings are London and New England, and the minor supernatural element is peripheral and incidental to the plot. "The Door" followed a few months later, and was another acceptable work, this time dealing with the post-mortem experience of a young man who does not realise that he is dead.

Both "Tea Leaves" and "The Door" were rather typical of Whitehead's earlier tales, which tended to be satisfactory but lightweight. They were fairly short and almost anecdotal in nature, and while their themes were interesting and the writing competent, they hardly warrant any undue attention. But as Whitehead's self-confidence as a writer grew, so his fiction became longer and more powerful. To illustrate this, "West India Lights", published in 1927, is neither overly memorable nor chilling; but rewritten as "Seven Turns in a Hangman's Rope", the 1932 version is longer and very much more effective. The jaunty tone of the original is replaced by a darker, more unsettling mood, and the romantic sub-plot is removed entirely. Whitehead was clearly maturing as a writer, honing his craft and developing his ideas, and perhaps his regular visits to the Virgin Islands were also providing fuel for his imagination.

The West Indies series, steeped in the supernatural and usually of a macabre nature, only got seriously under way in 1926 with the publication of "Jumbee", to be quickly followed by the first of some twenty or more Gerald Canevin tales, "The Projection of Armand Dubois". Subsequently, the bulk of Whitehead's fiction was set in the Caribbean, and Gerald Canevin featured in nearly all of them.

Canevin's adventures are certainly diverse. He encounters a sentient tree in "The Tree-Man"; a haunted piece of music in "The Ravel Pavane"; a vengeful ghost in "The Projection of Armand Dubois"; and psychic possession in "Mrs Lorriquer". He thwarts an obi-man in "Black Terror"; battles ghouls in "The Chadbourne Episode"; and uncovers miscegenation in "Williamson" (this latter story does incidentally have a rather clever title, but this only becomes apparent on the final page). He also ventures where few people would dare to go: in "The People of Pan", for example, this is the arresting first sentence:

I, Gerald Canevin of Santa Cruz, have actually been down the ladder of thirteen hundred and twenty-six steps set into the masonry of the Great Cylinder of Saona; have marvelled at the vast cathedral underground on that tropical island; have trembled under the menacing Horns of the Goat.

IN HIS INTRODUCTION to *Jumbee and Other Uncanny Tales*, Robert H Barlow indicated that Whitehead started writing short stories in 1921 for markets such as *Outdoors* and *Adventure*, but began concentrating on the eerie when he discovered *Weird Tales* in 1923. However, Whitehead's writing career was actually longer; his first story, "Not to the Swift", appeared in December 1905 in *Outdoors Magazine*. His known literary productivity – some forty short stories in the last nine years of his life – suggests that he was not a speedy writer, but his relatively low output was probably due to the fact that there were other considerations on his time; in particular, he was a full-time priest.

Devout though he presumably was, there is no question of Whitehead using his fiction to get any sort of "message" across, although he did write one very good effective religious piece called "The Tabernacle", which poignantly deals with the effect of the consecrated Host on a hive of bees. This remarkable and powerful story was initially rejected by Farnsworth Wright on the basis that *Weird Tales* readers would not understand what it was about, but it was eventually published with an Author's Note explaining the religious background.

Elements of spirituality also occur in "Cassius", with Canevin giving the malignant homunculus a Christian burial. His reasoning is that as it was originally a part of Brutus Hellman, who would have been baptised, it was thus "a child of God", and should be treated accordingly. At the very end of the story Canevin says, "It may have been – doubtless was, in one sense – a grotesque act on my part. But I cherish the conviction that I did what was right". This is a somewhat unconventional ending, bearing in mind the reign of terror conducted by the spiteful creature over the preceding few days, and it adds an unusually thought-provoking element to the tale. There are few authors who would have covered this particular aspect, or who could have so adeptly drawn attention to the basic humanity of the malevolent Cassius, subtly changing the reader's response from repulsion to compassion.

"Cassius" was published in November 1931, and over the next eighteen months such superior stories as "The Trap", "The Great Circle", "Seven Turns in a Hangman's Rope" and "The Chadbourne Episode" appeared. Presumably "The Ravel Pavane", "Scar Tissue" and "Bothon" also date from the same period, fine stories that had been completed at the time of the writer's death, but which for some reason did not appear until many years later.

Whitehead did occasionally use non-Caribbean locales in his work, most notably in "The Shut Room", an excellent Canevin tale set in England. This particular story, of the spirit of a highwayman haunting a coaching inn in a rather strange manner, has a nicely expressive passage where Canevin and Carruth encounter the ghost: "...he turned upon us, with an audible snarl and baleful, glaring little eyes like a pig's, deep set in a hideous, scarred face, and then he spoke – he spoke, and he had been dead for more than a century!"

"The Shut Room" represents a distinct departure from the norm in the Canevin *oeuvre*. Apart from being non-West Indian in setting, it is reminiscent of the tales in William Hope Hodgson's *Carnacki the Ghost Finder* (a book that is actually referred to in the story), with Gerald Canevin and Lord Carruth as the psychic investigators. "The Napier Limousine" also has an English location, and again features Canevin and Carruth. Although this second story is very much a minor piece, the two tales taken together are possibly indicative that Whitehead could have been intending to expand the scope of Canevin's adventures.

But the warranted popular success of the fiction set in the Caribbean may well have side-tracked any such intentions. By 1931, tales like "Passing of a God", "The Black Beast" and "Cassius" were amply demonstrating a fulfilment of the promise of the previous few years. Whitehead had adroitly succeeded in merging those aspects of West Indies folklore that so clearly intrigued him with a style of writing that was at the same time both deceptively uncomplicated and genuinely macabre. His straightforward storytelling technique deftly combines with a convincing local authenticity and colour, clearly reflecting the author's captivation with the Islands and their people. Whitehead's direct, unembellished prose heightens the disturbing effect of his tales with its realism, as does the fact that the bleakest of the stories sometimes conclude with a volte-face return to the innocuous and the commonplace.

In "Passing of a God", for instance, there is Dr Pelletier's grim description of the "thing" that he removes from Arthur Carswell, which is supposedly dead but opens its eyes and stares at the Doctor:

They were the eyes of something more than human, Canevin, something incredibly old, sophisticated, cold, immune from anything except pure evil, the eyes of something that had been worshipped, Canevin, from ages and ages out of a past that went back before all known human calculation, eyes that showed all the deliberate, lurking wickedness that has ever been in the world.

But the tale having been told, the final page dextrously and reassuringly lightens the mood – with dinner served, the story ends: "I nodded in agreement and resumed my soup. Pelletier has a cook in a thousand".

Several individuals reappear in the stories. Apart from Dr Pelletier, there are also Nils Hansen, Colonel Lorriquer, Arthur Carswell and Andrew Penn. This gives a neat sense of continuity to the tales, although sometimes there are unconscious oversights – Colonel Lorriquer's widowed daughter is Mrs Spencer in "Cassius", but her name mysteriously becomes Preston in "Mrs Lorriquer". All of these characters are, like Canevin, down to earth, solid people and they all accept that there are mysteries in the Islands that cannot be rationally explained. Their attitudes heighten the effect of the stories, strengthening the illusion that the author is recounting actual experiences, as many of the tales assert. In reviewing *Jumbee and Other Uncanny Tales* in the *New York Times*, Orville Prescott said:

With deceptive gentleness and clerical decorum, Dr. Whitehead wrote of voodoo spells, fiendish manikins and other terrors to be found in the tropic nights of the Virgin Islands. So quietly did he edge up on his horrors that his stories seem quite like the truthful reminiscences they purport to be, which means they are pretty good.

It is interesting to note that some of Whitehead's fiction *is* based on fact. "Hill Drums" tells of the way in which William Palgrave, the unpopular British Consul in St Thomas, is driven out of his post by means of a hypnotic song. The tale is only minor, but Palgrave really *was* the Consul at the time in question, and *had* been transferred from Trebizond, as the story states. The basic details are therefore correct, although whether Palgrave was "magicked" out of St Thomas is of course another matter – he evidently did fail to mention his tenure in the Virgin Islands in what was apparently an otherwise all-embracing account of his consular career in the book *Ulysses*, and one might wonder as to the reasons for such reticence...

A CORRESPONDENT OF Lovecraft, Whitehead was one of the relatively few *Weird Tales* authors who actually met HPL, and they collaborated on a story called "The Trap", published in 1932. This tells of an inter-dimensional mirror that draws people into its clutches, with Gerald Canevin finally defeating it. The theme is certainly Lovecraftian, but the styles of the two authors blend surprisingly well when one bears in mind their contrasting techniques. There is no jarring transition where one writer finishes and the other starts, although Lovecraft's style is noticeable in the central section, which he wrote in its entirety.

Lovecraft also provided the synopsis for "Bothon", originally entitled "The Bruise". This is a story of ancestral memory, dealing with the destruction of Atlantis, and was almost certainly written at around the same time as "Scar Tissue", to which it is thematically similar. Both of these tales incorporate vivid and exciting action scenes, and the same can be said of Whitehead's two major novelettes of 1932, "The Great Circle" and "Seven Turns in a Hangman's Rope". This may again be suggestive of the areas of fiction into which the author intended to progress; it is certainly a fact that his pieces were increasing in length, and they were also getting more ambitious. "The Great Circle", as well as being by far the longest of Whitehead's published tales, is also the most imaginative in its scope – Canevin quite literally confronts a demigod in this story, which ends with his evocative reflection: "...that cosmic entity of the higher atmosphere, presiding over His element of air; menacing, colossal; His vast heart beating on eternally as, stupendous, incredible, He towers there inscrutable among the unchanging stars".

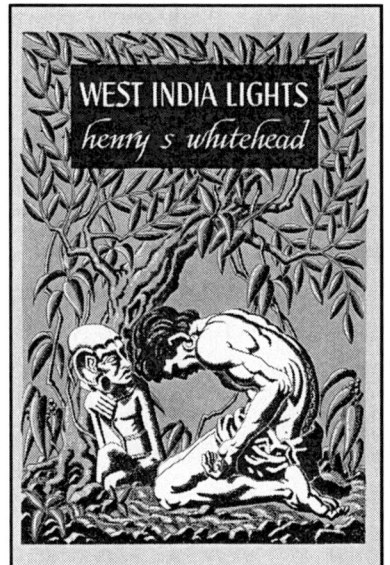

It is intriguing to ponder just what Whitehead might have produced, and what he had in mind for Gerald Canevin, had he lived a full span. It may well be that he was thinking in terms of extended formats for his fiction, and of expanding into more swashbuckling arenas, but we will never know. As with many other writers of weird fiction, he did not survive to old age, dying at fifty on 23 November 1932. We do know that at the time of his death he left an unfinished novel called *The Good Wine*, although its content and whereabouts are now a mystery, and are presumably likely to remain so.

After Whitehead's death, two further stories appeared within the next three months, the unimpressive ghost story "The Napier Limousine", and the far better tale of Canevin battling ghouls, "The Chadbourne Episode". There was then a hiatus of thirteen years, when 1946 saw the appearance of no less than five new stories which, with one exception (the mediocre "In Case of Disaster Only"), were all up to the standard that had been set by their author during his published lifetime.

There was speculation, about "Bothon" in particular, that August Derleth could have edited or rewritten some of the "new" material, although again we will probably never know. There was a similar rumour about the later Carnacki stories by William Hope Hodgson that were published by Arkham House, but Sam Moskowitz discovered the original manuscripts of two of them and found that Derleth had not changed a word, and he also convincingly demonstrated that a third tale was almost certainly genuine as well.

It is something of an indignity that much of Whitehead's work is currently available. It is admittedly true to say that some of that work might be considered inappropriate today because of the use of racial stereotypes and words now considered to be offensive, but we need to remember that when these stories were written such terminology was presumably not as distasteful and unacceptable as it is now. It is highly unlikely that Whitehead himself was writing with the deliberate intent of disparagement, but was simply reflecting the accepted attitudes of his time and his environment.

However, there is light in the literary darkness. Ash-Tree Press has announced a three volume complete collection of the author's work, and the first of these – *Passing of a God and Other Stories* – appeared in 2007. Additionally, *The Compleat Fiction of Henry S Whitehead* in three trade paperback volumes is due from The Battered Silicon Despatch Box at some point in the future. These books should serve to acquaint a new generation of readers with some fine and creative writing, for at their best Henry S Whitehead's stories are an excellent contribution to the genre of imaginative fiction, and are as enjoyable and absorbing today as they were to the readers of *Weird Tales* eighty years ago.

SELECTED BIBLIOGRAPHY

"Tea Leaves" – *Weird Tales*, May/June/July 1924

"The Door" – *Weird Tales*, November 1924

"The Fireplace" – *Weird Tales*, January 1925

"Sea Change" – *Weird Tales*, February 1925

"The Thin Match" – *Weird Tales*, March 1925

"The Cunning of the Serpent" – *Adventure*, May 1925

"The Wonderful Thing" – *Weird Tales*, July 1925

"Across the Gulf" – *Weird Tales*, May 1926

"Jumbee" – *Weird Tales*, September 1926

"The Projection of Armand Dubois" – *Weird Tales*, October 1926

"West India Lights" – *Mystery Magazine*, April 1927

"The Left Eye" – *Weird Tales*, June 1927

"The Shadows" – *Weird Tales*, November 1927

"The Cult of the Skull" – *Weird Tales*, December 1928

"The People of Pan" – *Weird Tales*, March 1929

"Black Tancrède" – *Weird Tales*, June 1929

"Sweet Grass" – *Weird Tales*, July 1929

"The Lips" – *Weird Tales*, September 1929

"The Tabernacle" – *Weird Tales*, January 1930

"The Shut Room" – *Weird Tales*, April 1930

"Passing of a God" – *Weird Tales*, January 1931

"The Tree-Man" – *Weird Tales*, February/March 1931

"Hill Drums" – *Weird Tales*, June/July 1931

"The Black Beast" – *Adventure* July 1931

"Black Terror" – *Weird Tales*, October 1931

"Cassius" – *Strange Tales*, November 1931

"The Moon-Dial" – *Strange Tales*, January 1932

"The Trap" – *Strange Tales*, March 1932

"Mrs Lorriquer" – *Weird Tales*, April 1932

"The Great Circle" – *Strange Tales*, June 1932

"Seven Turns in a Hangman's Rope" – *Adventure*, July 1932

"No Eye-Witnesses" – *Weird Tales*, August 1932

"The Sea-Tiger" – *Strange Tales*, October 1932

"The Napier Limousine" – *Strange Tales*, January 1933

"The Chadbourne Episode" – *Weird Tales*, February 1933

"The Ravel Pavane" – *Who Knocks*, June 1946

"Scar-Tissue" – *Amazing*, July 1946

"Bothon" – *Amazing*, August 1946

"Williamson" – *West India Lights*, 1946

"In Case of Disaster Only" – *West India Lights*, 1946

THE PASSION, THE MAGIC, AND THE OUTRAGEOUS THEODORE STURGEON

STARTING IN 1939, when "Ether Breather" was published in *Astounding Science Fiction*, Theodore Sturgeon (1918-1985) wrote short stories, novelettes and novels that ran into the hundreds, becoming one of the most popular writers of his time. As far as quantity was concerned, the majority of his work fell within the category of science fiction, but in quality it was fantasy that predominated. This is by no means a belittlement of Sturgeon's science fiction (such titles as "Microcosmic God", "Extrapolation", "Maturity", "Killdozer", and many others more than demonstrate his superlative abilities in that field) but there is an allure about the fantasy stories that sets them apart as matchless and wholly individual contributions to the genre.

As with certain other superior fantasy authors – Jack Vance and Roger Zelazny for instance – Sturgeon's reputation was founded principally on his science fiction and yet, in common with those other two writers, one gets the impression that it was the fantasy-oriented stories for which he reserved his real affection and to which he devoted his skills to the fullest. Some of his science fiction may have seemed a little uninspired or stilted, but there was always a refreshing originality of concept and treatment in the fantasy tales.

Sturgeon's range was considerable both in mood and setting, but his fantasy could, broadly speaking, be broken down into three groups: the humorous, the horrific, and the gentle (sometimes deceptively gentle). Such labelling is necessarily not exclusive as some of the stories defy classification and others overlap, but it does represent a broad guideline to the primary types of story in the author's canon, although it was the latter category that outnumbered the first two in the fullness of his career.

THE HUMOROUS ELEMENT expressed itself in what could best be described as *Unknown*–type fantasies, after the magazine in which most of them appeared. Two of the finest, both originally published in 1941 but still enjoyable today with no sign of dating, are "Shottle Bop" and "Yesterday was Monday". The first deals animatedly with some bizarrely amusing events in a grim old haunted house and ends with the storyteller himself dead and becoming responsible for the haunting, while the second concerns itself with the premise "all the world's a stage" and tells of a man who inadvertently wanders onto the wrong set and finds himself in Tuesday when he should be in Wednesday.

These stories are droll and tongue in cheek, infused with a dry wit, a uniquely enjoyable and observant type of fiction that Sturgeon mastered completely. Other notable tales in this category are "The Ultimate Egoist", where solipsism becomes reality and leads to an unexpected but very appropriate ending, and "Brat", with its memorable changeling.

Sturgeon was one of the most popular of all *Unknown*'s contributors and most of the stories that he wrote for the magazine have been anthologised more than once. As an interesting aside, two Sturgeon tales appeared in *Unknown* under the pseudonyms E Hunter Waldo and E Waldo Hunter; Edward Hunter Waldo was the name he was born with and legally changed on the remarriage of his mother. A reader wrote in praise of one of these stories, commenting on its similarity to Sturgeon's work, to which "Waldo" solemnly replied that it was indeed written "consciously in the style of Sturgeon".

IT WAS A very different Sturgeon who put his name to such stories as "It" and "Bianca's Hands". These are tales of genuine horror, an area which the author visited comparatively rarely but never without chilling effect. "It" is a prime example about the unnatural formation and awakening of a bestial monster and its murderous depredations until it is finally destroyed. This is one of Sturgeon's darkest pieces, with the fruition of the "thing" in the backwoods and the horrific events that follow unnervingly well depicted. The final lines are cheerless and downbeat, entirely fitting to the overall tone of the narrative: "So the Drews had a new barn and fine new livestock and they hired four men. But they didn't have Alton. And they didn't have Kimbo. And Babe screams at night and has grown very thin"

Such bleakness is far more prevalent in the conclusions of these stories than happy endings, which are sparse indeed. Of "It", Sturgeon said: "Possibly it was catharsis – in other words, I was feeling so good that I took what poisons were in me at the moment and got rid of them in one pure plash of putrescence".

That could also be so of "Bianca's Hands", the unpleasant but undeniably powerful story of an ugly, imbecilic girl with beautiful hands and one man's fatal obsession with them. This unsettling story was not to everyone's taste, and Sturgeon later recalled that one editor had said that "he would never buy a story from a man who wrote the likes of 'Bianca's Hands'".

Of his other horror stories, "The Professor's Teddy Bear" is a fine demonstration of how to produce an incisive and memorable narrative within a mere ten pages or so, with an ending that is again unremittingly bleak. "The Music" is also a remarkable piece which in less than 600 words produces an aura of malevolence and irrationality hard to forget, while "The Other Celia" tells of a particularly strange woman and the fatal consequences of the interference of an inquisitive neighbour.

There is no denying the force of these tales. In the shorter form Sturgeon repeatedly managed to instil a wealth of atmosphere and impact, although he also excelled at longer lengths. The novelette "Bright Segment", for instance, is another fine work, not strictly speaking a horror story although very graphic in its descriptive passages. It tells of an ignorant, lonely man who finds a girl – a drug dealer – who is near to death, having been brutally beaten and slashed. He carries her back to his apartment and with the aid of reference books and his medicine cabinet he saves her life and nurses her back to health. It is the one time in his life that he has ever been needed, the one "bright segment" in his dreary existence, and when the girl is well and about to leave, the man realises that he cannot let her go; he attacks her savagely with an iron, and sets about saving her life once again.

This latter story does highlight one of Sturgeon's major attributes, its compassionate treatment of the lonely or abnormal man who has never known kindness or affection and who is forever an outsider. The individual concerned may be repellent but he is not fundamentally evil, with his worse fault an amoral nature, and Sturgeon draws him with a humanity and understanding that alleviate the grosser aspects and gain the reader's sympathetic attention.

THE THIRD MAIN category of Sturgeon's fiction, and the one which tended to dominate his later work, is typified by a combination of both expressive prose and an empathy with the many varieties of human feeling; the characters have depth and there is a passion to the writing that communicates itself to the reader. The best of these stories are effective on a dual level, being strongly plotted and incorporating a strong sense for character and emotion, as in such fine examples as "The Other Man" and "When You Care, When You Love". With "A Saucer of Loneliness", one of the most moving and exhilarating of all Sturgeon's stories, all of the power is in its emotive force and evocative atmosphere, with the plot of secondary importance in what is fundamentally a very simple tale.

Similar in mood is "The Graveyard Reader", a masterful tale exploring the meaning of loss and loneliness. A man is obsessed by his wife's apparent faithlessness and her resultant death, and learns to "read" graves, which tell everything about their occupants in various ways perceptible only to those who know what to look for. He finally finds consolation and inner peace in an unexpected way that is Sturgeon at his understated and gentle best; but the story also emphasises a further aspect of his writing, namely the perceptive observation. As an example, here is an illustration of the difference between "the truth" and "the whole truth":

An old lady who was walking along the street minding her own business, when a young guy came charging along, knocked her down, rolled her in a mud puddle, slapped her head and smeared handfuls of wet mud all over her hair. Now what should you do with a guy like that?

But then you find out that someone had got careless with a drum of gasoline and it ignited and the old lady was splashed with it, and the guy had presence of mind enough to do what he did as fast as he did, and severely burn his hands in the doing of it, then what should you do with him?

Yet everything reported about him is true. The only difference is the amount of truth you tell.

Such thought-provoking viewpoints occur in many of these stories, including "A Way of Thinking", about retribution in the form of reverse Voodoo, a tale in which a man has a way of living his life that involves extreme lateral thinking as compared to the straightforward orthodox approach.

Both "A Way of Thinking" and "The Graveyard Reader" are stories with, not *twists*, but *turns* in the final paragraphs that take the reader unexpectedly; not as unexpectedly as the savage surprises in "Fluffy" or "Scars", but in a way that heightens the effect of what are already fine tales. This knack of taking the reader unawares, but quietly, is also apparent in "Twink", where a telepath is assumed to someone specific and is – but that someone's status comes as a surprising and fascinating plot development.

In "Take Care of Joey", the narrator's search for a genuinely altruistic action is incidental to the main thrust of the narrative but is still cleverly woven into the fabric of the story to provide an excellent final paragraph. There is also an exhilarating ending to "Suicide", where a man finds redemption in struggling against the death that he had so deliberately sought; and in "A Touch of Strange", it is an encounter with a mermaid that leads to a satisfyingly unexpected conclusion.

AS WELL AS his impressive list of short fiction, Sturgeon produced a number of novels, three of which were genuinely exceptional. The first of these was *The Dreaming Jewels*, the story of a young orphan who runs away from his foster-parents and joins a Carnival, eventually discovering the secret of his existence and the power that is inherent in him. The theme is that of paranormal abilities and learning their application. The book is gripping and well paced, developing some intriguing ideas about the nature of "freaks". It also innovatively presents such stock characters as the lecherous and corrupt judge and the madman who wants to destroy the world he hates. Additionally, there is a remarkable seduction scene which ends in a manner that the reader cannot possibly anticipate and which does not remotely resemble anything the judge involved had in mind.

More Than Human is a novel which leaves an indelible impression both descriptively and emotionally. It has an array of characters that appear to be unprepossessing: an idiot, the neglected six-year old daughter of a prostitute, twin four-year old coloured girls with a speech impediment, and a mongoloid baby. But each has a special talent and they "mesh" together to form the beginnings of a gestalt, or group entity, each one having a distinct and essential function within it. Basically, the three part story covers the formation of this entity and its progression to the ultimate form of *Homo gestalt*, the next step up from *Homo sapiens*, but it is in the inner evolution and conflicts of the gestalt that the book's effect lies. There are many memorable sequences in the novel, and Sturgeon explores the depths of feeling in and the experience of his characters to a greater extent than in any of his other fiction.

More Than Human is a stunning work which has of course received an abundance of praise and won the 1953 International Fantasy Award, being rightly regarded as a classic of its kind. It has an originality and impact from its opening sentence – "The idiot lived in a black and gray world, punctuated by the white lightning of hunger and the flickering of fear" – that is sustained through to its moving closing lines, with the attainment of a fundamental morality elevating the gestalt into its final "more than human" phase.

Both this novel and *The Dreaming Jewels* can be described as "science-fantasy", incorporating elements of both science fiction and fantasy, but the later *Some of Your Blood* is a modern vampire tale written as a series of reports, letters and taped interviews. The book tells the story of George Smith, an unrefined and coarse man who has an overwhelming thirst for blood, human or animal. He eventually meets Anna and finds that with her there is a particular way he can satisfy his vampiric lust without the need to kill. Clumsily handled, the theme could easily result in the book falling to the nadir of taste, but it is *not* clumsily handled.

Throughout the whole story, Smith's simple-minded candidness about his life and crimes, and the gradual revelation of the nature of his "periodic aggressive acts" induce more sympathy than revulsion, as he is seen to be the victim of his derangement rather than the callous killer which he may initially appear to be. *Some of Your Blood* is a very good book in which the author pulls no punches, but there is a subtlety in the plot and an intricacy in the relationship between the characters that belies the apparently straightforward story line.

STURGEON WAS A master at tackling subjects that were considered "daring" at the time. He wrote of all kinds of love with an insight and compassion that is sincere without being condescending or glib. There is a particular skill in handling sexual themes in a meaningful way, and he displayed this to perfection in such stories as "The Silken Swift", with its love and its lust and its unicorn, and in "The Wages of Synergy" in which the theme is *liebestod*, or death by orgasm. "If All Men Were Brothers Would You Let One Marry Your Sister?" is an intelligent study of incest; "The World Well Lost" is a sad and double-edged tale of homosexuality; and "Scars", with its misleadingly rough Western dialect, has a real sting in its gently reached tail – impotence this time.

Yet paradoxically the full length novel *Venus Plus X* (1960), which Sturgeon said came about because he "wanted to write a decent book about sex" is unimpressive. About an artificially created unisexual society, the book dwells too long in its "travelogue" stages and seems stylistically flawed in parts. The climax, with its admittedly surprising revelations, is handled well but the novel must be classed as an ambitious failure overall, rather incongruously so in light of its author's preceding and subsequent writing.

A few years after *Venus Plus X* Sturgeon evidently started on the novel *Godbody*, although it was not published until 1986, when it appeared posthumously. Replete with graphic sex scenes and explicit language, it tells of a Christ-like figure who appears in a small American town and changes peoples' lives. It is not amongst the author's best work but it does have its points of interest and is very readable; there are some sharp characterisations and interesting developments, but overall the book tends to be a little too fervently preachy.

The significance of love and the resolution of loneliness did play a large part in Sturgeon's writing, but he covered a lot of other ground as well. Telepathy was one of his favoured themes, as is evidenced by such titles as "Twink", "Nightmare Island" and "Prodigy"; while the sixth sense outlined in "Need" revolves around a man who can mentally feel the needs of other people and seems to exploit them financially, although his true nature and his selflessness do ultimately become apparent. A similar concept of accurate intuition is used in "The Girl Who Knew What They Meant", which has a pragmatic ending far from characteristic of its author, although the sacrifice leading up to that ending is certainly typical.

Ghosts feature in a number of Sturgeon's stories, from the benign and helpful kind in "Cargo" to the malevolent ones of "The Haunt", in which the narrator seems powerless to prevent invisible hands strangling the life from his girlfriend. In "Ghost of a Chance", there is a persistent poltergeist which is ultimately thwarted with shrewd ingenuity, while the problems set by another in "Blabbermouth" are pragmatically solved and turned to financial advantage. There are some unusual hauntings as well: in "Fluke", for instance, it is the victim's continuing effect on others that persists, an effect in no way vengeful but so *beneficial* that it finally drives his killer to his own destruction.

Another theme which received Sturgeon's astute attention was that of revenge. In "Largo", a composer destroys the man he hates and the woman he once loved by means of the murderous ultimate in music; and in "The Bones", someone meets his deserved end in an intriguing way – dying in an accident at which he was not present and which happened a week before. The vengeance meted out in "Take Care of Joey" is just as subtle, with a man forced to spend his life close to the victim of his violence to ensure that no harm comes to him.

Those seeking revenge do not always find it: "The Hag Seleen" fails fatally as the result of the intercession of a little girl whose ingenuous innocence is more than a match for the evil that confronts her; while one of Sturgeon's last stories, "Vengeance Is", is a short piece which forcefully deals with sexual revenge. A placid beginning progresses quickly into a grim narrative of brutal rape with an even grimmer aftermath for all of the parties concerned, roles being disconcertingly reversed.

Syzygy, in the sense of the complementary pairing of opposites, was also a subject that clearly intrigued the author, and there are some exceptional examples of this theme. "It Wasn't Syzygy", "The Perfect Host", and "The Sex Opposite" all stand out (despite the title of the first one!), while the novel *More Than Human* provides an instance of what can only be described as multi-Syzygy.

Sturgeon may have had the time to unfold ideas and characters in novels but as evidenced by the relatively small number of these, he appeared to be more content with shorter fiction. He was certainly very capable in the novel form, to which he was able to resort with facility where necessary, as is demonstrated by the quality of the titles mentioned earlier, but of the longer lengths it was the novelette that evidently attracted him more. Indeed Sturgeon was a writer who was able to put as much into 20,000 words as can be found in three or four times that length by some other authors. His dexterity was such he often did not need anything longer to encompass the whole of the tale he had to tell.

STYLISTICALLY, IT IS difficult to pin Sturgeon down. He ranged with equal facility from the descriptive lyricism of "The Silken Swift" to the breathlessness of "To Here and the Easel", a frenzied tapestry of the mind and of myth becoming reality that suggests an influence on the early works of Roger Zelazny, and *The Dream Master* in particular. Then there is the semi-pidgin English of "The Clinic" compared to the carefully built prose of "Largo", while the smooth flow of "The Graveyard Reader" contrasts with the deliberate disjointedness of *Some of Your Blood*.

Sturgeon rarely repeated himself; the only common factor in his stories was their excellence. It is hard to believe that the man who wrote the witty "Yesterday Was Monday" also penned the grisly "It", the tender "A Saucer of Loneliness", the surreal "To Here and the Easel", and such classic science fiction as "Microcosmic God". The author himself, in his comments to the 1964 collection *Sturgeon in Orbit* said that it is "...the shining machines, the passion, the magic, and the outrageous which have always moved the undersigned and made him write", and these are indeed elements that do feature largely in much of his work. But the real wonder of Sturgeon was the way that whatever its theme or structure, his writing so often transcended its apparent limitations and reached levels of meaning and relevance that other writers rarely approach. In achieving this he consistently maintained a high standard of storytelling that seldom failed to enthral and which had a flair that was inimitably the author's own.

Theodore Sturgeon died in 1985, and in the two decades prior to his death his output had fallen considerably compared with what had been the prolific heyday of the 1940s and 1950s. Even so, that last period of his life saw the publication of such excellent tales as "The Man Who Learned Loving", the award winning "Slow Sculpture", "Occam's Scalpel" and "Case and the Dreamer", stories sustaining a quality that had hardly faltered in a literary career that lasted for more than forty years.

Early on, Sturgeon had attained the status of a master of his craft, having fulfilled all of his considerable potential, but he then proceeded to enhance his reputation with a diversity of skilled fiction. If *More Than Human* perhaps represented the pinnacle of his literary art, his subsequent efforts did not disappoint and many came close to matching the force of that novel. He gave his readers much to remember and to savour, and his contributions to the realm of imaginative fiction will not be forgotten.

SELECTED BIBLIOGRAPHY

"Ether Breather" – 1939

"It" – 1940

"Cargo" – 1940

"The Ultimate Egoist" – 1941

"Shottle Bop" – 1941

"The Haunt" – 1941

"Microcosmic God" – 1941

"Yesterday was Monday" – 1941

"Nightmare Island" – 1941

"Brat" – 1941

"The Hag Seleen" – 1942

"Ghost of a Chance" – 1943

"The Bones" – 1943

"Killdozer" – 1944

"Blabbermouth" – 1947

"Maturity" – 1947

"Fluffy" – 1947

"Bianca's Hands" – 1947

"It Wasn't Syzygy" – 1948

"The Professor's Teddy Bear" – 1948

"The Perfect Host" – 1948

"Fluke" – 1949

"Prodigy" – 1949

"Scars" – 1949

The Dreaming Jewels – 1950

"The Sex Opposite" – 1952

"The Clinic" – 1953

"The Music" – 1953

"A Saucer of Loneliness" – 1953

"A Way of Thinking" – 1953

More Than Human – 1953

"The Silken Swift" – 1953

"The Wages of Synergy" – 1953

"The World Well Lost" – 1953

"Extrapolation" – 1954

"To Here and the Easel" – 1954

"Bright Segment" – 1955

"Twink" – 1955

"The Other Man" – 1956

"The Other Celia" – 1957

"The Graveyard Reader" – 1958

"A Touch of Strange" – 1958

"Need" – 1960

Venus Plus X – 1960

Some of Your Blood – 1961

"When You Care, When You Love" – 1962

"If All Men Were Brothers Would You Let One Marry Your Sister?" – 1967

"The Man Who Learned Loving" – 1969

"Slow Sculpture" – 1970

"The Girl Who Knew What They Meant" – 1970

"Suicide" – 1970

"Occam's Scalpel" – 1971

"Take Care of Joey" – 1971

"Case and the Dreamer" – 1973

"Vengeance Is" – 1980

Godbody – 1986

A FORGOTTEN DISCIPLE
C HALL THOMPSON

HP LOVECRAFT'S CTHULHU Mythos was particularly attractive to those seeking to emulate him, and many authors have contributed to that sub-genre. In the main, they were either friends of Lovecraft, who actively encouraged them, or people who had permission through his publisher Arkham House, in particular from August Derleth. Others produced unauthorised pastiches and consequently met with opposition that led them to change or discontinue their efforts.

One of these was C Hall Thompson, whose first published story seems to have been "The Shanghaied Ruby" in the Winter 1945 issue of *Fight Stories*, and who had also appeared in several Western magazines during 1946. It was when he turned his attention to *Weird Tales*, which published four of his stories between 1946 and 1948, that problems arose. Two of his contributions – "The Spawn of the Green Abyss" and "The Will of Claude Ashur" – were so close to Lovecraft in theme and execution that they prompted August Derleth to take action.

In *The Weird Tales Story* (1977) editor Robert Weinberg says, "Derleth made *Weird Tales* stop from publishing them. Derleth maintained a stranglehold on all Lovecraftian ideas, though it was doubtful that he had any legal right to do so". In his anthology *Tales of the Lovecraft Mythos* (1992), Robert M Price elaborates on this by saying "…the story goes that August Derleth intimidated Thompson into dropping the Lovecraft pastiche hobby, apparently because Thompson was working Derleth's side of the street (and selling a better product)", and ST Joshi in his *Icons of Horror and the*

Supernatural (2007) states that "Derleth was reportedly incensed by the 'outsider' making use of the Mythos, and he demanded that Thompson write no more such stories".

Derleth was very possessive of all things Lovecraftian, and his correspondence on this particular matter shows that he did indeed object to Thompson's fiction. This is detailed in *Arkham's Masters Of Horror* (2000), edited by Peter Ruber, who had access to much of Derleth's correspondence, and confirms that Derleth wrote to Lurton Bassingame, Thompson's literary agent, on 3 May 1947. He maintained that "the use of certain literary properties of the late HP Lovecraft" involved "illegal borrowing" and asked that "all further use of such literary properties in Mr Thompson's stories cease". He went on to say that

...if Mr Thompson would like to use the literary properties of Mr Lovecraft his work ... would have to clear through us first. We feel that Mr Thompson is a competent writer, and his use of the Lovecraft properties is wholly unnecessary to the success of his stories, which seem to us otherwise well-written and plotted.

As for the four stories themselves, they are indeed as Derleth stated, the product of a competent writer and are well-written and plotted. It is only the first two that show a really distinct Lovecraft influence, and these were in fact the only ones that had been published at the time of Derleth's letter to Bassingame. All of Thompson's four published weird stories are of interest and while the first two represent his best work, each is of considerable merit in its own right and not simply because of their status as Lovecraftian curiosities.

The first was "The Spawn of the Green Abyss" which appeared in the November 1946 issue of *Weird Tales*. The novelette relates how a man marries a woman of mysterious lineage only for her to unwillingly revert to type, unable to resist the lure of her alien heritage. The reader is immediately made aware that he is in Lovecraftian territory in the second paragraph of the story, where we find "...there are things beyond the veil of human understanding, strange, antediluvian monstrosities that stalk the shadows, preying on dark, lost minds, waiting at the rim of the Great Abyss to claim their own...".

After ably setting the scene in this way, and making his literary inspiration quite clear, Thompson proceeds to utilise elements from a number of different Lovecraft stories, predominantly those concerned with the Cthulhu Mythos. The theme of the "The Spawn of the Green Abyss", which are a race exiled to the depths of the ocean having been "banished from the earth for its evil practice of black magic", is of course a staple of the Mythos, as is the fact that they are awaiting their chance to return; and the concept of humans interbreeding with them and taking on ichthyoid characteristics is a feature of "The Shadow over Innsmouth".

Then there is the setting of the coastal town of Kalesmouth, isolated and run down, which obviously suggests Innsmouth itself. It is also a town that has its own garrulous old inhabitant in the shape of Solly-Jo, who warns the narrator about Lazarus Heath and Heath House and who thus takes on the Zadok Allen role from "The Shadow over Innsmouth", using much the same sort of localised dialect (and with much the same unconvincing effect!).

A part of the back story tells of how Heath was shipwrecked on an uncharted island which appeared to have risen from the depths of the sea, as in "The Call of Cthulhu". There is also a strong echo of the latter story and the disturbing wrongness of the proportions of R'lyeh in Thompson's description of the undersea world: "A submarine, slime-choked empire of strange geometrical dimensions, a city whose architecture was somehow 'all wrong'". And when Cassandra is talking of her pregnancy, she says "My father was human; I was born in the image of that father. But think of the child I must bear… Suppose … suppose he is born in the image of *his* father", thus reminding us of the final sentence of "The Dunwich Horror". There is also a Great One called Yoth Kala, a name which appears to be an amalgam of Yog Sothoth and Cthulhu.

Despite these many similarities (but not because of them) "The Spawn of the Green Abyss" is actually a rather good story, peopled by sympathetic and rounded characters and using just the right amount of florid prose, which surprisingly never includes the word "eldritch". Thompson treads a fine line between pastiche and parody, but he treads it expertly and never lets the story get out of control. Thus, descriptions such as "the slobbering gelatinous horror that seethed by night from sightless, watery depths to reclaim its own" and "the stench was something from the bottomless watery depths of the sepulchre, a vile effluvium that was somehow the embodiment of every malevolent terror that stalked Heath House" do not seem out of place at all, and add to rather than detract from a narrative which is absorbing and compelling.

The structure of the story is such that the ending is given away almost at once – it starts with the narrator awaiting execution for the murder of his wife – but the journey towards that ending is a rewarding one. From its intriguing opening paragraph to its chilling final lines, a mood of unsettling strangeness is expertly sustained.

Thompson's next story was "The Will of Claude Ashur" (July 1947), and this makes an even closer approach to Lovecraft than "The Spawn of the Green Abyss". Early on there is this description

At a certain point in the road that fingers its way along the lifeless, Atlantic-clawed stretches of the Northern New Jersey coast, the unsuspecting traveller may turn off into a bramble-clotted byway. There is (or was, at one time), a signpost pointing inland that

proclaims: 'INNESWICH – ½ MILE'. Not many take that path today. People who know that part of the country give wide berth to Inneswich and the legends that hang like a slimy caul over the ancient coastal village.

No reader could have missed the tenor of those descriptive passages, even without the place name that plainly combines two of Lovecraft's famous creations, Innsmouth and Dunwich.

The premise of the novelette is very similar to "The Thing on the Doorstep", with Claude Ashur seeking to prolong his existence by sorcerously exchanging his consciousness with another person, switching from his own diseased body into a healthy one. Arkham is mentioned, and Ashur attends the Miskatonic University, where he has access to the *Unaussprechlichen Kulten*, the *Book of Eibon* and of course the *Necronomicon*. The prose is rather more restrained than that of "The Spawn of the Green Abyss", although there is still room for such phrases as "A stench of immeasurable age swirled upward to me as I bent to decipher the ancient hieroglyphics that crawled like obscene insects across the paper", and "Even as I watched, strangled with loathing, those corrupt lips curled slowly in a malevolent grin".

If its basic plot elements derive from "The Thing on the Doorstep", and its writing style again owes a clear debt to Lovecraft, "The Will of Claude Ashur" is nevertheless another well-written story, atmospheric and gripping, with nicely shaped characterisations. It ends on a similar note to "The Spawn of the Green Abyss", highlighting the fact that while this particular tale may be over, its root remains and is more than capable of resurgence. This was of course a literary device that Lovecraft had used in such titles as "The Call of Cthulhu" and "At the Mountains of Madness", and it is not therefore surprising to find it here.

But with his first two efforts Thompson had accomplished what few writers, before or since, have fully achieved: writing under a palpable Lovecraftian influence but producing fiction of high quality and which remains eminently readable today. If the stories were deficient in originality in perhaps too many respects, they were stylishly written and infused with atmosphere and colour.

Thompson's subsequent tales did see his horizons widen, but he did not quite recapture the lingering aura of foreboding that he had managed to instil into "The Spawn of the Green Abyss" and "The Will of Claude Ashur", both of which were significantly longer than his succeeding efforts. "The Pale Criminal" appeared in November 1947, and is a quite different type of story to its predecessors, taking place in the Black Forest, in Castle von Zengerstein. This setting seems to emphasise that Thompson apparently had difficulty with coining original names – one immediately thinks of the story "Metzengerstein" by Edgar Allan Poe.

The tale itself is forceful and interesting, of a brilliant surgeon who is blinded in an accident and who is desperate to recover his sight by any means, including murder. His ultimate fate is the result of guilt manifesting itself as an imagined horror, which probably irrelevantly was also the case in Poe's "The Tell-Tale Heart".

The plot may owe nothing to Lovecraft but the start of the "Markheim Manuscript", which constitutes the bulk of the narrative, reads:

...I should feel safe. I should know that there can be no truth in the

unholy phantasms that have come to haunt my every waking moment. The doors are locked. Nothing could penetrate those ponderous panels. Nothing human. Yet, at every whimper of the wind in the grate, I start; the howling of the wolf-hounds gnaws at my nerves...

and later in the same paragraph:

...There is no escape. Soon, the time will have run out. And then, the slash of the scalpel, the pale face pressed close to mine – and death. The same death that monster brought to Simon Conrad short weeks ago.

This is of course reminiscent of the start of Lovecraft's "The Hound", and indicative of the continuing Lovecraftian effect on the writing.

"Clay" was Thompson's final contribution to *Weird Tales*, appearing in May 1948. It again uses a curiously unimaginative name for the location of the action, "Dunnesmouth", although beyond that there is only the prose to suggest any Lovecraftian inspiration. The opening scene, set in Wickford House Asylum, ably establishes the tone:

These men stood in the soundless chapel, and remembered mouldering death discovered in its dim alcoves; they passed the room once occupied by Jeremy Bone, and saw again the foul liquescent thing that rose from lost hells to defy the reasoning of normal minds.

The story tells of the curse of the Mark of Clay: when twins are born to the Bone family, one murders the other prenatally and is then haunted by his victim's presence and forced by it to kill, while bearing the marks of graveyard clay on his hands. The idea is intriguing and the plot compelling, and the air of irrational horror is sustained well, with an ending that is in keeping with the author's three previous tales, entirely satisfactory but at the same time having little cheer.

The four stories mentioned above represent the whole of Thompson's known weird fiction. Each of them has its own considerable strengths and while some of the writing and ideas may be lacking in creativity, the tales are all memorable and leave a lasting impression; it is a pity that there are not more of them. Ironically, in *Arkham's Masters of Horror,* Ruber indicates that "Derleth said he would have given Thompson permission to write the pastiches had he simply asked" – this information deriving from a letter from Derleth to Ramsey Campbell "early in their correspondence".

Campbell had of course contacted Derleth before trying to market his Mythos stories and had received much help, culminating in Arkham House publishing his first collection, *The Inhabitant of the Lake and Less Welcome Tenants* in 1964. That initial correspondence with Campbell was admittedly some fifteen years after "The Spawn of the Green Abyss" first appeared in *Weird Tales,* but it does not seem unlikely that had Thompson sought Derleth's approval he would have obtained it in much the same way that Campbell did. Derleth probably had no valid legal right to demand that the stories stop, and interestingly he had been involved in the same sort of thing himself by pastiching Sherlock Holmes with his character Solar Pons. That had resulted in him receiving correspondence and threats from the legal representatives of Arthur Conan Doyle's Estate in September 1946, but Derleth maintained that they had no case in law and continued to unabashedly write his pastiches.

Thompson certainly seemed to be a good enough writer to have produced fiction that was not derivative, and in his last two pieces he had been moving away from the Lovecraft influence that had so marked his initial tales. As it was, he evidently chose to abandon the field altogether. The following year, 1949, saw him appearing in such periodicals as *The Saturday Evening Post, Argosy* and *Esquire* with Western short stories and novelettes. He subsequently had four Western novels published – *A Gun for Billy Reo* (1955), *Montana* (1959), *Under the Badge* (1966) and *The Killing of Hallie James* (1969) – as well as some thirty short stories in various magazines. It appears likely that Thompson was a part-time writer; there is no trace of anything else published under his name, although he may of course have written pseudonymously.

It could well be that after his initial enthusiasm for HP Lovecraft and weird fiction had waned, he decided that higher profile markets such as *Argosy* and *Esquire* were more to his liking. They would almost certainly have been more profitable, although if he *was* a part-time writer, that would have been an aspect that was presumably of secondary importance. That he wrote Westerns for over twenty years does suggest that he must have had an affinity with that type of fiction, and perhaps that was where his real affection lay.

C Hall Thompson himself is something of a mystery man; little is known of him, although various sources list him as having lived between 1923 and 1991. He would therefore have been in his early twenties when he wrote his Lovecraft pastiches, perhaps captivated by the imaginative power of the writing in the same way as many another young author.

He may have grown out of his fondness for the weird tale, or he may have left the field disgruntled at Derleth's reaction to his stories. But if he had simply followed up on the suggestion that was made – "If Mr Thompson would like to use the literary properties of Mr Lovecraft his work … would have to clear through us first" – and if permission had been forthcoming, as Derleth later indicated it would have been, then the weird fiction genre could just perhaps be the richer as a result.

SELECTED BIBLIOGRAPHY

Appearances in *Weird Tales*

"Spawn of the Green Abyss" – November 1946

"The Will of Claude Ashur" – July 1947

"The Pale Criminal" – November 1947

"Clay" – May 1948

ANOTHER FORGOTTEN DISCIPLE CLIFFORD BALL

THE PAGES OF *Weird Tales* in the 1920s and 1930s saw the emergence of several writers who were to become key figures in the formation of modern-day imaginative literature, and whose importance cannot be overestimated. One in particular was Robert E Howard, whose work not only displayed a thematic originality that was to have a far-reaching influence on fantasy as a whole, but which was also to inspire a host of later writers.

One of the earliest of these was Clifford Ball, whose work began to appear in 1937 but which attracted little attention. His career as a genre author was short-lived, but his stories were enjoyable, and while they admittedly do not rank amongst the higher echelons of the field, they are certainly worthwhile.

Ball's inspiration was the Conan series, and as the very first writer to pastiche Conan he became the unsuspecting forerunner of what was to become a veritable deluge in later years. Robert E Howard, with his creation of Conan of Cimmeria and the "Hyborian Age", fashioned something genuinely innovative in the fantasy domain, something which was to have a major and enduring effect, and which eventually came to be called "sword & sorcery". The latter term was coined by Fritz Leiber in 1961, and it represents tales that are primarily action-oriented and which generally feature a powerful barbarian warrior as the main hero; they also incorporate distinctively dark supernatural elements and are usually set in a wholly invented land.

The first of Robert E Howard's Conan stories was "The Phoenix on the Sword" which appeared in the December 1932 issue of *Weird*

Tales, and it was quickly followed by more. Howard was adept at both historical fiction and weird fiction, but generally utilised a familiar background. His tales of series characters such as Francis Xavier Gordon were action-packed but lacking any sorcerous ingredients, while those of Solomon Kane and Bran Mak Morn did have some such elements but kept to accepted historical settings. Howard had come close to producing an amalgam several years earlier in 1929 with "The Shadow Kingdom", featuring King Kull and set in the legendary realm of Atlantis, but the fantasy trappings – the shape-changing abilities of an ancient race of Serpent Men – harkened back to the "lost race" type of fiction, notwithstanding the garnish of magic he introduced.

Having failed to sell another 1929 story featuring Kull, "By This Axe I Rule", Howard rewrote it with a potent supernatural sub-plot, changed the setting to the invented Hyborian Age and the hero to Conan of Cimmeria, and thus produced "The Phoenix on the Sword". This caught readers' attention in a way that "The Shadow Kingdom" had failed to do, perhaps because Conan was such a dominant character and perhaps because the more prominent weird element was not subsidiary to the narrative but represented its driving force. The immediate success of "The Phoenix on the Sword" prompted Howard to produce many more such tales and was in effect the creation of the sword & sorcery genre, although its creator would have little realised what he was setting in motion and what a lasting contribution his writing was to make.

Inevitably there were other writers who were attracted to this ground-breaking area of fantasy fiction, but surprisingly it took several years for the first Conan pastiche to appear. Other authors had made use of the basic premise, the first being Nictzin Dyalhis with his story "The Sapphire Goddess", which appeared in the February 1934 issue of *Weird Tales*. This included much swordplay and some sorcery but bears little resemblance to Howardian writing, owing more to the basic traditions of interplanetary pulp fiction. Dyalhis had simply written a straightforward adventure story of that type with swords replacing ray-guns and magic replacing science.

The next author to publish a sword & sorcery story was CL Moore, whose "Black God's Kiss" appeared in *Weird Tales* in October 1934. This introduced the character Jirel of Joiry, who was to be the heroine of several subsequent tales, a barbarian swordswoman battling magic in a medieval fantasy world. Moore made use of the sword & sorcery scenario to produce fiction that was uniquely her own, establishing a niche that is still warmly and justifiably remembered today. She had already skirted the field with her earlier Northwest Smith tales, starting with the impressive "Shambleau" in the November 1933 issue.

But the first story that specifically simulated Conan and his environment was "Duar the Accursed" by Clifford Ball, which appeared in the May 1937 issue of *Weird Tales*. The plot is certainly derivative, its basic premise taken from the Conan story "The Tower of the Elephant", and its protagonist is very similar to Howard's hero. Duar is a tall and muscular blue-eyed barbarian, once a slave, once a mercenary, once a pirate, and more recently a king, and is brought in chains before the beautiful Queen Nione before being imprisoned in the Pits of Ygoth. After making his escape he enters the Black Tower, which is rumoured to hold a magnificent jewel called the Rose of Gaon guarded by a demon. Duar triumphs and wins the love of Nione – "What more could a barbarian wish than a powerful kingdom and a beautiful Queen?"

Although showing little originality, the story is readable enough even if Ball does fail to wholly capture the forceful narrative flow that was so symptomatic of Howard's prose. Duar also seems to lack the pre-eminence of Conan, being helped both in his escape from the Pits and in his battle with the demon by a magical being called Shar, one of the Elder Race. The reason for this is that Duar has the blood of the

Elder Race in his veins and has lived multiple lives, with Shar now striving to draw him back to his birthright and guide him to ruling the whole world rather than just one relatively small part of it. This idea of past lives had itself been used by Howard in such earlier titles as "The Valley of the Worm" and "The Garden of Fear".

"Duar the Accursed" did not seem to make much of an impression. Such a close approach to the storytelling style of the Conan series and the use of such a similar character in a familiar plot was unlikely to produce a long-lived career in *Weird Tales*, and Ball seemed to realise this. He may in fact have simply been feeling his way with this first piece, with no intention of making Duar an ongoing character, because his next contribution to the magazine, a mere two months later, featured a different hero, this one called Rald.

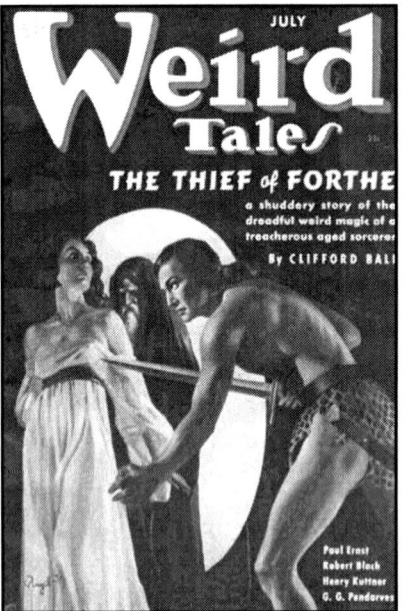

The story in question was "The Thief of Forthe", which appeared in the July 1937 issue. The style of writing still owed much to Howard, and the atmospheric opening paragraph is very reminiscent of the beginning of Howard's *The Hour of the Dragon* (1935/36), starting, "The crude stone chamber was lighted only by the flickering flame of a single torch thrust into a crevice in the wall". Rald is a barbarian thief (another of Conan's early occupations) rather than a barbarian warrior, although there is little subtlety in the way that he goes about his work, and even when relaxed he "still gave the impression of a creature ready to spring into snarling, ferocious battle".

Persuaded by the mysterious wizard Karlk to steal the Necklace of the Ebon Dynasty and thus dethrone the reigning King of Forthe, Rald succeeds in the theft with what must be said is surprising ease, but belatedly discovers where his true loyalties lie and realises that the cost of taking the throne is too high. There are some pleasing and unforeseen twists in the plot, and while Rald is not quite the Conan clone of Ball's first piece he still comes very close both descriptively and in his actions.

Next was "The Goddess Awakes" (February 1938) in which Rald has forsaken thievery and become a mercenary, choosing the wrong side in a war and fleeing from the conquering army in the company of his boon companion, Thwaine. They find themselves in a hidden land peopled by female warriors and enslaved men, and ruled by a priest whose "daughter" is an incarnation of a cat-goddess who takes the form of a monstrous black panther, a statue by day but coming to ravening life by moonlight. In what is perhaps the best of Ball's three sword and sorcery stories Rald and Thwaine do of course ultimately triumph, although their victory is again perhaps a little too easily accomplished.

The pair, who "were a dangerous combination and held reputations of note in many widely scattered countries", with Rald "huge" and Thwaine of "small stature", interestingly foreshadow Fritz Leiber's characters Fafhrd and the Gray Mouser. There is not, however, any question of Leiber having been influenced by Ball's tale, for although the first in the Nehwon series did not appear until the following year ("Two Sought Adventure", which was published in *Unknown*, August 1939), Leiber had been working on the idea in collaboration with Harry Fischer for several years prior to that, possibly as early as 1934.

"The Thief of Forthe" and "The Goddess Awakes" were solidly situated in the same Hyborian Age-type of world as "Duar the Accursed", where there are warring kingdoms, dark magics, beautiful women and outlandish creatures. In "The Goddess Awakes" Ball curiously refers to the River Nile (in a "far off land") and to Egyptian mythology, and there is also a passing reference to Buddha, allusions that seemingly represent an attempt to establish the setting as being in the "real" world. This is rather counter-productive, jarring the illusion of a created fantasy milieu and making the reader wonder exactly *where* the numerous independent kingdoms such as Forthe, Livia, Fuvia and Sorjoon are supposed to be if they are purportedly historical.

Be that as it may, having begun to establish something that could have held interesting possibilities for the future, Ball discarded sword & sorcery fiction altogether (although the mantle was taken over by Henry Kuttner, whose Elak of Atlantis stories began to appear in 1938). He may have decided that the format was too restrictive and that he would be unable to widen its scope to any extent, or he may simply have preferred to move into other areas; in any event his remaining three contributions to *Weird Tales* were all quite different to what had gone before.

The first was "The Swine of Aeaea" (March 1939), an atmospheric tale of a tramp-steamer coming across an uncharted island and discovering it to be the legendary abode of Circe, the enchantress who turns men into pigs. This well-written and satisfying story is certainly the most accomplished of all of the writer's offerings and again introduces a character who could have featured in further tales but who was never used again. Next came "The Little Man" (August 1939), which is a fairly commonplace account of post-mortem revenge told in a standard hard-boiled pulp detective style, and which works quite well.

Ball's *Weird Tales* swansong was "The Werewolf Howls" in the November 1941 issue, a short and competent piece, but it suffers from what is intended to be a surprise ending that comes as no surprise at all. In fact, all of these last three tales have a final paragraph revelation that fails to have the impact that it should, not simply due to it being telegraphed long before, but also – particularly in the cases of "The Swine of Aeaea" and "The Little Man" – because it is unnecessary in properly concluding the narrative, which has already capably achieved its intended effect without the need for any additional emphasis.

After his tenure of a little more than four years as a *Weird Tales* contributor, Clifford Ball appears to have had nothing further published anywhere else. Although he is thought to have lived between 1896 and 1947, even that sparse information does not seem capable of confirmation. If the dates are correct, then Ball was not a young writer beginning to make his way when "Duar the Accursed" was published, and he could of course have written under different names in different fields of fiction. He may have seen the Conan character and his colourful setting as an opportunity to break into *Weird Tales*, and then decided to move on to other areas, though it would appear that he only lived a further six years after the publication of "The Werewolf Howls", dying at a relatively young age.

At this late date, we are probably unlikely to ever learn Ball's full story. What we do know is that he was an author who was significantly influenced by his renowned predecessor and initially made no attempt to do anything other than follow faithfully in footsteps that had already left a considerable imprint. However, what little originality there may have been in his fiction was at least partially outweighed by the fact that he did produce stories that are readable and entertaining, even these many decades later, and ultimately that is a literary epitaph that should satisfy any writer.

SELECTED BIBLIOGRAPHY

Appearances in *Weird Tales*

"Duar the Accursed" – May 1937

"The Thief of Forthe" – July 1937

"The Goddess Awakes" – February 1938

"The Swine of Aeaea" – March 1939

"The Little Man" – August 1939

"The Werewolf Howls" – November 1941

TALES IN A MAJOR KEY
C L MOORE

CATHERINE LUCILLE MOORE was born in 1911 and became fascinated with imaginative fiction during prolonged periods of childhood illness, when she turned to the escapist literature of the day to pass the time. After being forced to leave university for financial reasons she began to write fiction, and submitted the story "Shambleau" to *Weird Tales*, where it appeared in the November 1933 issue as by CL Moore. Such masking of gender by an author was not uncommon, with fantasy fiction being very much a male domain – up to that time, less than ten percent of the stories published in *Weird Tales* were by female authors, although that minority produced many outstanding contributions.

CL Moore's "Shambleau" made an immediate impression on readers, representing a remarkable beginning to the author's literary career. It was the first of many of her works that were to appear in the pages of *Weird Tales* before the end of the decade, and was an outstanding debut, distinguishing itself not just by virtue of its imaginative premise but also by the sophistication of its writing. At a time when there was a plethora of garishly written melodramatic tales appearing in the pages of pulp periodicals, Moore's initial work was especially notable for its subtlety and atmosphere as well as for its originality and understated element of sensuality. These were all features that were to become hallmarks of Moore's subsequent weird fiction, which was consistently enjoyable and far from mundane.

The *Weird Tales* stories were all parts of two separate series which featured the charismatic characters of Northwest Smith and Jirel of

Joiry, the former in science fiction tales of the future and the latter in fantasy set in the past. The lines between the two genres did tend to be blurred as far as Moore was concerned, with Smith and Jirel actually meeting up in one of the later stories.

The Northwest Smith tales owed little to contemporary interplanetary fiction apart from such standard and accepted locales as the rust-red dry-lands of Mars and the swampy, humid forests of Venus. These worlds held little glamour in Moore's fiction – they were hard and harsh, with no place for the weak, where only the strongest thrived, and where illicit trade represented a significant part of the economy. Although Smith involved himself in various illegal activities, including gun-running and smuggling, these aspects of his life were not the ones that Moore was interested in relating. Dark gods and ancient alien beings were the powerful and mystical creatures that Smith had to contend with. His adventures were always exciting and death-defying, but never commonplace.

Smith himself is an Earthman exiled from his home planet, someone who lives his life outside the law; he is a man with a reputation, sought by the authorities, an outlaw hunted by the Patrol. Tall and leather-brown, the colourless eyes in his scarred face have seen many strange things in untoward places, and his experiences have hardened him although he still has wistful thoughts of Earth in unguarded moments. He can be a cold-blooded killer, but is also a man who will protect the weak and defenceless without too much thought if he comes across a situation in which they are threatened. And if the "weak and defenceless" is in the form of a beautiful woman, then he will leap to her defence with absolutely no thought at all...

He has acquaintances but his only real friend is the Venusian Yarol, a character who appears in several of the stories including the very first one, "Shambleau". This is set on Mars in the bleakly unfriendly town of Lakkdarol, and tells of how Smith rescues an exotically attractive woman from a mob seeking to kill her. What he does not realise is that she is actually a Medusa-like creature who lures the unwary into her clutches and feeds on their life-force with the red worm-like appendages that emerge from her head. Her feeding is symbiotic in that it gives the victim intense and addictive pleasure, and soon Smith is totally enmeshed and dying slowly.

"Shambleau" is an adroit and seamless fusion of science fiction, fantasy and horror, incorporating a subtle sensual aspect throughout its narrative. It is unusual in that the hero has to be rescued from the Shambleau's clutches by Yarol, and is clearly reluctant to be released, demonstrating a fallibility that was to recur in later tales. The story is not flawless, with the ending a little drawn out, and some of the writing overwrought; for instance, there are seven separate uses of the words "obscene" and "obscenity" in describing the creature within just a few pages. But overall it was a very impressive debut, and readers may have doubted the author's ability to follow such an exceptional story without a sense of anticlimax.

However, "Black Thirst", which followed a few months later, was another fine tale which lingered in the memory. In the second story, this time set on Venus, Moore does a good job of creating a claustrophobic and haunting atmosphere in the stronghold of the Minga, with its maze of passageways and strange denizens. Smith finds himself within the Palace after agreeing to help one of the maids of Minga, and eventually confronts the dread Alendar, a millennia-old vampire-like being who feeds on the essence of beauty.

In "Scarlet Dream", which appeared a year later in May 1934, Smith is again on Mars. He is drawn into a dream-land by means of the hypnotic allure of a red scarf, before discovering that he is unable to leave. There is horror beneath the veneer of the languid and luxuriant world that he finds himself in, with a bitter price to be paid for the ease with which the inhabitants live. He only escapes through the self-sacrifice of his lover in what is again a very effective tale demonstrating Moore's undeniable power in generating a distinct aura of strangeness in her compelling and a well-written stories.

There was a discernable pattern in the Smith series even at this relatively early stage – a restrained sensual subtext was evident, where all of the stories featured a beautiful woman to whom Smith was attracted, and as a result found himself in harm's way. This was not a flaw in the stories, but rather the highlighting of a fundamental weak spot in Smith's character; nor was the repetition tiresome, for it was always framed in narratives that were consistently gripping and imaginative.

"Dust of the Gods", from later in 1934, was the exception in that there were no female characters. Smith and Yarol are hired to retrieve the millennia-old dust that is all that is left of the corporeal form of the all-but-forgotten Pharol, one of the three archetypal gods of which all other gods known to Man are echoes. The dust is reputed to be found amidst the buried ruins of an isolated Martian city so old that its very name has been totally forgotten, dating from a time when the planet was green and verdant. But although it is no longer even a memory, the city still has its guardians…

Moore impressively and convincingly evokes a feeling of the almost inconceivable antiquity that pervades the ruins, and Smith and Yarol's underground journey to the throne room is well paced and tense, with some finely wrought confrontations and a gripping climax. She also uses the sense of smell to emphasise descriptive aspects of her story: "…that nameless dry salt smell of eon-dead seas", "An odour of unnameable things very faintly spread upon the air – the smoke of dead gods". Such allusions draw understated attention to the alien setting in both physical and cerebral terms and skilfully highlight its outré nature.

AFTER THESE FOUR outstanding tales of Northwest Smith, Moore then turned her attention to a new character, that of the swordswoman Jirel of Joiry, who first appeared in "Black God's Kiss" in the October 1934 issue of *Weird Tales*. This was something that was genuinely ground-breaking in that it was the first bona-fide sword & sorcery tale to be published by an author other than Robert E Howard, who had introduced the sub-genre in the December 1932 issue of the magazine with "The Phoenix on the Sword", the first of many stories featuring Conan of Cimmeria.

Moore had already approached the theme with the Northwest Smith tales, but in these she was combining science fiction and fantasy, while "Black God's Kiss" and the subsequent Jirel titles were completely true to the central Howardian sword & sorcery premise in that they featured a powerful warrior as the main character, incorporated characteristically dark otherworldly elements, and were set in a land which had only a passing acquaintanceship with past history, a land in which magic was most definitely *real*. Moore's writing was nothing like that of the Conan author and bore more resemblance to Clark Ashton Smith in its atmospheric power, but if it lacked the dynamic cadences of Howard's prose, it had a compelling and haunting appeal that established a lasting niche in the field.

As well as being the very first female sword & sorcery heroine, Jirel's involvement with the supernatural is far more direct than Conan's, and she confronts Evil in a variety of guises. She obviously lacks the physical abilities of a male barbarian hero, although her skill with weapons and her leadership qualities are unquestioned; tall and slim, with red hair and yellow eyes, she is not a stunning beauty but can rely on her wits and mental toughness to weather most storms, although sometimes her emotions can overcome her, as is demonstrated in the very first of the tales in the saga.

"Black God's Kiss" is primarily an action-oriented narrative which begins with Jirel captured after the usurper Guillaume has won the battle for Joiry. Jirel is so consumed with hatred that when she escapes she travels to the dark realms in search of a weapon to use against the despised Guillaume. She returns with the Black God's Kiss which she then bestows on Guillaume in a scene of tense foreboding, and watches him die horrifically; however, her triumph proves to be dismayingly hollow as she discovers too late her real feelings in what is a notably downbeat ending. Jirel's journey to the black temple is descriptively quite excellent, capturing the bleak ambience of the dread land particularly well and instilling an impression of menacing danger and forces beyond human experience. Moore's depiction of the unknown consistently displayed this latter facet, her prose conveying unfathomable mystery in a convincing and telling manner.

"Black God's Shadow", the sequel to "Black God's Kiss", appeared in December 1934. Haunted by the anguished ghost of Guillaume, Jirel sets out to rescue him from the doom into which she cast him, and consequently returns to the dark realms. The land is different on this journey, and so the reader is not simply presented with a reworking of the first story – if anything this tale displays even more imaginative force. There are shadows cast that do not resemble their owners, rivers and streams that murmur words that are on the very edge of an unsettling comprehension, and completely inhuman inhabitants that act and react in dangerously impenetrable ways. The tale ends completely satisfactorily and was a splendid follow-up to its predecessor. It was Moore's sixth published story in little more than a year, and all six of them had been excellent, confirming the author's mastery of the weird tale at the age of only twenty-three.

Another Northwest Smith story – "Julhi", again set on Venus – followed within a few months, good enough that it did not suffer by comparison to the two outstanding Jirel stories that had preceded it. Julhi is perhaps the most alien of all the creatures that Northwest Smith confronts, and it is to Moore's credit that she conveys this alienness very convincingly – alluring and beautiful, the eponymous creature uses a psychic girl as a conduit to travel from her own alternate dimension and enter Smith's world, where she feeds on sensations that she draws from her victims.

Smith reappeared in "Nymph of Darkness" in 1935, a story written in collaboration with Forrest J Ackerman. In the dark and forbidding Venusian streets of Ednes, also the location of the earlier "Black Thirst", Smith rescues an invisible girl from her pursuers, the dour Nov, dwellers beneath the city and worshippers of the god known as the Darkness. The girl, Nyusa, is the half-human daughter of that god, and is used by the Nov in their rituals. Captured by them and facing death, Smith is saved by the vengeful actions of the Darkness as its daughter finally attains her powers and returns to her father.

MOORE NOW BEGAN to alternate stories featuring her two charismatic characters. "Jirel Meets Magic" appeared later in 1935, with the swordswoman pursuing a mage whom she has sworn to destroy, and finding herself in the realm of Jarisme the Sorceress. Jirel proves to be an instrument of fate, fulfilling a prediction that someone will defy the Sorceress three times and cause her death; but Jarisme is not prepared to surrender her life so easily and attempts to change destiny. But Fate is inexorable, although Jirel's survival is actually due to something that Jarisme seeks to use as a weapon of exquisite torture against her – the memory of the death of Guillaume. But this is something that has such emotional strength that it unfetters Jirel's mental shackles and enables her to focus the whole of her being on escaping from the psychic grip that is holding her.

In "The Cold Gray God", also from 1935, the setting is the pole city of Righa on Mars, with Smith hired by a beautiful Venusian woman to steal a primeval artefact. He is double-crossed and has his body taken over by an acolyte of an ancient and evil nameless god who is seeking to open a gateway to allow it access to the living world, where it will then exact a murderous toll. With his consciousness still functioning separately, outside his body, Smith engages in a grim battle to regain control as the essence of the Unnameable God begins to seep through the gateway…

"The Dark Land" (1936) begins with Jirel near death after a battle. Her journeys in forbidden realms have come to the attention of the dark beings that inhabit those places, and one of them – Pav – wants her as his bride. He restores her failing life-force and transports her to his own sombre dominion of Romne, where all is not as it seems and where "space and matter are subordinated to the power of the mind".

Jirel is tricked by a witch into making Romne – and Pav, the two being one – revert to the Darkness which they actually are, but her rescue from oblivion comes via an unexpected source. There is impressively vivid imagery in this well-told tale, with the initial representation of Pav as a huge black statue with a crown of lambent flame particularly memorable.

Moore then seemed to abandon Jirel, and she was not to reappear until the following year, with only two more stories to come. However, Smith was back in "Yvala" the month after "The Dark Land"; this is set on Mars initially and then on a Jovian moon where Smith and Yarol – hired by slavers to investigate the rumours of a new source of women – are confronted by what appears to be Beauty Incarnate and are totally entranced. The creature is an ageless alien entity that vampirically feeds on the devotion of its victims, and as in "The Cold Gray God" Smith battles to regain his body and escape from the clutches of evil. This story emphasises Smith's ambiguous morality and his pragmatic approach – while accepting that slaving is disagreeable he is still prepared to get involved in it on the basis that if he doesn't, someone else will.

"Lost Paradise" is the first story set on Earth – in New York – with Smith psychically transported back many hundreds of millennia to when the Moon was a beautiful and fertile world, protected by the Three in One – three dread gods who cast but one ravening shadow. The price for their protection is high, with them taking free rein to prey ruthlessly on the inhabitants. The cleverly-shaped tale demonstrates the inflexibility of fate, as the long ago destruction of the Moon's forgotten civilisation is seen to have its roots firmly and unalterably in the present.

Moore's last 1936 appearance was with "The Tree of Life", which finds Smith on Mars, in the ruined city of Illar. He is lured into another dimension by a beautiful priestess, and is trapped in the realm of the dread Thag, which feeds on its denizens. As in "The Cold Gray God" and "Yvala", it is Smith's inner strength and his aggressive core that see him survive and best his opponent. Again there is an expert depiction of a creature that is totally alien, and while the reader is well aware that the hero is going to ultimately triumph this does not detract from the tense narrative.

As Moore was becoming a successful writer, in 1936 she met Henry Kuttner, whom she was to marry in 1940. Kuttner had been unaware of her gender when he wrote to her expressing his admiration of her fiction, and their relationship blossomed not only personally but professionally as well. The first of many collaborations was "Quest of the Starstone" in 1937, which had the intriguing premise of Northwest Smith meeting Jirel of Joiry, with the many centuries that lay between them resolved by the expedient of time travel.

The warlock Franga recruits Smith and Yarol to go back in time to the year 1500 and retrieve the Starstone that Jirel had taken from him. Sensing betrayal and drawn to Jirel, Smith reneges on the agreement, but then all three humans are cast adrift in a strange timeless world until Smith saves the day. There is certainly an attraction between Jirel and Smith and at the very end she seems to be trying to make her feelings known, but the two are then inextricably pulled apart as they return to their respective worlds. Despite the attentions of a pair of very good writers, the story disappoints – it is too short to fully explore what should have been a more fascinating interaction between the two characters, and its conclusion leaves the reader somewhat dissatisfied.

"Werewoman" from 1938 is a Smith tale that appears to be set on Earth. In the aftermath of a losing battle, he wanders through barren wastelands in an area where a great city once stood but whose enemies brought it down and sowed the land with salt, as well as laying a dire spell on it. Smith is ensnared within the spell and loses his human consciousness, joining and running with a pack of werewomen stalking a desolate and haunted landscape. He eventually regains his rational mind and breaks the curse by destroying the sorcerous symbol that sustains it, and consequently recovers his humanity. It is an interesting but incongruous Smith tale, one that reads much more like Jirel and which would have slotted far more comfortably into that other series.

The last Jirel story, and one of the very best, was 1939's "Hellsgarde". To save the lives of twenty of her men held captive by Guy of Garlot, Jirel agrees to enter the shunned and ghostly castle of Hellsgarde, which only appears at sunset. She has to recover the treasure that its vindictive lord Andred died to protect. She meets a remarkable group of people within the castle, seekers of the undead and surely the strangest assembly of ghost-hunters ever seen. Their intent is not what it at first seems, and Jirel is unwillingly used as bait to ensnare the long-dead lord. The powerful tale ends with the swordswoman anticipating her forthcoming revenge on Guy, and knowing that this time there will be no regrets.

"Hellsgarde" was followed by just one more fantasy, with Northwest Smith's weakness for beautiful women the subject of the short "Song in a Minor Key" (1940). This vignette is set on Earth with Smith remembering the violence and destruction of twenty years before, events that drove him into his lawless life. There had been a sole fleeting reference to these incidents in "Julhi", when the "deep-buried memory had burnt like a heat-ray". Inevitably there was a woman involved, but Smith reflects that if things had not happened as they did then they would still have happened at some other point in time – it was his fate and it was unavoidable. The tale is an interesting coda to the Smith series and does indirectly signal that there are to be no more of his adventures, which was of course true.

All of the Smith and Jirel stories were first published between 1933 and 1940, and Moore never returned to their fascinating worlds again. She went on to produce some fine science fiction both in her own name and primarily in collaboration with Henry Kuttner under various pseudonyms. After Kuttner's death in 1958 she concentrated on television scripts for several years before retiring from writing on remarrying in 1963. She died in 1987 and her legacy was impressive. As well as providing much entertainment for readers of the 1930's pulp magazines, her creative settings and intriguing characters influenced many later writers, who in turn were to become masters of the field. The realm of imaginative fiction really would have been the poorer had CL Moore never decided to contribute to it, and her standing in the genre is such that her tales of Smith and Jirel will long be read and long savoured.

SELECTED BIBLIOGRAPHY

The Northwest Smith stories

"Shambleau" – *Weird Tales*, November 1933

"Black Thirst" – *Weird Tales*, April 1934

"Scarlet Dream" – *Weird Tales*, May 1934

"Dust of the Gods" – *Weird Tales*, August 1934

"Julhi" – *Weird Tales*, March 1935

"Nymph of Darkness" (with Forrest J Ackerman) – *Fantasy Magazine*, April 1935

"The Cold Gray God" – *Weird Tales*, October 1935

"The Tree of Life" – *Weird Tales*, October 1936

"Lost Paradise" – *Weird Tales*, July 1936

"Yvala" – *Weird Tales*, February 1936

"Quest of the Starstone" (with Henry Kuttner) – *Weird Tales*, November 1937

"Werewoman" – *Leaves*, 1938

"Song in a Minor Key" – *Scienti-Snaps*, February 1940

The Jirel stories

"Black God's Kiss" – *Weird Tales*, October 1934

"Black God's Shadow" – *Weird Tales*, December 1934

"Jirel Meets Magic" – *Weird Tales*, July 1935

"The Dark Land" – *Weird Tales*, January 1936

"Quest of the Starstone" (with Henry Kuttner) – *Weird Tales*, November 1937

"Hellsgarde" – *Weird Tales*, April 1939

SHAPES AND SOUNDS
M P SHIEL

IT IS GENERALLY acknowledged that MP Shiel's principal claim to literary fame lies with his novels, and understandably so. They overflow with extraordinary events and intriguing plots, with dramatic invention and startling denouement, and the unique prose style that suffuses them all is as compelling as the headlong pace of their action.

The Purple Cloud is undeniably Shiel's magnum opus. This book is one of the genuinely great works of imaginative fiction, telling of Adam Jeffson's return from the North Pole to discover that he is the last man left alive after a cloud of cyanogen gas had killed everyone else. Jeffson's gradual realisation of the extent of this apocalypse leads him on a twenty-year rampage across the dead world, burning city after city in an orgy of destruction: "...leaving in my rear reeking regions, a tract of ravage, like some being of the Pit that blights where his wings of fire pass".

The vibrant, gripping prose, particularly in the middle third of the book, will be indelibly etched on the mind of any reader, but in fact Shiel maintains interest right up to the end, which, while predictable, is still uplifting.

The Purple Cloud has rarely been out of print since initial publication in 1901, and unlike many of its contemporaries is still thoroughly readable well over a century later. Superb as it certainly is, Shiel aficionados may place it only slightly ahead of those other outstanding novels, *The Lord of the Sea* and *The Isle of Lies*. Not too much further down the scale is a cluster of additional fine works, including *The Last Miracle, Cold Steel, The Weird o'It, Unto the Third Generation, The Dragon, Children of the Wind, The Yellow Danger, How the Old Woman Got Home, This Knot of Life, The Yellow Wave* and *The Man-Stealers*.

That Shiel was a great novelist is beyond doubt, but this was just one aspect of his ability to work wonders with words. It is perhaps unfortunate that his shorter fiction has been overshadowed, to the extent that he is regarded as having only incidentally written some fine short stories. He was a writer whose talent manifested itself equally in both the long and short form, with the one complementing the other. His position in the world of creative fiction would be as secure had he never written a single novel, with short stories such as "The House of Sounds" and "Dark Lot of One Saul" as outstanding and enduring as are the novels *The Purple Cloud* and *The Lord of the Sea*. Reviewing *Prince Zaleski and Cummings King Monk*, Richard Lupoff said:

They are among the most bizarre and mind-bending tales I've ever read: Shiel could write like a satanic scripturalist on an amphetamine jag, and some of the stories will leave you positively reeling around the room, searching for a chair to grab onto. By no means is Shiel fare for all readers, but I suggest you try at least the first two or three paragraphs of "The Race of Orven", and if you're not hooked by then, just put down the book and go in peace. But if Shiel grabs you the way he did me with that story, you'll be a goner for sure.

These enthusiastic comments refer to Shiel's early, Poe-influenced fiction, and his technique did change considerably in later years. The power of his writing remained undiminished throughout a long career spanning more than fifty years, encompassing twenty-six novels and more than seventy shorter pieces, a number of which are uncollected. Five volumes of Shiel's short fiction did appear in his lifetime: *Prince Zaleski* (1895), *Shapes in the Fire* (1896), *The Pale Ape and Other Pulses* (1911), *Here Comes the Lady* (1928), and *The Invisible Voices* (1935). There were several posthumous collections: *The Best Short Stories of MP Shiel* (1948), *Xélucha and Others* (1975), *Prince Zaleski and Cummings King Monk* (1977) and volume one of *The Works of MP Shiel* (1979), which included fifteen short stories off-printed from their original magazine sources and complete with period illustrations. *Prince Zaleski* and *Shapes in the Fire* have been republished in a number of different editions, but with the exception of *The Invisible Voices* in 1971, none of the other books have ever been reprinted. Although there have been infrequent appearances in various anthologies over the years, and the two excellent collections in more recent times – *The House of Sounds and Others* (2005) and *Haunts & Horrors* (2012) – the fact remains that Shiel's substantial contribution to the short story genre remains unappreciated.

This may in part be due to difficulties in the categorisation of his work, and the only adequate way of describing it is to say that each and every story is distinctly "Shielian". They range from the romantic to the macabre, and from the humorous to the fantastic, with equal gusto. There are detective stories, adventures, thrillers, mysteries, and even one erotic tale. Shiel's scope was the whole province of fiction, with the chilling and cold-blooded tale of supernatural revenge no less representative than his account of a clergyman's difficulty in writing sermons.

Shiel revelled in his versatility, not only through the variety of his plots and settings, but also in the style and structure of his writing. Never seeming to be fully content with his work, he continually looked to improve upon it, rewriting many of his novels and short stories; and this revision was on occasion quite extreme. *The Purple Cloud* exists in three separate and distinct versions; it initially appeared as a serialised fifty-five page novelette in the first half of 1901; it was then published as a much-extended 463 page novel later that year; and reprinted in 1929 in a significantly shortened 288 page edition. But none of the alterations made to that novel come anywhere near the considerable changes in style and language that transformed the classic weird tale "Vaila" into "The House of Sounds".

These changes seemed to be a conscious attempt on the part of the author to put his theories on the Art of Writing into specific practice, and consequently result in two distinctly different versions of the same story. Each of them is an astounding tour-de-force in its own right, and while one or both *may* represent the very best of Shiel's short fiction, there are various other contenders, and it is not easy to single out individual titles.

MANY OF MP Shiel's finest stories were published prior to 1900. The twentieth century found him adopting a less elaborate, less adjectival form of prose, although a form uniquely his own. The studied, arabesque approach that characterised the early collections *Prince Zaleski* and *Shapes in the Fire* was discarded, and was reproduced only once more to any significant effect with "Dark Lot of One Saul", in 1912.

This could have been a reflection of Shiel's self-conscious maturity as a writer, his feeling that the Poesque fantasies of his formative years needed to be effaced by the adoption of a more fundamental literary approach. As early as 1900, he said of *Shapes in the Fire*, "I pronounce (it) good in its way, well wrought: but I did not see then, what I see now, how much is to be said for lucidity and simplicity of manner", and he was lightly regarding the book as "juvenilia" by 1924, presumably juvenilia in the sense that a younger, different self had produced it. He was also dismissive of *Prince Zaleski*, attributing the book to the transient influence of Poe, saying "...on writing more, I decided that writing English ... was given me to do". Yet, by any standards, the tales in both *Shapes in the Fire* and *Prince Zaleski* are excellent examples of inspired writing, fully deserving the praise they have received from various sources since their initial appearance.

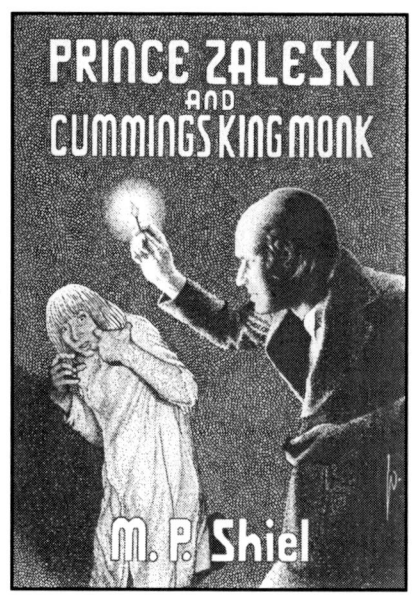

SHIEL'S FIRST PUBLISHED story was "The Doctor's Bee", which featured in the 14 December 1889 edition of the periodical *Rare Bits*. *Prince Zaleski* appeared just over five years later, in March 1895. The period between that volume and *Shapes in the Fire* at the end of the following year was marked by the publication of such fine pieces as "Huguenin's Wife", "Wayward Love" and "The Spectre Ship". The later stories are far more skilfully written than that first example, and demonstrate a finesse and faculty that were not at all evident in 1889. In those few years, Shiel matured rapidly as far as his literary abilities were concerned, and it would be interesting to chart that progress by studying his contemporary writing.

However, no published fiction has been traced between 1889 and 1893, when the well-forged "Guy Harkaway's Substitute" appeared, a story polished enough to emphasise the growth in Shiel's skills since his initial effort. There are at least two other pieces that were written during the early 1890s, "Maddelena's Lovers" and "Two Fogs", titles mentioned in a letter dated April 1892, but where or even if they were ever published is unknown. It is probable that there are further stories from the period in question, but searches through many of the periodicals of the time have been unsuccessful, and the passage of time makes it less likely that any new discoveries will be made. Even magazine appearances of novels have proved to be elusive. Shiel indicated several times in correspondence that *The Lord of the Sea* was written for serial periodical publication, but it has never been traced.

While "The Doctor's Bee" is a frankly minor piece, it does nevertheless have its points of interest when considered in the light of the author's later fiction. A recurrent theme in much of Shiel's writing, up to and including his last novel *The New King*, was the concept of the "Overman", and in his first published story there is the low-key harbinger of just such a person, unrefined but still identifiable.

Shiel's Overmen were often individuals who accomplished astonishing deeds and attained great heights, but who were ultimately brought down – heavily – by their own flaws. The doctor in "The Doctor's Bee" inherits a vast sum of money and uses it to set up an unusual and revolutionary college of education; he becomes successful but finally meets his end through a rather unscientific oversight on his own part. In essence, then, the story is a sure microcosm of the rise and fall of later Overmen, such as Richard Hogarth in *The Lord of the Sea* and Hannibal Lepsius in *The Isle of Lies*, illustrating that this particular idea had taken root with the writer at a very early stage.

PRINCE ZALESKI WAS Shiel's first major character and the title of his first published book in 1895, a collection of three short stories. An eccentric and unfathomable individual, the reclusive Zaleski enters a self-imposed exile in a gloomy, half ruined old mansion (his abode is in fact referred to as an abbey in "The SS", although the descriptions in the previous stories are not at all reminiscent of an abbey). He is attended only by his Libyan servant Ham, and surrounds himself with various exotic appurtenances. Only the most complex of problems can kindle any sort of enthusiasm in him, whether a mysterious crime or something along the lines of "co-ordinating to one of the calculi certain new properties he had discovered in the parabola".

The Prince solves the most bizarre cases by pure reasoning; given all the facts, he proceeds to deduce the truth of what is presented to him without needing to leave his antique dwelling. He does rouse himself from his languid inaction on one occasion, to put an end to a series of murders, but this is *after* he has successfully solved the matter.

Each of Zaleski's cases has its own particular element of strangeness. In "The Race of Orven", a double murder is the problem, *double* in the sense that the victim has been shot and stabbed; and although an apparent murderess is found on the scene, knife in hand, the cause of death was a bullet – but there is no gun and the room is securely locked. "The Stone of the Edmundsbury Monks" tells of a fabled jewel, reputed to herald its owner's demise by changing colour, which disappears and reappears bewilderingly, leaving deaths in its wake. The final story, "The SS", deals with a wave of murders that resemble suicides, engineered by the Society of Sparta, an organisation devoted to ridding the world of the unfit and unhealthy. All three of these adventures are unusual, thought-provoking and memorable, and the brooding, melancholy Prince is a powerfully drawn and commanding figure.

As to Zaleski's forbears in detective fiction, there is little of Holmes in him and not very much of Dupin. The stories do reflect the stylistic influence of Poe, but it is clear that in the creation of the Prince, Shiel was more indebted to Eugene Sue's Prince Rodolph (in *The Mysteries of Paris*) and Prince de Hansfeld (in *Paula Monti),* both of whom pre-date Zaleski by more than fifty years.

But if the character of the Prince is derivative, his essence is uniquely Shiel. The similarities in background and disposition with Sue's Princes, which it must be said are very similar indeed, are superseded by both the powerful personality of Zaleski and the outré nature of the events with which he is concerned. These combine to place the stories in a "dedactive" niche that warrants its importance in the early history of the literature of detection. The term "dedaction" seems to have been coined by Shiel's latter-day collaborator and literary executor John Gawsworth, and presumably means deduction by proxy.

Five Zaleski stories plus an incomplete fragment were published, including three "posthumous collaborations" with John Gawsworth. The first of these was "Lend Lease", also known as "The Murena Murder", apparently written solely by Shiel in 1945 but eventually revised by Gawsworth and printed as "The Return of Prince Zaleski" in 1955. This is a somewhat unsatisfying story; its mediocre beginning and end are such that it would be easy, but perhaps unkind, to assume that these were the areas of collaboration. At its core, the tale does have much of the feel of the 1895 stories, with the Prince deciphering a cryptic message from a mass murderer and uncovering the solution to a series of killings. The plot is not as similar to "The SS" as it may sound in summary.

"The Missing Merchants", the fifth story and the second collaboration, was first published in 1980 and is very different. Apart from the storyline, itself taken from the 1909 novel *By Force of Circumstances* by Gordon Holmes (a pseudonym of Shiel and Louis Tracy), several paragraphs are lifted almost word for word from "The Return of Prince Zaleski". Additionally, the location Hargen Hall is borrowed from "The Pale Ape", and two of the characters in the story are Edward Denman and Walter Teeger, names originally used in *Unto the Third Generation* and "The Bride" respectively.

There is more of the same in the unfinished third collaboration, "The Hargen Inheritance", published in the 2002 Tartarus Press edition of *Prince Zaleski*, which collects all of the Prince's tales. "The Hargen Inheritance" is a sequel to "The Missing Merchants", and that it was never completed need not concern anyone who admired the original book.

The faults in these later stories may not be of any real consequence but, as well as being so uncharacteristic of Shiel, they do alter the whole nature of the Prince. At one point in "The Missing Merchants" he is even found in the grounds of Hargen Hall "with a magnifying glass at his eye, staring intently at every sign", clear evidence that his role had been downgraded to that of a surrogate Sherlock Holmes. Zaleski was most certainly *not* a detective in the mould of Holmes; he did not seek to solve crimes, but could be persuaded to do so if the fancy took him to exercise his deductive powers. A complicated mystery was as acceptable as a mathematical problem, either challenge being a passive defence against ennui.

Similarly, Cummings King Monk, whose initial adventures appeared in *The Pale Ape* in 1911, was far from being an orthodox detective. Unlike Zaleski, Monk needs little persuasion to become entangled in investigative matters; rather he actively seeks involvement. Shiel described him as "...a new sort of detective-hero, not thinking but acting, using synthesis instead of analysis..."

A restless multimillionaire, Monk has a keen analytical interest in all things that bear upon the human condition. This naturally includes crime, not to any all-consuming extent but simply as one aspect of the greater whole. His approach varies: he creates the illusion of robbery in "He Meddles with Women" in order to observe and manipulate the consequences; he seeks out murder and its perpetrator in "He Wakes an Echo"; he discourses philosophically in "He Defines Greatness of Mind"; and he is righting the wrongs of social injustice in "The Corner in Cotton".

Monk is a dynamic, larger than life character, but his presence never detracts from the action. The absolute opposite of Zaleski in almost every respect, he is just as fascinating an individual, and is involved in adventures that are equally unusual. In particular, "He Meddles with Women" and "He Wakes an Echo", with their compellingly readable prose and their intriguing plots, are examples of Shiel approaching his outlandish best.

Only "He Wakes an Echo" is properly a tale of detection. A bored Monk decides that a big crime would be just the thing to rouse him, and his way of getting involved is a unique one: "…first conceive the crime, construct it, then find someone who is somewhere committing it in the world, and mix ourselves up generally in the trouble". The story develops very quickly into an incident-packed, melodramatic adventure that is breathlessly paced, even by Shiel's standards.

Monk is very much a background figure in "The Corner in Cotton", published in the collection *Here Comes the Lady* in 1928. He does, however, retain his charisma, which was not the case in the later collaborations with John Gawsworth, of which there are two: "The Master" (1936), a slightly revised version of "The Doctor's Bee" with Monk as the narrator, and "The Return of Cummings Monk" (1980). The detective is back to sleuthing in this latter story, which although better than its predecessor is disappointing. It includes whole paragraphs from earlier Monk tales, a plot that derives largely from "The Return of Prince Zaleski", and an ending that again uproots entire sections from a much earlier work, this time "The Case of Euphemia Raphash" (1896). The story does little for the reputation of either Monk or the authors, and Shiel's participation in both this and the last two Zaleski pieces must be questionable. His literary integrity was such that he would surely never have actively condoned such distinct character changes, or the use of borrowed plots and prose.

But despite the liberties taken with both Zaleski and Monk in later years, the two are undoubtedly amongst the most remarkable of all crime solvers, and the tales in which they initially featured are a fine tribute to their creator's inventive powers.

SHIEL'S UNUSUAL STYLE certainly lent itself readily to unusual concepts. This is perhaps why his tales of the bizarre make the most impression, although in Shiel's hand even the apparently unprepossessing plot is entertainingly readable. Nonetheless, it is the more fanciful writings that stay longest in the memory, and some of the best of these are found in the *Shapes in the Fire* collection, first published in 1896. These stories are sensual and sumptuous, with an elaborate Gothicism and an exotic imagery that distantly resemble Poe in effect, but which remain uniquely and exhilaratingly Shiel at his most pervasive and most forceful.

Of the seven pieces in the book, each has its own rare quality. "Tulsah" and "Xélucha", for instance, are stories dealing with the mysteries of death. In the former, there is a dramatic resolution in a sealed chamber far beneath the ground, with the narrator solving the great mystery for himself in unenviable fashion. We are told that he is a man "not unloved by the gods, but loved, you perceive, in *their* peculiar fashion". The ending of "Xélucha" is of equal power as a slowly mounting atmosphere of horror culminates in awful revelation. There is no question in the reader's mind about the true identity of the woman who is so morbidly obsessed with death and the grave, but the piece is no less potent for that. Shiel was not the sort of writer who relied on a climactic surprise for impact, although as in "Xélucha" his final paragraphs could be both terse and effective: "Sudden memory flashed upon me. I scrambled to my feet, and plunged and tottered, bawling, through the twilight into the street".

"Phorfor" is another carefully constructed and ornate story, of a love triangle that is actually quadrilateral. Numa's possession of the lovely Areta is thwarted not only by the veiled and forbidding figure of the Elder Theodore, but also by the omnipresent Sergius, dead but mummified. "Phorfor" is also noteworthy for quite another reason: it has the extremely uncommon Shielian trait of repetition. At one point we read, "As the spaces of the night marched by, the tapering flames began to leap duskily..." and then further on, "We sat together silent. The spaces of the night marched by us". And there is an echo of the same here: "Grey spaces of the morning now shivered past, like home-turning ghosts". But repetition can be forgiven when it produces such evocative phrases.

One of the most admired of all Shiel's stories, in its original form, appears in *Shapes in the Fire*: "Vaila", which was later extensively revised and published as "The House of Sounds" in *The Pale Ape* (1911). The strength of this fine story lies in its depth, in the creation of a mood at once brooding and malevolent, grim and disturbing, with Haco Harfager's house of brass an interface that isolates the irrationality within from the normal world without. Harfager is a memorable character, as is the murderous Aith. The mental and physical disintegration inevitably portended by the constant tumult of Vaila is as impressively depicted as any scene in Shiel's fiction. Indeed, the incessant noise assaulting the mansion is so vividly portrayed that the reader is left feeling exhausted and deafened. The effect of the story is startling in its intensity, skilfully evoking a mood that is as unnerving as it is unremitting.

Of the remaining pieces in *Shapes in the Fire*, "Maria in the Rose-Bush" recounts how the burning of a Dürer portrait caused a House's downfall in the Middle Ages; "The Serpent Ship" is an eerie effective poem in blank verse (not to be confused with "The Spectre Ship", published earlier in 1896, and featuring the same characters in a quite different story); and "Premier and Maker" is a philosophical essay structured as fiction. It describes the meeting of the "Premier" and a certain writer called "Mr Phipps" and their subsequent discussion on the subject of Art. The result is actually far more entertaining and readable than it may sound.

IT IS INTERESTING to note that in these earlier stories there are a number of mysterious and intimidating figures of questionable origin: Aith in "Vaila", Theodore in "Phorfor", and Ul-Jabal in "The Stone of the Edmundsbury Monks", for example. There are also varying degrees of fiery destruction in "Vaila", "Phorfor", Huguenin's Wife", "The Spectre Ship", "Tulsah" and "Maria in the Rose-Bush". It is tempting to idly wonder whether there was any significance in this. Could the shadowy, menacing figure have had any symbolic relevance in Shiel's own experience? Did the conflagrations represent a form of literary catharsis for him? If so, then one assumes that it was successful, because characters of the enigmatic stature of Aith and Theodore do not reappear after *Shapes in the Fire*, and devastating holocausts also become less common, with one notable exception in *The Purple Cloud* (1901).

A simpler explanation may be the waning of the influence of Poe. Shiel's recourse to the innate characteristics of stories such as "The Fall of the House of Usher" and "The Masque of the Red Death" correspondingly declined. Be that as it may, as already mentioned, after the turn of the century Shiel only rarely revisited the decorous realms of his early writing. Later stories tend to be complete contrasts in the way they are written, but are just as powerful despite their less figurative prose.

"The Bride", for example, is written in a deceptively light tone although it is gruesome to the extreme in its implications. In the story, Walter Teeger discovers that the passionate woman sharing his bed and his embraces on his wedding night is actually his new wife's jealous sister ... the sister who died two days earlier. The final sentences are succinct and straightforward: "After two days Walter, still unconscious, died. His disfigured body they placed in a grave not far from Rachel's".

This tale highlights a feature that Shiel utilised expertly in his treatment of the macabre. The horror here is inferred rather than explicit, with the use of the one word "disfigured" far more unsettling in its suggestiveness than any graphic description. Similarly, in "The Place of Pain" we are never told exactly what it was that Podd saw that drove him to madness, except that it was on the Moon and that "the souls in that place live in pain". It was not convention or any lack of ability that dictated this apparent reticence on Shiel's part. He knew precisely how to impart the maximum effect in his stories and exactly *when* to be explicit, as is shown in both "Huguenin's Wife" and "Xélucha", two fine examples of unmasked horror.

Dramatic prose also marks "The Tale of Henry and Rowena", with its vivid and detailed description of Henry Darnley cutting off his own arm to save Rowena from an escaped panther. When her love proves to be ephemeral, the now dead Henry exacts revenge. Again, the closing lines are chilling: "...the fingers of the strangler (if there was a strangler) were of such a species as to leave not the faintest trace or impression on the snow of the lady's throat".

Horror of a different sort is found in "Dark Lot of One Saul", a tale that ranks very high in the Shiel canon. Saul is placed in a cask and thrown overboard, ending up in a lightless, lonely land *beneath* the ocean. The darkly majestic descriptive passages and pseudo-archaic narrative style admirably convey an atmosphere of claustrophobic terror, and instil a feeling of isolation and nightmare. There are similarities in both style and theme between this story and William Hope Hodgson's *The Night Land*, but such similarities are coincidental; "Dark Lot of One Saul" was published in February 1912, six months before Hodgson's epic novel appeared.

Isolation in its varying forms is a recurrent topic in much of Shiel's short fiction, whether it is the physical isolation of the castaway Saul; the mental isolation of Harfager or Podd; or the isolation of the dead from the living. Many stories are concerned with vengeance from beyond the grave; besides "Xélucha", "Huguenin's Wife", "The Tale of Henry and Rowena" and "The Bride", other notable examples of post-mortem revenge include "The Great King" and "The Spectre Ship". Retribution, grim but not necessarily supernatural in nature, is also featured in "The Bell of St Sépulcre" and "The Primate of the Rose". Sometimes it is tinged with irony, as in "The Flying Cat" and "A Night in Venice", and then again it can be light-hearted, as in "The Whirligig". This latter story has another characteristic popular with Shiel: impersonation – people are not always who or what they may seem to be, although the reader normally has a fairly good idea of what is going on. Other instances of this include "No16 Brook Street", "Wayward Love", "Guy Harkaway's Substitute", "Family Pride"; and in a more grisly vein "The Pale Ape", and of course "Xélucha".

Shiel successfully turned his hand to areas of fiction that would perhaps not normally be thought of as his forte, as with "Maymia and M'Toma", which at just under 700 words is the shortest piece that the writer attempted. Written in 1936 and intended as the preface to a collection of John Gawsworth's poems, it was not published until

1965, when it appeared as "The Tigress' Cave". The tale is unique in the Shiel catalogue by virtue of its particularly overt sexual content, although it is so well written that nobody is likely to find it offensive.

Another example – and a sharp contrast – is Shiel's one known juvenile story, "The Awful Voyage of Ralphie Hamilton", which passably succeeds on the level intended, even if it is difficult to reconcile with the tales that he was producing in other areas at around the same time (1898). It is perhaps indicative of the writer's professionalism that he was producing work for specific markets and adapting them accordingly. The stylishly florid prose of "Phorfor" would hardly have been appropriate in the pages of the Easter Double Number of *The Boy's Friend*!

PROFESSIONALISM IS ALSO apparent in that Shiel was a compulsive revisionist. This seems to have been more from aesthetic considerations than commercial dictates, and his revisions could veer between the minor and the drastic. One of the more drastic is "The House of Sounds" in *The Pale Ape* (1911), a rewritten version of the 1896 "Vaila". In the later story, the events and the characters are unchanged (although the name Vaila becomes Rayba), but the prose is substantially altered. As an example, here is a passage from "Vaila":

A dense and dank seaborne haze now lay, in spite of the vapid breezes, high along the water, enclosing the boat in a vague domed cavern of doleful twilight and sullen swell. The region of the considerable islands was past, and there was a spectral something in the unreal aspect of the silent sea and the sunless dismalness of sky which produced on my nerves the impression of a voyage out *of nature, a* cruise *beyond* the world.

And this is the same passage from "The House of Sounds":

A mist now lay over the billows, enclosing our boat in a dome of doleful gloaming, and there was a ghostly something in the look of the silent sea and brooding sky which produced upon my nerves the mood of a journey out of nature, a cruise beyond the world.

Such condensations occur throughout the story, but the nature of the revision is not simply to reduce wordage. Certain scenes are in fact lengthened, and although "Vaila" is some 2,000 words longer than "The House of Sounds", the compression is nowhere near as extreme as with the 1920's versions of such early novels as *The Purple Cloud*, *The Lord of the Sea* and *Cold Steel*.

Despite that no more than fifteen years separate the respective stories, there is a considerable amount of modernisation in the second version. Such words as "discerned" are replaced by "seen", "purview" by "survey" and "eschew" by "escape". There are also numerous deletions or alterations of adjectives, adverbs and phrases, although sometimes the changes do seem to be for the worse, as when "the excess of lunacy possessed her" becomes "she was as mad as a March hare".

These individual aspects are constituent parts of the revision, which radicalised the stylistic approach. It is particularly pertinent that two years before *The Pale Ape*, Shiel published an essay called "On Reading" as the preface to his 1909 novel *This Knot of Life*. The essay set out the author's thinking on literary technique, and "The House of Sounds" appears to be the practical application of those ideas. It can therefore be seen as a unique experiment in style, one that demonstrates the writer's unification of his concepts of Matter, Expression, Harmony and Tone, the four ingredients that for Shiel constituted the "Art" of good writing.

In particular, the comments in "On Reading" concerning harmony and tone can be appreciated with phrases such as "no doubt profoundly drowned in the world of surge without…" and "a gust of auguster passion galloped up the mansion…" or again in "the monstrous racket of the crackling of a cosmos of crockery…" and "the blush of that bluish moonshine". These are newly-added passages that do not appear in "Vaila", and by comparison the earlier prose can seem flat and lifeless, as when "I looked forth upon a spectacle of weirdly morne, of dismal wildness…" is transformed into this example of alliterative magic: "I gazed forth upon a scene no less eerily dismal than some drear district of the dreams of Dante".

"The House of Sounds" is a fascinating insight into Shiel's philosophy of writing and the gulf that he envisaged had arisen between "real" writing and the efforts of his literary youth. Whether the story is better than "Vaila" is difficult to say. The two tales may have the same plot, but they are nevertheless distinctly different, and if "Vaila" lacks the Art that Shiel took such pains to instil into its rewritten version, then it does have a baroque effect that is all its own. If its prose is less compelling, then it does create a more intense aura of insidious menace. Each version has its own considerable merits and its own points to savour, and each is unquestionably a masterwork of weird fiction.

Some people definitely preferred the later version. In a letter to August Derleth, HP Lovecraft said:

I know you will find "The House of Sounds" to be one of the most powerful weird tales you have ever read […] It is obviously the result of great care and frequent re-writing on the author's part – for an earlier version is extant, in which the style is more or less cluttered up with the flashiness and showiness of the spectacular nineties.

To describe "Vaila" as being cluttered up with "flashiness and showiness" is rather harsh, and Brian Stableford, in his perceptive introduction to the Tartarus Press reprint of *Shapes in the Fire* (2000), is more accurate when he says "...there is no doubt that the earlier and more pyrotechnic version of 'Vaila' wears its wildness very well". And he is not alone: Clark Ashton Smith was one of the many admirers of "Vaila", describing it as one of Shiel's "masterpieces of Poesque weirdness ... it is indeed a tremendous and memorable thing".

One can fully appreciate Lovecraft's fulsome praise for "The House of Sounds", which is indeed quite stunning, and which he described as "the most haunting thing I have read in a decade". However, his comments about "Vaila" were perhaps more of a reflection of his boundless enthusiasm for the new tale rather than a serious criticism of the earlier one. He did extol "Xélucha" as a "noxiously hideous fragment" and this tale is no less elaborately written than "Vaila"; we must assume that he was so overwhelmed by "The House of Sounds" that as far as he was concerned, no alternative version could possibly match it and therefore could only be inferior.

THERE IS A further story in *The Pale Ape* collection that was also extensively revised for re-publication. "Huguenin's Wife" involves a nemesis from beyond the grave in the form of a monstrous cat-like creature. Surprisingly, although the changes made to the later version of this fine tale are at least as numerous as those made to "Vaila", the basic style of the story remains the same, without the close attention to "harmony" and "tone" that so mark "The House of Sounds". The pulsating rhythms are evident only rarely in such passages as "...while he slept his damp trances I started my tramp on the track of the scarlet thread", which replaced the comparatively stilted "...while he slept his damp, unquiet, opiate slumbers, I started out on the track indicated by the scarlet thread". Overall though, the revision seems to be more concerned with "expression" and there is a muted, almost timid, feel to it when compared to "The House of Sounds" and such bravura sentences as "He was like some poor wight into whose eyes in the night have pried the eyes of affright".

Shiel was clearly attracted to certain turns of phrase. It is interesting to note that in the story "The Pale Ape", which relates the strange events at isolated Hargen Hall, the narrator says "the stare of eyes of affright in the night was ever present in my imagination". Presumably the author so liked this particular combination of words that he could not resist re-using them – as was the case with "the spaces of the night marched by" in "Phorfor".

John Gawsworth said of Shiel's revisions: "…it was clear that on occasions he revised down, generally to suit some inferior momentary market. Such versions, forced upon him by economic necessity ... often debasing his unique genius".

Other critics have also picked up on this idea, but it seems unlikely that Shiel's prime motivation would have been financial. As far as he was concerned, he was not revising "down", but expressing his evolving ideas of the way in which to write creatively.

Those ideas may have been considerably re-thought with the passage of time. What must have been one of his last revisions – the "Xélucha" of 1896 for inclusion in the Arkham House collection *Xélucha and Others* – finds the prose only slightly altered, with just a single phrase completely removed and the other changes minor. The one deletion is the sentence "A belch of pestilent corruption puffed poisonous upon the putrid air", and while the passage may not have been completely satisfactory to the author of "On Reading", it does have an alliterative harmony that should have appealed to his perceptive ear.

Xélucha and Others was Shiel's own selection of tales with "a more or less weird twist". Although the book did not appear until 1975, August Derleth was discussing its publication with Shiel in the mid-

1940s, and as well as asking the author to provide an Introduction, he also requested that the title story be revised. Shiel duly obliged, saying, "I agree with you that 'Xélucha' is 'florid', but I will modify..." As mentioned above, the modifications were very minor indeed – but Derleth did not seem to notice!

THE LATE REVISION of "Xélucha" was done when the ageing writer was concentrating on what he saw as his masterwork, *Jesus* (unpublished and apparently un-publishable), and perhaps his enthusiasm for fiction was hard to rekindle. Despite such novels as *This Above All* (1933), *Say Au R'Voir But Not Goodbye* (also 1933), *The Young Men are Coming* (1937) and *The New King* (c1945), Shiel's later years were not truly productive, and perhaps in some ways counterproductive. The mid-1930s had seen a series of collaborations with John Gawsworth that in the main fell a long way short of the standards set by Shiel's preceding work. Seven of the eight collaborations were to have been collected as *The Seven Limbs of Satan*, which is a reasonable enough title, but the contents would have been very slight. That the book has not yet been published is no great loss.

Hardly any of the joint efforts can bear comparison with the superlative fiction that Shiel produced up to the end of the previous decade, and even the best of them tend to make use of ideas taken from previous books. This latter trait was a hallmark of most of the collaborations, including the later Zaleski and Monk tales.

Shiel himself did think highly of at least one of these stories. When selecting the contents of *Xélucha and Others*, his list contained "The Globe of Goldfish", which was included in the Arkham House collection. He gave no indication that the tale was a collaboration and its original publication date of 1934 is early enough in his association with Gawsworth to suggest that the story is likely to be primarily

Shiel's. Even though its central idea admittedly owes something to the 1903 novel *Unto the Third Generation,* "The Globe of Goldfish" is a clever and enjoyable mystery, and is markedly superior to any of the other "seven limbs".

Shiel's literary output slowed by the 1930s and it was probably only the enthusiasm of Gawsworth, who despite his many failings was a good friend to Shiel, that prompted the collaborations and the few new stories. But at this same time, Shiel was at work on his penultimate novel *The Young Men are Coming*, and was also completing shortened versions of several of his earlier books. At least three date from 1936/37: "The Phantom Man o'War" (a condensation of *Contraband of War*), "China in Arms" (*The Yellow Danger*) and "The Innocent Hands" (*The Weird o'It*). There are a further four novelettes that could well have been finalised during the same period, adaptations of *Cold Steel*, *The Lord of the Sea*, *The Lost Viol* and *The Black Box*. Apart from extremely limited printings of "The Innocent Hands" by JDS Books in 1995 and "China in Arms" by The Vainglory Press in 1998, these titles remain unpublished, which is a pity. In their original form they are all fine books, and it would be interesting to see how Shiel converted them into shorter format.

By way of comparison, *The Purple Cloud*, of novelette length in its original 1901 magazine serialisation, was much expanded in its book publication. The first version is not, however, a short novel, nor is the book in any way padded. The two variants are equally effective at their respective lengths, and the seven abridgements mentioned above would almost certainly be similarly "new" to readers, demonstrating yet another aspect of Shiel's literary abilities.

Widespread publication of the shortened novels is unlikely; we must instead be content with what *has* been published, and there is much to appreciate in that. The best of MP Shiel's short stories are outstanding examples of his matchless ability, and even those that do not rank in the upper echelon are eminently readable.

Novels such as *The Purple Cloud* and *The Lord of the Sea* are quite unforgettable, but many of the shorter pieces have a potency which ensures that they too will remain permanently in the reader's memory. In the gallery of Shielian fiction, the major portraits may well be those of Jeffson, Hogarth and Lepsius, but the images of Zaleski, Harfager and Saul also loom large.

POSTSCRIPT

IN HIS 2010 biography *MP Shiel: The Middle Years 1897-1923*, Harold Billings reveals a number of unpleasant and unpalatable aspects of Shiel's life that have recently been uncovered. For instance, it seems astonishing that he flagrantly plagiarised Stewart Edward White's 1907 story "The Two-Gun Man", published as "One Man in a Thousand" by Shiel in 1914, but there is no question that he did. This was perhaps due to his need for money – something that was a constant problem throughout this whole period. Remarkably, it seems to have had no effect on his reputation, even though it was well publicised in *The Bookman* in 1915.

There was also his seemingly compulsive womanising, which produced at least three "love children", involving adultery and the relentless pursuit of married women. But there was something far, far worse... The womanising pales into insignificance beside the reason for his sixteen-month term of imprisonment in 1914, when he was forty-nine years old: he had a sexual relationship with a twelve-year-old girl, the daughter of his common law wife, an action which he admitted to and which he tried to defend at his trial. He never showed any remorse and felt "outrage" at his imprisonment, claiming – apparently in all seriousness – that he had "copulated, as a matter of course, from the age of two or three with ladies of a similar age in lands where that is not considered at all extraordinary". Even if such a preposterous statement were true, it conveniently overlooks the fact that in 1914 Shiel was a middle-aged man taking predatory advantage of a young girl, and there can quite simply be no justification at all for such behaviour.

Even more disturbing is that this incident may not have been an isolated one. There is a desperately sad little note to him from another girl, in which she apologises for her "foolish act", the inference being either attempted suicide or abortion. The letter in question is dated June 1908, when the girl was about seventeen, although it seems likely that Shiel's relationship with her had started several years earlier. And even as late as the 1920s he was "showing too much interest" in the fourteen-year-old niece of his wife Lydia, according to a member of the family.

In his 1933 novel *This Above All*, the immortal Ruth has to live her endless life in the form of twelve-year-old girl. Her depiction as an object of desire and her carnal nature has caused an element of unease on the part of many readers, and now we can perhaps understand the appeal of such a characterisation as far as the author was concerned. These revelations are troubling to say the least, and it is difficult to view Shiel with the same warmth as before.

MP Shiel's literary talents are unquestioned, and yet it is apparent that his sense of morality was negligible. Should the writer who entertained us be separated from the man with a dark nature? Should the wonder of *The Purple Cloud* be forgotten and we only remember that its author was a paedophile? Should we brush aside these disquieting revelations and concentrate solely on the literary quality of "The House of Sounds"? These are difficult questions to answer, and while it is impossible to overlook the appalling faults in Shiel's character, he was responsible for an outstanding body of fiction, and that should not now be dismissed.

SELECTED BIBLIOGRAPHY

Short story collections

Prince Zaleski – John Lane, 1895

Shapes in the Fire – John Lane, 1896

The Pale Ape and Other Pulses – T Werner Laurie, 1911

Here Comes the Lady – Richards Press, 1928

The Invisible Voices – Richards Press, 1935

The Best Short Stories of MP Shiel – Victor Gollancz, 1948

Xélucha and Others – Arkham House, 1975

Prince Zaleski and Cummings King Monk – Mycroft & Moran, 1977

The Works of MP Shiel Volume 1 – Reynolds Morse Foundation, 1979

Prince Zaleski – Tartarus Press, 2002 (an expansion of the 1895 edition)

The House of Sounds and Others – Hippocampus Press, 2005

Haunts and Horrors – Coachwhip Publications, 2012

THINGS OF DARKNESS
G G PENDARVES

IN ITS FIRST decade of publication, *Weird Tales* featured around 1,400 stories from many different authors, but its main themes of horror and the supernatural seemed to be primarily a male domain. No more than ten percent of the stories were written by women, and of those there are very few who are remembered today. The likes of Elizabeth Adt Wenzler, Effie W Fifield and Margaret McBride Hoss are as forgotten as their sole contributions to the magazine, which were respectively "The Demons of Castle Romnare", "The Amazing Adventure of Joe Scranton" and "The Weird Green Eyes of Sari". That such tales have sunk into oblivion may or may not be a good thing. However, there were other female writers who became regular contributors to the magazine and who produced excellent work.

The most notable early examples of this small group were Greye La Spina, CL Moore and Mary Elizabeth Counselman. Other less-known female authors whose work certainly had merit also proved to be popular with readers, including Everil Worrell, Eli Colter, Bassett Morgan and Allison V Harding. It is interesting to note that of these only Harding's gender is immediately apparent from her name. Equally popular but similarly reticent was Gladys Gordon Trenery (1885-1938), whose tales were published under the name of GG Pendarves (although on one occasion she did use the pseudonym of Marjorie E Lambe).

Pendarves appeared in the pages of *Weird Tales* between 1926 and 1939, and the smooth style of her prose and its narrative flow made her dark tales of the occult never less than highly enjoyable, with two of her stories – "The Eighth Green Man" and "The Sin-Eater" – being reprinted twice in the magazine, an achievement shared by few other writers. There are recurrent themes throughout her work that include family curses, vengeful revenants and psychic duels, but although there is admittedly a minor element of repetition the stories are all well written and eminently readable.

An English author, Pendarves set much of her fiction in the British Isles. She was born in Liverpool and lived for most of her life in that area, although her ancestry was Cornish, and it would appear that she had a partiality for where her roots lay. Cornwall, a south-western county of England, is a place of considerable beauty with wild moorland and a rugged coastline. It is an area that is steeped in folk-lore, with King Arthur's Camelot popularly thought to be located within its boundaries. Its standing stones and other ancient archaeology speak of millennia of history, and these elements seem to have caught Pendarves' imagination, for several of her tales utilise this evocative locale. Another favoured location was the East, and particularly the desert, which also featured in a number of the non-weird tales she sold to such markets as *Oriental Stories*, *Magic Carpet Magazine*, *Argosy All-Story Weekly* and *Hutchinson's Adventure-Story Magazine*.

Her early weird fiction appeared in *Hutchinson's Mystery-Story Magazine*, a popular British pulp; her first published work was "The Kabbalist" in the November 1923 issue. Over the next two years a further eight of her stories appeared in the same periodical, and her first two contributions to *Weird Tales* were pieces that had originally appeared there: "The Devil's Graveyard" and "The Return". She went on to appear a further seventeen times in *Weird Tales*' pages, and while some of her contributions had splendidly pulpish titles ("From the Dark Halls of Hell", "The Whistling Corpse", "The Laughing Thing", "Werewolf of the Sahara"), her fiction was in the main capable and literate, remaining enjoyable these many decades later.

"The Devil's Graveyard" marked her first appearance in *Weird Tales* in the August 1926 issue although, as mentioned, it had previously been published in *Hutchinson's Mystery-Story Magazine*. A very good tale, it features a character called Sir Donald Fremling, a worldly occult expert who was to also appear in several of the author's ensuing works, and whose help is enlisted to combat the ancient family curse that is coming to its fulfilment after seven hundred years. With his expertise in arcane matters, Fremling is able to confront and defeat an Elemental which is animated by an ancient hatred and driven by the evil of Gaffarel the Mighty and the Four Ancient Ones. The story served as a good introduction for American readers to Pendarves, although it must be said that her next two appearances were less than outstanding.

The first of these was "The Return", the second reprint from *Hutchinson's Mystery-Story Magazine:* a short, competent, but undistinguished story of a man spending the night in a haunted room only to find that the ghost is someone whose death he had been responsible for eight years earlier. The second was "The Power of the Dog" and again the story is short and unexceptional, with a last line revelation that would hardly have come as a surprise to any reader.

Her next appearance was with "The Lord of the Tarn", and this was a much better work, reverting back to both a longer format and the promise that had been evident in "The Devil's Graveyard". She reintroduces Sir Donald Fremling from the latter tale, and he plays a pivotal role in the story of a girl who is earmarked for sacrifice at Monk's Rock by the evil and long-dead Father Ambrosius, the eponymous Lord. The tale is told in the form of a series of letters, an unusual narrative structure for Pendarves but one that works well in introducing the major players and quickly establishing the plot, which builds up to a climactic battle between Fremling and the Lord of the Tarn.

This story served to set the scene for much of what was to come from Pendarves, heralding a succession of fine tales. The next to feature Fremling was "The Doomed Treveans", which tells of a curse that strikes at a Cornish family once each century. The curse is maintained by hatred and spite, transcending death, and there is a tense and well-depicted psychic duel at the climax in which the curse is broken and its perpetrator finally destroyed.

After this, Fremling appeared in just one more story, "From the Dark Halls of Hell", and then only briefly. It appeared that Pendarves had perhaps wisely seen that the tales involving him were becoming formulaic and the plots too confining. All three of the pieces that featured Fremling revolved around the perpetuation of ancient hatred throughout the years and the dead seeking a final revenge, only to be thwarted at the last by Fremling's intervention. It may or may not also be significant that in "The Devil's Graveyard", Fremling defeats his adversaries by repeating "the terrible name which could command even the Ancient Four themselves"; this would appear to make him omnipotent against the forces of evil, which means that he could never lose. Indeed, one has to wonder why he did not invoke the same name when confronting Ambrosius in "The Lord of the Tarn" and Jabez Penhale in "The Doomed Treveans"…

Pendarves may not in any event have been concentrating on developing Fremling into a long-term series character. He had not appeared in the story immediately prior to "The Doomed Treveans", "The Eighth Green Man", which was quite different in tone to anything that the author had produced before. It does feature another occult expert, Raoul Suliman d'Abre, but his presence fails to affect the grimly inexorable fate that befalls Nicholas Birkett in a story that is effective and chilling, with a surprisingly downbeat ending which sees evil triumphant.

"The Doomed Treveans" had been set in Cornwall, and so too was the first part of "The Grave at Goonhilly", which also features a fascinating supernatural battle at its climax. The two stories are, however, quite different, with the latter telling of haunted golf tee under which an evil man is buried, his spirit eventually taking possession of the body of a young golfer. A third specifically Cornish story was "The Sin-Eater", and there are others where the location might be Cornwall ("The Devil's Graveyard", "From the Dark Halls of Hell", "The Footprint"). The north-west of England, where the author lived for most of her life, was also utilised for a number of stories and, as has already been mentioned, the East was another setting that Pendarves was fond of, as in "The Power of the Dog", "The Altar of Melek Taos", "Werewolf of the Sahara" and "Abd Dhulma, Lord of Fire".

These "desert tales" are fairly straightforward adventure stories with a weird element, fast-paced but lacking the bleak tone that the author could so capably instil in less exotic surroundings when relating narratives of undying hatred, family curses and hauntings from beyond the grave. All but one of her remaining stories after "Werewolf of the Sahara" revisited the traditional locale of Britain, the one exception being "The Whistling Corpse", which is the quite atmospheric but ultimately implausible story of a haunted liner. But succeeding efforts, starting with "Thing of Darkness", saw her return to the format with which she was most familiar and with which she had produced her most memorable fiction.

"Thing of Darkness" tells of a haunted house and the fate of its new inhabitants, culminating in a gripping confrontation between Good and Evil. The malevolence of Thomas Werne is depicted well, as is the eerie atmosphere of darkness that pervades the troubled Troon House, which although finally vanquished still leaves its tarnish, with the House a "shell of death". This was the last story to be published during Pendarves' lifetime, although there were still several tales to come, having been submitted prior to her death.

The first of these was "The Black Monk", a short but noteworthy tale about the ghostly priest of Chaard Island who has supposedly protected a cache of riches since the Fifth Century. A sceptic light-heartedly tests the veracity of the legend and pays a bitter price for discovering the truth. Interestingly, Pendarves had made reference to the Black Monk of *Caldey* Island in "The Whistling Corpse", published the previous year; Caldey Island is off the southern coast of Wales and it has a legend of a powerful ghost who has guarded a treasure since the Tenth Century. The concept presumably appealed to the author, and she eventually used the idea, with minor changes, in "The Black Monk".

"The Whistling Corpse" also mentions Lord Saul, "a terror and a mystery since the days of Atilla, who tried to kill him by fire and by the sword, and failed. Lord Saul lives to this day". This is a theme that would perhaps have been incorporated into a story at a later date had Pendarves lived. As it was, there were only two further stories that were to appear under her by-line, both of them superior works.

In "The Sin Eater", the penultimate tale, Mark Zennor seeks to perpetuate his evil existence through black magic by using his wife and his nephew as the Perfect Sacrifices to complete a mystic Triad and possess the Key of Thoth. The final scenes in a dark chapel beneath Lamorna House, as the dread ritual draws to an inexorable climax, are tense, compelling, and satisfyingly well rounded, its occult detail convincingly depicted. The character of Zennor was almost certainly inspired by Aleister Crowley, who actually lived in Zennor, a village in Cornwall, for a short time early in 1938.

Pendarves' final tale appeared in November 1939 and was one of her best. "The Withered Heart" describes an impoverished landowner's discovery of an ancestor's heart and directions on how to resurrect his dead flesh in return for whatever he wishes. The lure of wealth to replenish his fortunes – and to satisfy his beloved but selfish young wife – leads him to undertake the required rite, but there are tragic and unforeseen consequences. His wish is granted, but it brings him no satisfaction as the story ends on a note of bleak despair.

There does seem to be an unresolved aspect to this story, with the ancestor – Count Dul – succeeding in his malignant plan, this being one of the very few instances in Pendarves' fiction of evil triumphing. The narrator's final vow to seek out and destroy the Count – "it will be all that remains worth doing in a world of fear and shadows" – may suggest that the author was thinking in terms of a sequel which was never to be written, a sequel in which there would have been a final reckoning.

Such a confrontation between the powers of darkness and the powers of light was a common theme in much of Pendarves' fiction. Those confrontations, although used frequently (in well over half of her *Weird Tales* stories) are never mundane or repetitive – they are intriguingly different each time. On occasion, victory can only be gained by willing sacrifice ("Thing of Darkness", "From the Dark Halls of Hell") while at other times the battle is purely one of willpower ("The Doomed Treveans"); trappings such as pentacles do occur, but infrequently ("Werewolf of the Sahara"); while love can be the powerful force that finally triumphs ("The Dark Star"), although hate is also an emotion that has its own dark strength ("The Devil's

Graveyard").

The relatively straightforward tale of revenge, as in "The Return" and "The Laughing Thing", is unusual in the Pendarves canon, although vengeance is a motive that animates elemental evil in such tales as "From the Dark Halls of Hell". The dead seldom rest in peace but seek to claw their way back to the land of the living, sometimes at the expense of their own relatives, family ties being tenuous, to say the least. In "The Footprint", "The Sin-Eater" and "The Withered Heart" there is no sentiment on the part of the revenants who seek to callously use their kin to fulfil their grim purposes.

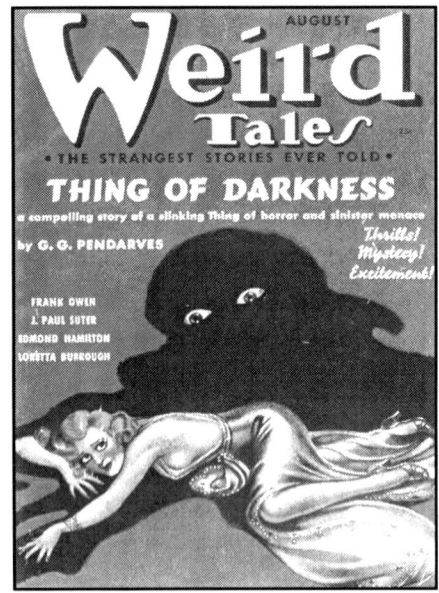

In both "The Devil's Graveyard" and "The Eighth Green Man", the entity Gaffarel is mentioned, and Pendarves may have been looking to populate her fiction with her own literary pantheon of magical beings. Apart from the reference to Gaffarel in these two stories, there were also The Four Ancient Ones in "The Devil's Graveyard", and the being Chavajoth in "From the Dark Halls of Hell", which incorporates a Lovecraftian sounding formula: *Vaa Chavajoth! Chavajoth! Chavajoth! Vaa! Vaa! Vaa!* However, as was the case with Donald Fremling as a prospective series character, she did not pursue the idea to any significant extent, possibly deciding in both cases that it would be too restrictive.

Subsequent fiction did on occasion include allusions to her mystical creations, including The Four Ancient Ones in "The Sin-Eater".

Chavajoth is referred to as a "demon-god" in "Werewolf of the Sahara", and Gaffarel is designated as the "Watcher in the House of Mercury" in "The Altar of Melek Taos". In both of the latter stories the beings in question do seem to have been incorporated into the devil-worshipping cult of the Yezidees, a real-life Arabian sect that had also been featured in Robert W Chambers' novel *The Slayer of Souls* as well as in fiction by E Hoffman Price and Seabury Quinn, while Robert E Howard used the premise in his short story "The Brazen Peacock".

Pendarves was writing and publishing her fiction in *Weird Tales* during a period that saw many outstanding works appear in its pages, a period that many consider to be its "Golden Age". As well as the famous triumvirate of Lovecraft, Smith and Howard, she was also competing with such popular authors as Henry S Whitehead, Seabury Quinn, Edmond Hamilton, August Derleth, E Hoffman Price, David H Keller and Frank Belknap Long. A measure of her success is that her work was never overshadowed by those other writers. She quietly produced a solid body of absorbing weird fiction which has been underrated and overlooked and which is deserving of more recognition.

GG Pendarves died following a heart attack on 1 August 1938 at the relatively young age of fifty-three. Her writing career was thus brought to a premature end at a time when her fiction was gaining power – the last four of her stories published had each demonstrated that her imaginative prowess was undiminished, and clearly indicated that there was much more to come. That alas was not to be. There were to be no more families haunted by dire curses, no more psychic battles and no more Things of Darkness.

SELECTED BIBLIOGRAPHY

Appearances in *Weird Tales*

"The Devil's Graveyard" – August 1926

"The Return" (as by Marjorie E Lambe) – April 1927

"The Power of the Dog" – August 1927

"The Lord of the Tarn" – November 1927

"The Eighth Green Man" – March 1928

"The Doomed Treveans" – May 1928

"The Laughing Thing" – May 1929

"The Footprint" – May 1930

"The Grave at Goonhilly" – October 1930

"From the Dark Halls of Hell" – January 1932

"The Altar of Melek Taos" – September 1932

"Abd Dhulma, Lord of Fire" – December 1933

"Werewolf of the Sahara" – August/September 1936

"The Dark Star" – March 1937

"The Whistling Corpse" – July 1937

"Thing of Darkness" – August 1937

"The Black Monk" – October 1938

"The Sin-Eater" – December 1938

"The Withered Heart" – November 1939

THE FINAL RESTING PLACE
LORD DUNSANY

THERE ARE SURELY no fantasy enthusiasts who are unaware that Lord Dunsany was one of the most important writers of all time. His influence on authors as diverse as HP Lovecraft, Clark Ashton Smith, Arthur C Clarke and Jack Vance is unmistakable, and one might ponder whether JRR Tolkien would ever have written about Middle Earth had Dunsany not paved the way with his own matchlessly imaginative fiction.

The Gods of Pegâna was the first of his fantasies, appearing in 1905, and was genuinely ground breaking in its originality. There had quite simply not been *anything* like that slim volume *ever* published before. The subsequent books over the next ten years or so – notably *Time and the Gods, The Sword of Welleran, A Dreamer's Tales, The Book of Wonder,* and *Tales of Wonder* – confirmed the vast sweep of Dunsany's creative talent as well as his outstandingly graceful literary technique. Not only are his books and his style of immense importance to the field, his writing is wonderfully *accessible*.

Good though they undoubtedly were, Dunsany's forbears – William Morris and George MacDonald, for instance – do not lend themselves to being read with ease. Their work generally tends to be long, complex and heavily descriptive, whereas Dunsany's is straightforward, with a natural rhythmic flow that carries his readers enthusiastically along regardless of plot. "Idle Days on the Yann", for example, is a story in which hardly anything happens – it has no climax and seems to end more or less where it began – but once read how many readers are ever going to forget its masterful prose or its richly evocative tone? And *The Gods of Pegâna* quite literally has no plot at all, and yet remains an astonishing achievement, a scene-setting collection that not only paves the way for the writer's subsequent collections, but which is also a remarkable and unique work in its own right.

Not that Dunsany struggled with plotting – the splendid novel *The King of Elfland's Daughter* belies any such thoughts, as do numerous other stories – but for him the creation of a particular mood was of paramount importance, and he was perhaps more successful in achieving that aim than any other fantasy writer has ever been. Those created moods could vary with effortless nonchalance between the mordant wit of "Chubu and Sheemish" to the disquieting chill of "The Probable Adventure of the Three Literary Men" and "The Hoard of the Gibbelins", with many stops along the way, from the dramatic verve of "The Sword of Welleran" and "The Fortress Unvanquishable, Save for Sacnoth" to the sad poignancy of "Carcassonne". He could write with simple directness or with delicate irony, of heady adventure or unadorned romance, and was fully at ease with whatever approach he chose to adopt.

Many of the tales have a sardonic edge, with an emphasis on the transient nature of what appears to be eternal, a theme that is particularly effective in "Time and the Gods" and "In Zaccaranth". And who else could have written the excellent "Mlideen", which in a mere 700 words recounts how the forbearance of the gods is not infinite, and which also demonstrates that some lessons are never learned. Such miniature tours-de-force, often with similarly unforeseen twists in the tail, also include "How the Gods Avenged Meoul Ki Ning" and "The Jest of the Gods", tales amply demonstrating the fallibility of the deities in question.

Dunsany wrote numerous books; only a relatively small proportion of these were fantasy. As well as his superb collections of short stories, there were four excellent novels and a number of plays. I had only recently discovered the latter, via two slim volumes from Wildside Press, *Five Plays* and *Plays of Gods and Men*, and was delighted to find that this was another format in which the author excelled. In particular, "The Laughter of the Gods" and "The Gods of the Mountain" are incomparably atmospheric pieces, while "The Glittering Gate" lingers long in the memory for its unremittingly bleak ending. Perhaps the most impressive of all the plays is "King Argimines and the Unknown Warrior", a creative magnum opus which succeeds not only as an entertainment in its own right but also as a multi-layered and thought-provoking fable.

Dunsany's versatility was remarkable, covering many facets of fiction, and he seemed to almost casually master everything that he touched. Ghost stories were another field in which he excelled: "The Return" is a near classic. The non-fantasy writing is equally skilled, with the well-known tall tales of Jorkens at the Billiards Club perhaps the most renowned, as well as *The Little Tales of Smethers*, which includes a particularly fine example of the macabre in "Two Bottles of

Relish". This story was apparently rejected by some publishers as being "too gruesome", but gruesome though it certainly is, it is tempered by a light-hearted approach that culminates in a wonderful final line that leaves the reader unsure whether he should shudder or laugh.

For all his wonderful writing in so many distinct areas, Dunsany remains the undisputed master of the fantasy form; the imaginative scope of his work has never been approached, let alone equalled. He is, of course, one of the few writers whose very name has become an adjective – references to *Dunsanian* fiction are not uncommon, and such allusions very clearly describe the style to be expected (but not necessarily its quality).

The writer himself seems to have been a fascinating character. A veteran of the Boer War, he wrote with a quill pen, was known as "the worst dressed man in Ireland", was an inveterate sportsman and world traveller, a lecturer, a chess champion, and a hugely successful writer. At one point there were *five* of his plays running in New York at the same time, and many of his books apparently went through multiple printings.

Lord Dunsany's final years were spent in England, at Dunstall Priory near Shoreham in Kent, and after his death on 25 October 1957 he was buried in the Parish Church of St Peter and St Paul in Shoreham. Although he died at Dunsany Castle in County Meath in Ireland, he had indicated that he wished to rest in the Kentish surroundings that had meant so much to him.

SHOREHAM IS A pleasant little village about twenty miles from London, fairly close to where I live. I had been meaning to visit the Church for quite some time. A few years ago, I was intrigued to discover that Peter Russell, an old friend of mine and someone with whom I now work, had actually *met* Dunsany in the 1950s. Peter is not a reader of fantasy at all, and consequently we had never discussed the subject. How it eventually cropped up I cannot recall, but I was astonished to find that here was someone who for all these years had somehow kept from me the fact that he had been face to face with *the* master of fantasy.

Peter was one of a group of Boy Scouts who were looking for somewhere to set up camp for a few days, and the grounds of Dunstall Priory looked ideal to them. They knew that a peer lived there, but assumed that he was Lord *Dunstall*; it was not until many years later that Peter realised that the Lord Dunsany who he had subsequently heard of as a famous writer was one and the same as the supposed Lord Dunstall.

The Scouts were amiably received, and allowed to stay in the grounds of the Priory for the weekend. They returned on several occasions, and were made welcome each time. Peter remembers Dunsany as very tall and bearded, an imposing individual with a wide brimmed hat and tweeds, accompanied by a spaniel-type dog. To the young boys he seemed to be the archetypal eccentric English peer, and they were all a little in awe of this striking figure; however, the warm and jolly welcome that they received soon put them at their ease, and this was so on each of their visits. I have read that in his latter years, Dunsany was supposed to be tetchy and irascible, but Peter does not remember him in that way at all.

This Dunsanian discovery prompted the two of us to visit Shoreham on a dull and rather misty New Year's Eve, to firstly find Dunstall Priory and then to pay our respects at the grave. Peter remembered exactly where the Priory was, and after explaining our interest to the present owner, we were graciously allowed to take some photographs.

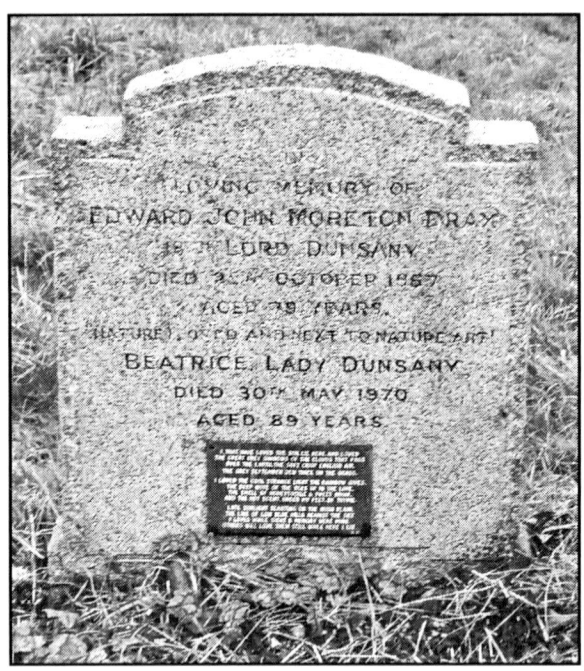

The impressive six-bedroomed house, set in the most beautiful countryside, was designed by Robert Lugar and built in 1806. It has apparently not changed very much over the last sixty years, and it is easy to imagine a pensive Dunsany taking his ease in the lovely gardens, perhaps sipping a glass of a particularly fine vintage of wine before again taking up his quill pen.

We eventually moved on to the Church, which is on the outskirts of the village. The Visitors Guide indicates that "A church has stood on this site from Saxon times, and the North Wall is said to be eleventh century. Therefore you stand on ground hallowed over many centuries". The entrance is through a fifteenth century porch formed from an enormous upended oak tree. The Church has a gentle, restful atmosphere. The sense of history is pervasive – there is a board on the

North Wall that details the names of all the Rectors, Vicars and Curates since the early thirteenth century; these include two Cardinals, a Dean of Westminster and an Archbishop of York.

The grounds of the Church are pretty and tranquil, the unpretentious grave is easy to find, and both Lord Dunsany and his wife Beatrice rest there. The headstone reads:

IN
LOVING MEMORY OF
EDWARD JOHN MORETON DRAX
18TH LORD DUNSANY
DIED 25TH OCTOBER 1957
AGED 78 YEARS.

'NATURE I LOVED AND NEXT TO NATURE ART'

BEATRICE, LADY DUNSANY
DIED 30TH MAY 1970
AGED 89 YEARS

The quotation on the seventh line is from Walter Savage Landor's "Dying Speech of an Old Philosopher". The full 1849 poem reads as follows:

> *I strove with none; for none was worth my strife;*
> *Nature I loved, and next to Nature, Art;*
> *I warmed both hands before the fire of life;*
> *It sinks, and I am ready to depart.*

There is a plaque at the foot of the headstone, and this has the following verse:

> I, THAT HAVE LOVED THE SUN, LIE HERE, AND LOVED
> THE GREAT GREY SHADOWS OF THE CLOUDS THAT PASS
> OVER THE EARTH, THE SOFT CRISP ENGLISH AIR,
> THE GREY SEPTEMBER DEW THICK ON THE GRASS.
>
> I LOVED THE COOL STRANGE LIGHT THE RAINBOW GIVES,
> THE DEEP NOTE OF THE BEES UP IN THE LIME,
> THE SMELL OF HONEYSUCKLE & SWEET BRIAR,
> AND THE HOT SCENT, UNDER MY FEET, OF THYME.
>
> LATE SUNLIGHT SLANTING ON THE IRISH PLAIN,
> THE LINE OF LOW BLUE HILLS AGAINST THE SKY
> I LOVED WHILE SIGHT & MEMORY WERE MINE
> OTHERS WILL LOVE THEM STILL WHILE HERE I LIE.

I have been unable to trace the source of these lines, but they are credited to "BD", and I assume that this *may* stand for "Baron Dunsany". Although he was of course *Lord* Dunsany, he was actually the eighteenth *Baron* Dunsany; the title *Lord* is applicable to all five ranks of the nobility (Duke, Marquess, Earl, Viscount and Baron). I have virtually none of his poetry, but from what little of it I have seen, this does appear to be in his style. The one problem with this supposition is that I cannot find any evidence that he ever used the title "Baron" rather than "Lord" for any of his writings.

There is of course the possibility that "BD" is Beatrice Dunsany, but this seems unlikely on the basis that utilisation of that name would have been incorrect usage. However, I have seen reference to a 1943 letter that is apparently signed "Beatrice Dunsany", so perhaps she did use that name on occasion, although there does not appear to be any record of any poetry attributed to her.

Dunsany published six volumes of verse during his lifetime, amongst the seventy or so titles with which he is credited. He never returned to fantasy and the "kingdoms at the edge of the world" after his early efforts, as they were not overly well-received critically, and his popular fame was to be achieved in other literary fields. Yet it is those fantasy works for which he is now most renowned, while his other work is largely forgotten – an irony that may well have caused a twinkling in his Lordship's eye had he but known, and which ultimately would have been something which would have delighted him, given the enormous and far-reaching impact those few books were to have.

The setting of his final resting place, with its quiet dignity and unassuming beauty, has a definite appropriateness to the writings we so relish. The heart of the peaceful Kent countryside has no unicorns to be hunted, but one instinctively *knows* that Lord Dunsany is completely at peace here.

SELECTED BIBLIOGRAPHY

The classic fantasies

The Gods of Pegāna – Elkin Matthews, 1905

Time and the Gods – William Heinemann, 1906

The Sword of Welleran – George Allen, 1908

A Dreamer's Tales – George Allen, 1910

The Book of Wonder – William Heinemann, 1912

Tales of Wonder – Elkin Matthews, 1916